AF581222

The Last Road Rebel—
and Other Lost Stories

"Gilberg's memoir is a vivid portrait of the American mid-west in the 1950s. *The Last Road Rebel* offers a ride down Memory Lane -- one in a fast car with the radio playing the songs of a generation. Readers will be sure to enjoy the ride."

T. Greenwood, author of, *Two Rivers, Bodies of Water, and Grace*

An explosive romp and wild joy ride through 1950s Ohio.

Larry M Edwards, author
Dare I Call It Murder?: A Memoir of Violent Loss

The Last Road Rebel— and Other Lost Stories

Growing Up in a Small Town— and Never Getting Over It

Robert Gilberg

THE LAST ROAD REBEL—AND OTHER LOST STORIES
GROWING UP IN A SMALL TOWN—AND NEVER GETTING OVER IT

Copyright © 2015 Robert Gilberg.

All rights reserved. No part of this book may be used or reproduced by any means, graphic, electronic, or mechanical, including photocopying, recording, taping or by any information storage retrieval system without the written permission of the publisher except in the case of brief quotations embodied in critical articles and reviews.

iUniverse books may be ordered through booksellers or by contacting:

iUniverse
1663 Liberty Drive
Bloomington, IN 47403
www.iuniverse.com
1-800-Authors (1-800-288-4677)

Because of the dynamic nature of the Internet, any web addresses or links contained in this book may have changed since publication and may no longer be valid. The views expressed in this work are solely those of the author and do not necessarily reflect the views of the publisher, and the publisher hereby disclaims any responsibility for them.

Any people depicted in stock imagery provided by Thinkstock are models, and such images are being used for illustrative purposes only.
Certain stock imagery © Thinkstock.

ISBN: 978-1-4917-5723-9 (sc)
ISBN: 978-1-4917-5724-6 (hc)
ISBN: 978-1-4917-5722-2 (e)

Library of Congress Control Number: 2014922797

Printed in the United States of America.

iUniverse rev. date: 01/30/2015

For my wife, Nikki, and mother, Delight Gilberg

Well, I was born in a small town
And I lived in a small town
Probably die in a small town
Oh, those small town communities

All my friends were so small town
My parents lived in the same small town
My job is so small town
Provides little opportunity

Educated in a small town
Taught to fear Jesus in a small town
Used to daydream in that small town
Another boring romantic, that's me

But I've seen it all in a small town
Had myself a ball in a small town
Married an LA doll and brought her to this small town
Now she's small town just like me
No, I cannot forget where it is that I come from
I cannot forget the people who love me

—John Mellencamp, "Small Town"

Contents

The Past in My Windshield 1
New Bremen, Ohio—the '50s 13
Duty Calls 19
The Carbide Cannon Incident 33
Polio 57
Summertime Blues 63
Dancing at the Opera House 85
Dead Man's Curve 89
Road Rebels: Just Because 99
The Little Race Car on the Corner 113
You're Going to Lose That Girl 133
The Last Road Rebel 143
Are You Crazy? 161
The Problem with Misty 165
Tragedy 187
Good-Bye, Columbus 195
Get a Job 205
Nikki 209
How Do You … 217
In My Rearview Mirror 225
October 2013, Southern California 231

Epilogue 2014 239
Afterword 249
Acknowledgments 253

The Past in My Windshield

Take me home, country roads, to the place I belong …
—John Denver, "Take Me Home, Country Roads" (J. Denver, B. Danoff, T. Nivert)

The silver Mustang convertible was slightly more than idling at 1,700 rpm along the freeway, northbound from the Dayton airport, poking along at the minimum speed limit of fifty-five miles per hour. I wasn't in a hurry. I had picked the car up in the rental lot with the top already down—waiting just for me, it seemed—not parked in one of the usual rental company numbered spots but instead next to the walkway so that travelers were sure to pass by, inviting someone to rent it.

I did. It was the perfect car to drive up to my old hometown and the two reunions I was going to attend—a Californian returning home to small-town Ohio. It was partly ego tripping and partly the car-guy in me. With the exception of my first three years in college when I didn't own a car, I've never been without a convertible since age sixteen, and I have never owned a four-door sedan.

I drove slowly because I wanted to take my time, soaking up the nostalgic feelings I was having as I drove to my younger brother Richard's house in Piqua, where I would stay for the several days I was in Ohio. I was thinking about what brought me back there, near the places I grew up and where I still had family, where I'd met the girl I'd married, and where I had spent my early career in electronics. It had all followed from a phone conversation I had with my old classmate and fellow Road Rebel Car Club member, Ray, when he was still up in Alaska in early summer of 2013.

"Ray, I haven't heard a thing from anyone about a fifty-fifth class reunion. We may not have too many of these left. Maybe we should do something simple: just sit around on someone's porch or in a backyard and drink a little wine and beer," I suggested. "No program, no speeches, no booklets; we all just hang out and BS."

"We could do that at our house in New Bremen," Ray said. "I've got a large backyard on the bank of the old canal. Joanne and I are leaving for Ohio in a couple of weeks, and I can pack along some salmon and a few other delicacies the folks in New Bremen will be intrigued by."

By *delicacies*, he meant bear and moose.

"Hey, that sounds really good! By the way, have you been in contact with any of the old Road Rebels? My brother Rich found a bumper plaque a while back and sent it to me. I can't stop thinking about those days. Maybe we should get those guys together too," I proposed. "We can have the first-ever Road Rebels Car Club reunion."

"Yeah, let's try to do it. I'll be back there in time to call some of the guys," Ray said.

"And I'll e-mail everyone I have an address for," I volunteered.

Two guys, one living in Alaska and one living in California, pulled the Ohio reunions together over the next month: the first-ever Road Rebels Car Club reunion on a Friday evening and the New Bremen High School class of '58 reunion the following Saturday.

After spending some time with my younger brother and his wife, I drove the Mustang up to New Bremen, Ohio, for that first Road Rebels reunion. It was a warm summer afternoon with the silhouettes of distant, dark thunderheads towering into the late-afternoon sky, dozens of miles off to the west—but I had the top down anyway. The soft, late-afternoon air was like a warm, humid blanket surrounding me as I settled comfortably inside the Mustang, cradled by the bucket seat, steering wheel in my left hand and floor-mounted shifter in my right. It felt perfect—plenty of horsepower under my gas pedal, five-speed tranny ready to drop into any gear I wanted, a fast-looking machine with bright metallic silver paint, and the top down. In spite of my graying, thinning hair blowing forward over my sunglasses in tangles, it was the perfect way to drive into my old hometown.

The sensation I felt as the Mustang glided along the northbound highway was one of floating along through nonstop Ohio greenery. Little traffic, few stop signs or traffic lights, and the smell of farms and vegetation everywhere—so different from Southern California. I knew the feeling; it was just like those I'd had on countless similar days in 1957 and 1958 when I drove around the same areas in my 1952 Ford convertible.

Going past miles and miles of those green farm fields up to New Bremen, twenty-five miles to the north, I traveled through the same small towns I had driven through more than fifty years before. Little had changed along that old two-lane highway. The farms all looked the same, and their fields probably bore the same crops. The towns seemed to have grown little, if any, with their tiny three-and four-digit population numbers printed on the city-limits signs; the numbers weren't much different from what they had been in the '50s. There were few new houses and few new roadside businesses—so different from California.

The route took me through Minster, Ohio, three miles to the south of New Bremen. As I reached the last few streets just before leaving Minster's northern city limit, I couldn't resist making a familiar turn onto Sixth Street and driving the short distance to Joanie's old house. Joanie—*the* love of my teenage life. Strong emotions from that teen love and long-ago disappointment swept over me as I parked there, across the street from her house, looking at the front door where I had kissed her for the last time in 1957. My feelings were no longer those of the broken heart from that time—I was over that long ago—but more the warm feelings I could now enjoy just knowing I had been touched by a girl, if only for a short time, and still have good feelings about her. Things hadn't worked out the way I had hoped back then, but in spite of that, I couldn't stop wondering where she was and what had happened to her.

I flashed back to a time when Minster and New Bremen were bitter rivals in high school sports—and religion. Minster was effectively an all-Catholic town, and New Bremen was essentially an all-Protestant town. Of course, Joanie was a Catholic, and I was a Protestant, and ours was a frowned-upon—if not nearly forbidden—relationship.

Dating between towns was almost unheard of; young people were supposed to date and marry boys or girls from their own hometowns—and wed within their parents' religions. There was a folktale around from the mid-1800s that travelers seeking land and new lives, when traveling by the old Miami and Erie Canal—which runs through Minster and New Bremen on its way from Cincinnati to Lake Erie—were advised that all Catholics should exit the boats at Minster and that Protestants should go on to New Bremen and debark there. Single-religion villages were not uncommon around our part of western Ohio in the '50s. Some things still hadn't changed much in the 150 years since that canal had been opened.

But religion really didn't concern me since my mother had told me that I should feel free, when the time came—like my father had been told by his parents when he reached eighteen—to choose my religion for myself. In our family, that choice had been made more than once based on love and marriage. It seemed a very modern concept for my father's family in the '30s, as it had for me in the '50s—and still does even now.

But the religion issue, which seemed like a decision I might have to make—and actually would have been ready to make at some point back then—never became our problem. It was unfortunate; I believed I had that one handled.

After a few minutes, sitting there watching that front door and almost expecting a pretty, seventeen-year-old girl in shorts would walk out and wave, I told myself, *Okay, Bob, enough of this. You have friends and relatives waiting just three miles up the road; that was fifty-five years ago. Come out of it. But someday, I'm going to find her.*

I returned to the highway and in another five minutes entered New Bremen. Almost immediately, I was driving toward the big house that had always been my favorite of the four houses our family had lived in there. It was a large, two-story place with a screened-in porch running all the way around from the front door on the west side to the kitchen door on the north side of the house. I loved watching summertime thunderstorms roll down the street from that porch, smelling the musty yet fresh scent of an approaching rainstorm and then watching the rain, in downward sheets, sweep the streets clean. I loved sleeping there on hot summer evenings, listening to the crickets and watching the gatherings of fireflies zigzagging over the lawns and streets until I fell into sleep.

And I loved that each of us three brothers had our own bedrooms in that house, which was a great luxury for our family. For the first time, we actually had the space that a five-person family needed. Better yet were our neighbors: next door to the south was where Linda—a girlfriend-to-be in a few years—had lived, and around the corner to the east was my beautiful classmate Judy's home. Next door to Judy was where my longtime friend and frequent date, Pat, lived at that time.

Parking just in front of my family's old house, I passed through a time portal. I recalled that in spite of how much I liked that house, and even with those wonderful girls living so close around me in those days, that house meant too much sadness.

It was where we lived when our family fortunes came crashing down with the beginning of my father's severe illnesses, which had the family moving to a rented apartment until things could get better. Through everything we experienced in that house, and over the next two to three years, the bright spot was my mother—as always. She managed to keep things going in spite of the worry and sleeplessness and exhaustion. She worked second- and even third-shift jobs—because the pay was better—and did whatever was needed to keep the family fed and sheltered. Three kids in school, and Mom working graveyard shift, Dad not able to work. But we all made it through those years.

Sitting there in my rented Mustang, I realized I had never given her enough credit and the gratitude she deserved for what she had done in those years. I was never strong enough to actually come out and say what I should have said to her. I would get too emotional, and my voice would falter. I'm still no good at saying some of the things I should be able to say by now.

But over the next thirty-some years, no matter where I had been working and living at any time until her death, if at all possible, I always called her every week. And I always scheduled a stop in to see her and Dad when my frequent business travel took me near Ohio. I believed, and hoped, that staying in contact through all the years was more important than any inadequate words I could have mumbled.

I finally forced myself out of that time and mood warp after sitting there, thinking for too long—or maybe not long enough—about the clouds we lived under in those days, and I continued my drive toward downtown. *Remember those days, and always remember that wonderful mother—but don't lose yourself in those memories, either.*

Things got better for Mom and Dad, but it took many years, and we kids had moved on to our own lives by then.

#

I drove the Mustang into the center of town and stopped at what had once been one of only two traffic lights in New Bremen in the '50s: the intersection of Ohio Route 66 and Ohio Route 274, with the old Miami and Erie Canal just yards away to my left, crossing under the Monroe Street Bridge. The old canal lock, Lock One, was behind and to my left; our old hangout, the Hollingsworth Hotel Bar and Grille, was across the canal on Monroe Street—the local street that doubles as Route 274 through town—and a city block farther on down Monroe was the burned-out shell of the old Boesel Opera House.

I was sitting at the center of the first twenty-two years of my life.

I had made the trip to Ohio and found myself at this intersection many times while my parents were still alive. But with them now both gone, along with so many of the rest of my close connections to the place, I had not been back for several years. Old memories began to come like a flood, wave after wave, washing everything else from my mind as I sat waiting for the light to change.

Other than earlier, short snapshot recollections from my very early childhood, the first significant memories I have of my times there are from when I was a twelve-year-old kid, traveling my newspaper route but looking forward to a real after-school job, a few years away from being able to drive a car, and so peddling myself around on a bicycle to get places, starting to wonder about girls and having dates, and thinking about the scarier things of the world at that time: the Cold War and atom bombs, the Korean War, and bad diseases like polio that, in 1952, still had no answers. And what to be when I grew up. It was a world of big questions in the mind of a small kid.

The light changed, and I turned left down Monroe Street, going the two blocks to a now vacant lot where my wonderful aunt, Ruth Ritter—a Gilberg by birth, but a Ritter by marriage—had lived until her death just a few years before at the age of ninety-eight. She had converted Dr. Fledderjohann's small, old single-story office building into an easier-to-manage home for her elder years, where she lived with her diabetes and degenerating vision. I stopped the Mustang in the alleyway next to that empty lot, letting it idle with the air conditioning on max, as I remembered her, our family, and the doc for a few minutes.

I had been born in my family's rented house in 1940 with Dr. Fledderjohann, our small-town country doctor, in attendance. Ruth was his nurse that day, as she was for many of the home births in that time. Dr. Fledderjohann, who started his practice in New Bremen in the first decade of the twentieth century, routinely made house calls to deliver new babies at home—in ordinary bedrooms, in ordinary houses, some without running water and indoor toilets even into the early 1950s. There were no IVs, no heart monitors, no ultrasounds, no x-rays, no fully equipped pediatric nurseries, and no drugs for pain or to induce birth. Just the doc, Aunt Ruth, my mom—and then me. My older brother and many of my friends and classmates were born in the same way, with the same doctor and nurse in attendance. Doc Fledderjohann was the town's doctor, and Ruth was the town's nurse.

The last time I saw Aunt Ruth was during a previous visit a few years before when, in spite of her near complete blindness, she had peeled apples for a pie that she baked and served to my wife and me when we visited her that day.

I've always thought of Ruth as New Bremen's Florence Nightingale.

#

I let the Mustang idle on through the alley for another one hundred yards and stopped at a lot with a large brick and wood building at one end and another large 2 story wood building at the other. My deceased uncle Paul Gilberg had used the two buildings as the family home and for his mortuary business and funeral parlor. Established originally in 1929 by Uncle Paul, the mortuary and funeral home business is still in the family with the family also still living in the residence.

I smiled at the contrast: at one end of that alleyway had until recently been the building that housed the medical practice of the doctor, and later the home of the woman who brought so many New Bremen people into the world. And very close, just a block away at this other end of the alley, was the business and home of the man who escorted so many out of this world. One Gilberg bringing them in and another taking them out, both with the same love and care.

The Gilberg Funeral Home has probably twice buried the equivalent of the entire town's residential population during its years in operation.

I turned the Mustang's engine off and sat there under the shade of a large, old tree and remembered our family. My parents were among the blue-collar working class in New Bremen, with both Mom and Dad working factory jobs. They each had completed their high school educations—not necessarily a common thing for folks of high school age during the Great Depression in farm country in the '30s. Stability was always a challenge for the Gilberg family, though; Dad had a long run of physical problems that kept him out of work or between jobs too frequently. Looking back now, I usually see him as a victim of events—someone who became a person unable to grasp and regain control over his life because of his lack of any additional education or specific, in-demand skills that would make it possible to find new work where his never-ending back problems were not an issue. He had been an expert in the repair of Pratt & Whitney bomber engines during World War II at Wright-Patterson Air Force Base, but that didn't help him around New Bremen, where there was no demand for that kind of skill. He tried auto mechanic work, which he was very good at, but his bad back made that an impossible career. Even as a kid, I understood his situation and felt badly for him. I can remember how strongly I vowed I'd never let myself be in that situation.

But for too long, I had no idea exactly what that meant and how I was going to accomplish something better.

Dad's health problems forced us to move from house to house as his health dictated our fortunes. The disruption our family went through during my high school years became a mental drag that was hard for all of us to shake. We kids all wanted desperately just to be able to go to school, enjoy our friends, and have a normal, satisfying home life. I'm sure Mom and Dad wished for the same kinds of things, but for most of my high school years it was impossible, and there frequently was tension in our home because of it.

Mom became the rock that our family was anchored against. She was always there to keep things going, staying upbeat and cheerful throughout around us kids. My mother and father were children of the Great Depression and never forgot the hard times and frugality they and their families had experienced. They knew how to live through difficult times. If she needed to, Mom could get up at 5:00 a.m. to drive me around my paper route in icy winter weather, butcher a live chicken in the backyard to prepare and serve for dinner that evening, go to her job, and—if she wasn't working the late shift—play card games or watch Milton Berle or Red Skelton on TV with us that night. It seemed the Great Depression was never very far back in the memories of most families in the '50s, and there was a persistent belief that there was another one—waiting—just around the corner to be wary of.

Dad's illnesses in the '50s became our own private Gilberg family Depression.

#

After restarting the Mustang, I slowly drove down quiet, shady streets and turned left onto Plum Street, traveling the two blocks to the previous site of our old municipal swimming pool. The pool had been one of the most important places to me and most of my friends in all of Auglaize County.

Of all the surrounding small towns, New Bremen had the only swimming pool. It was a Depression-era, FDR Works Progress Administration (WPA) project, and so it was not exactly a resort. It had a blunt, gray concrete building for the administration and changing rooms that even by the '50s looked old. Hoover Dam architecture comes to mind.

There are nearby lakes, but because they were muddy things that had been created by damming low-lying areas and were surrounded by farms and fed by farm runoff, even then—before the copious use of phosphate fertilizers—they were coffee-colored and opaque. Swimming in them was more than a little creepy. The lakes' original purposes had been as feeder reservoirs for the canal, but they were also handy for recreation. In the '50s, they were very popular for boating, water-skiing, fishing, and—for some people—even swimming. Grand Lake Saint Marys, just a few miles from New Bremen, was claimed to be the largest man-made lake in the world when it was completed in the mid-1800s. Oil was discovered beneath the lake in the late 1800s, and at one time, there were as many as 150 oil derricks in and around the lake. Not surprisingly, as time went on into the 1950s, for these and various reasons, ours were not lakes where one wanted to accidentally take in a mouthful of water while swimming or water-skiing. We didn't think about it, though; we fished, skied, and—sometimes—swam anyway. There were even what we optimistically called "beaches" along the muddy shores … imported sand spread over the real lakeshore—mud. Obviously, all of this was before the EPA and modern water-quality standards.

So it was good to have a clean swimming pool right in our own town that we could walk or ride our bikes to. There we learned to swim and dive, skinned our knees on the pool-area pavement or pool bottom, got a bloody nose from diving too deeply, or cut our heads on the diving boards with risky dives. Most importantly, it was also *the* place for boys and girls to meet. The pool was the social center for all the kids in our town, as well as many nearby towns, throughout our summers.

#

I drove the Mustang on up the hill and back over the Miami and Erie Canal Bridge toward the high school, stopping at one of the newer traffic lights installed since my days there. It was early evening; the town was falling into twilight. People were heading downtown to Bremfest, the town's yearly festival held each August in celebration of its citizens. As I sat at the light, four teenage girls waiting for the light to change waved and yelled at me, "Hey, mister, nice car!"

I'd have loved that fifty-five years earlier—but I didn't mind it then, either, even at my age of seventy-two. Back then, I surely would have pulled over to have a chat and ask them if they wanted a ride; but I just smiled and yelled back, "Thanks!" and dropped the transmission into first gear and accelerated around the corner, feeling a little guilty for not admitting that it was a rental.

I turned away from downtown and headed for Ray and Joanne's place at the south edge of town, along the east bank of the canal where we were holding the first-ever Road Rebels reunion. I was going to see people I hadn't seen since 1958—fifty-five years earlier. My mind was awash with memories of adventures, teenage loves, tragedies, unfounded hopes, and my time trying to find myself.

I pulled the Mustang into the driveway, shut the engine down, and went to meet many of the people who had shared my past and so many adventures and stories with me.

New Bremen, Ohio—the '50s

Home where my thought's escaping, home
where my music's playing …
—Simon & Garfunkel, "Homeward Bound" (P. Simon)

New Bremen, Ohio, was mostly like countless other small farm towns in that part of the state in the '50s. The primary business in that area at the time was farming—corn, wheat, hay, alfalfa, and soybeans, along with some dairy farming—and there were always cows and pigs in the fields. This was no gentleman's hobby-farm country; it was family, farm-for-a-living country. This is still the case today. The countryside's deep, rich soil attracted the original settlers who cleared the land, set up the farms, and built the towns. The land was wrestled by hand, with backbreaking manual labor, from the thick, hardwood forests that dominated the entire western part of the state in the early 1800s. Those settlers who founded New Bremen were primarily people from northern Germany, and a walk through the German Protestant Cemetery reveals names that clearly announce that background: Hogenkamp, Quellhorst, Meckstroth, Ziegenbush, Ruedebusch, Blanke, Klanke, Schulenberg, Schwieterman, Luedeke, Vogelsang, Vanderhorst, Wuebbenhorst, and so on. People were still speaking German, at home and sometimes even in public, during my high school years in the late 1950s.

New Bremen had about 1,800 residents then. There were two drugstores, two food markets, two medical doctors, three bars, five churches, six gas stations, and, until he retired, one dentist. The docs both made house calls. With the exception of one small Catholic church, the rest were of various Protestant denominations.

There was also one auto racing track, one public swimming pool, one movie theater, one bowling alley, and the Lock One North canal lock on the Miami and Erie Canal. Those first few things were what made New Bremen typical of the other surrounding towns. The last few things were what made New Bremen different, and they made all the difference to me and—probably to varying degrees—most kids growing up in New Bremen in those days.

Movies generally reached New Bremen months after the releases in the bigger Ohio cities, and big movies such as *Giant* and *Stalag 17* and *High Noon* didn't get there for up to a year later. Admission on Thursdays was fifteen cents, and the balcony was always open. Popcorn was a dime. And, in a remarkable concession to movie viewers' enjoyment mostly absent today, there was a glassed-in "crying room" with a speaker for mothers with babies.

The auto racing track had seen some glory years back in the '30s when big-name drivers came for the racing, but in an infamous and well-known episode around the area at that time, the drivers, disgusted by the day's purse, set fire to the grandstands and any wooden structure, and the place burned down. In the '50s, the track was just beginning its resurgence. It was an important part of my youth.

There was one high school and one grade school. Junior high classes were in the high school building. My senior graduating class had twenty-five students, eighteen of whom had started first grade together, and we had roughly 130 kids in the entire high school. Some of them had attended school in one-room schoolhouses in the surrounding townships before transferring into New Bremen's "bigger" system when the one-room schools began to close down.

There were two graduating students in my church's—the New Bremen Zion Evangelical and Reformed Church—confirmation class: my older brother and me.

In the very early '50s, milk, butter, and cream were all delivered to homes—in glass bottles—by a horse-drawn wagon every morning before seven o'clock. Ice, for those still using real iceboxes, as did my family, was also delivered by horse-drawn wagon. The milk bottles needed to be brought inside quickly in the winter to avoid freezing and popping the pressed-in cardboard stoppers. Bringing in the milk, along with the newspaper, was the first order of business in the morning.

Homes without plumbing, while not common, were still evident; we could tell by the wooden outhouses and the big cast-iron pump handles mounted on the backyard water wells or by seeing someone making the occasional backyard dash.

The canal was mostly abandoned by the turn of the twentieth century, but it was a main attraction and central point of kid activities in the 1950s when it had not yet become stagnant and unwanted. We found plenty of things to do around the canal: fishing, rowing boats, hiking along the towpaths, and even skating in winters when it froze over. We could sometimes skate to Minster, three miles away to the south, during hard freezes.

Surrounding towns were located on the county-state highway grid, with most just a few miles apart, linked together by arrow-straight, narrow, two-lane roads. The closest thing to an interstate highway was the Ohio Turnpike in northern Ohio, one hundred miles away, linking the industrial areas of northern Indiana, Ohio, and central Pennsylvania.

Most of the surrounding towns were as small as, or smaller than, New Bremen, generally between five hundred to two thousand people. Very few, if any, had movie theaters or swimming pools. It was farming community after farming community after farming community. Many of these towns were no more than the intersection of two county or state roads, with a gas station, a farm implement dealership, maybe a bar or café with a neon sign above the door saying EAT, the always-present church, and a scattering of houses.

Tall hardwood trees lined New Bremen's streets: oak, maple, ash, hickory, elm, and other species. On the older town streets, they were tall and wide enough to nearly meet over the center of the road. Walking or riding a bicycle down most of the town's streets was like going through quiet, leafy, shady, green tunnels. There was very little ambient noise. Ohio 66 was the only real highway through the town and carried little heavy truck—or, for that matter—automobile traffic. It was a very sleepy little midwestern farm town; there were no leaf blowers, Weedwhackers, power hedge trimmers, turbocharged lawn mowers, chain saws, or wood chippers. In those special years when they were active, the cicadas were sometimes the loudest noise to be heard.

There were some kids with dual exhausts and Cherry Bomb mufflers on their cars, though. And Bill Haley and the Comets were beginning to be heard on the radio, and "Rock Around the Clock" was just around the corner—but we didn't know it then.

There were no radio or TV stations within fifty miles, and TV reception was always marginal. The families who could afford it mounted TV antennas on forty-foot aluminum towers equipped with the antenna rotators made by a then small company in New Bremen. In the fancier parts of town, every house had a TV tower.

The only TV stations—all three of them—were in Dayton. The nearest radio stations in the early '50s were also located in Dayton, which was our metropolis: it entertained us, sent us the news, and was the nearest destination for upscale shopping, first-run hit movies, and, to the extent anyone from New Bremen was enthusiastic about theater, the nearest place for regional theater or big-time stage shows.

Tom Hamlin, the radio and TV celebrity and sports announcer from Dayton, frequently came to New Bremen to announce the big races at our speedway. When back in Dayton and on the air for his 11:00 p.m. wrap-up show that same Sunday night, he always said, "I've been up in God's country today to do the races at New Bremen."

New Bremen's population was extensively middle class—rural middle class. There were upper-middle-class families, but few, if any, really wealthy families. People could afford a new car every few years and sometimes had a second car for the fathers to drive to work or the kids to drive when they were old enough. The second car was usually an old, '30s- or '40s-something Ford or Chevy that sat out, year around—through all weather.

There seemed to be no poor or poverty-stricken families in New Bremen that we knew about. People were very proud and careful to disguise their financial difficulties. There was a spirit of helping men who were out of work to find jobs. I don't think the town would have ever let anyone be unable to feed their families or not have a place to live. There would be a job somewhere, and food would find its way to a doorstep.

There were no racial minorities in New Bremen until the late '40s, when a local company set up a factory to process alfalfa into livestock feed. The workers were mostly black and had moved in from Hope, Arkansas, in the Deep South. In the mid-1950s, a pretty girl from a family working for that business became the first—ever—African American student at New Bremen High School. Ethel began school at NBHS in my freshman class in the fall of 1954. Initially, this was quite a revelation for us, but our class and the other students handled it very graciously, and I've always believed Ethel was well treated, especially by the girls. She became, although probably somewhat distantly, just another member of our class. There was never any overt discrimination shown toward her, and our class—again, especially the girls—went out of its way to include her in activities. We had some—although limited—understanding of how tough it had to be for her. While we didn't know too much about the overt discrimination and segregation in the South, since the TV coverage of the '60s was still ten years away, we were vaguely aware of it. We knew enough to believe that things were probably better for her in New Bremen than whatever she had experienced in Arkansas.

Ethel finished high school and graduated with the other twenty-four of us in 1958—the first African American to graduate from NBHS.

That's not to say there wasn't subtle discrimination by some merchants and adults around town against those few black families living just to the north in the tiny homes provided by the agricultural business. New Bremen certainly wasn't perfect in that regard, but Fred—who owned the Lone Pine gas station where I worked part-time back then—allowed them credit when needed for gas in their cars and the kerosene used for their home heaters.

#

Growing up in that small, peaceful town surrounded by my parents, twelve aunts and uncles, fourteen cousins, two brothers, dozens of school friends and classmates and their parents, many helpful neighbors, and most of the rest of the town's 1,800 residents—all of whom seemed to know my name—was a nurturing environment hard to duplicate anywhere today. Kids could stray and get into trouble if they wanted to, but it was nearly impossible to stray too far or get too deeply into trouble—everyone looked out for everyone else. But in my case, it wasn't for lack of trying.

The number of high school students who graduated then, as well as now, was nearly 100 percent, and the number who immediately went on to some form of additional education, the military, or into a job was nearly the same 100 percent. During a class reunion several years ago, I listened as the high school principal described how the about-to-graduate senior class—with the exception of one individual—had all finalized their plans for either going on to college, joining the military, or had already found an occupation.

That one individual was undecided. He could have been me—forty years earlier.

Duty Calls

Ground Observation Corps Operation Skywatch, New Bremen, Ohio, 1952

Re, Mi, Do, Do, So …
—John Williams, "Theme from *Close Encounters of the Third Kind*"

The New Bremen Opera House burned out in February 2012, nearly destroying the one-hundred-plus-year-old village landmark. It was reported that an after-hours fire in the kitchen of the restaurant that occupied the bottom floor was the probable cause. But the sturdy external brick walls held, and hopefully the building someday will find a new life and purpose. It was another one of the common redbrick multistory-style buildings to be found in New Bremen, but with a stylish, fanciful facade that set it apart a little from most of the more business-oriented downtown buildings. Its official name was the Boesel Opera House, the name dating back to the earliest founders of the town by settlers from northern Germany. By the 1950s, the vaudeville acts, lectures, and operas or plays were things of the past, having been replaced by the movie theater just down the street. In our time, it became the American Legionnaires' hall and was used for meetings, weddings, the village's annual New Year's Eve Dance, our high school's teenagers' dances, and—importantly—the site of our Cold War Skywatch post.

In the early '50s, it seemed as if the skies were full of threats and pending terror. It was the height of the Cold War, and the Russians had nuclear weapons and long-range bombers. We believed that any day, the skies above New Bremen could be black with Russian bombers coming over from the North Pole headed to Dayton and Wright-Patterson Air Force Base, and maybe even Washington, DC. The newspapers talked about the threats every day and, on Sunday, somber-sounding newsmen on the national radio broadcasts talked in depressing tones about the impending threats to the country. Black-and-white television, which was still new then, added its own particular flavor of unpleasantness to it all. The national TV network news programs brought horrific threats—in those grim, grainy telecasts—into our living rooms every night.

The news anchormen—there were no women on the news back then—were all middle aged, not many years removed from their foxhole coverage of WWII and the Korean War, and they presented the news with their unsmiling, five-o'clock-shadow faces. Makeup seemed out of the question for men on TV back then; they always looked dead serious and like someone arriving to tell you about a relative who had just passed away. It seemed the networks placed a priority on somber, never-smiling men dishing out the bad news. Most movies were in Technicolor by then, and even horror movies like the *Murders in the Rue Morgue* seemed a little less terrorizing in color. But because of those grainy, colorless telecasts brooding into our living rooms, depressing things were even more depressing in black and white.

And it was the McCarthy era; Senator Joseph McCarthy was trying his best to scare us all to death. At times, it seemed to work: Russians were everywhere. Maybe our own neighbors were conspiring with them to help guide Russian bombers to important US targets. According to McCarthy, you couldn't trust your own townsfolk.

Say, doesn't that worker's cap on Mr. Jones look a little too communistic?

In addition to the Cold War problems, other things were going on in the skies. Flashing lights and streaking objects moved through the atmosphere at unheard of speeds and with unbelievable agility. They were being seen more commonly across the country and even the rest of the world. Notions of alien beings from distant planets surveilling Earth as a potential conquest were in the back of everyone's minds. It was the era of the UFO.

A new genre of science-fiction movie had evolved, and several were on the silver screens in the early '50s: *The Day the Earth Stood Still* had shocked us, *This Island Earth* had fascinated, and *When Worlds Collide* made us nervous about new ways to die. *The War of the Worlds* made us all understand that we may not have been alone in the universe, and *The Thing* made me distrust large blocks of ice for the rest of my life.

Against this backdrop, the federal government initiated a new civilian air defense project to observe the skies at thousands of points across the United States and provide a traceable monitoring system for enemy aircraft warning until the DEW (Distant Early Warning) Line, a string of long-range radar installations, was constructed across northern Alaska and Canada. Thousands of observation points were to be manned 24-7 by two-person crews working in two-hour shifts, constantly watching for and reporting the movement of all planes in the skies visible to each watch post.

The government was looking for five hundred thousand volunteers. About the only requirement was that the candidates needed to be at least eighteen years of age, have good vision, and be available for two hours each week—sober.

I guess they were having trouble finding the five hundred thousand volunteers. I was still twelve in the summer of 1952—but I would be thirteen and a "teenager" that fall—and they seemed happy to have me. The same was true with my brother, cousins, and other friends.

The specified ideal observation post was a tower twenty to thirty feet in height with a good field of view in all 360 degrees of the compass. I think some leeway was given on this point, however, in view of the fact that, for example, a Russian attacking force was unlikely to be flying from a southerly compass point northward over New Bremen on an inbound target run. So some limits on southern visibility were probably acceptable.

A New Bremen resident, Cliff Harris, who had some military aviation background, had been named Ground Observer Corps coordinator for New Bremen and was tasked with the responsibility of setting up an observation point and finding the manpower to staff the post. There was to be a temporary installation—a tent in his backyard—set up until a real, high-point post could be built.

Cliff had several children, including two daughters, Betty and Cecilia (Sissy), who were of my generation. They both participated in the Skywatch program. Betty was my classmate through all twelve years of my time in New Bremen's school system, and she was a great friend. Betty's older sister, Sissy, a well-known and important figure around town, was *the* person running the New Bremen municipal swimming pool. Sissy was the goddess of swim at the pool: lifeguard, manager, and all-around mother to a bunch of kids spending their days there and giving their moms a little relief.

And there was also a son, Niles, who later became famous for his adventures in Vietnam when he was with the 173rd Airborne and ambushed by the Cong just a few days after stepping out of his transport and arriving in country in Vietnam. The ambush and firefight he experienced that day was later made famous by the country music duo, Big and Rich, in a song titled "8th of November." Niles was just a little grade-school squirt hanging around the Observer Corps tent in those days—which is how I've remembered him—so I couldn't believe my ears one morning a few years ago, while eating breakfast at my home in California, when I heard Don Imus announce at the beginning of his morning MSNBC TV talk show that Niles Harris and the country music duo would be guests later in the show. Niles had been accompanied by Big and Rich back to that battleground in Vietnam so Niles could return to pay homage to his lost soldier mates, many of whom died there that day. He left his old combat boots there on that battlefield on that trip.

As I watched Niles on the Don Imus show that morning, I thought about the times I'd seen him in the summer of '52, a little kid hanging around the Observation Corps tent, wanting to be in on the important work we were doing. And I thought about how few people probably remember, or even now know about, the New Bremen Civilian Air Patrol Ground Observer Corps defending New Bremen and the nation from imminent Russian bomber attacks in those early '50s.

#

This is the untold story.

That first temporary observation post was simply an army surplus tent in Cliff Harris's backyard. Its official purpose was mainly as a training site. There were manuals that showed the various Russian airplanes we were to be looking for, how to tell the different sounds of single-, twin-, and multiple-engine airplanes, and instructions on how to report in on the occasions when we spotted suspicious planes in the vicinity. But there were tall trees nearby to the east, the north, and the south, and the Harris's two-story house was just over to the west, about sixty feet away. We didn't have much in the way of views toward any of the horizons, but we did have a really good view straight up; that is, if it wasn't cloudy or raining—a frequent thing during Ohio summers. But this was only to be a temporary location; an observation post with real, 360-degree views was yet to be set up.

The entire Harris family was, in one way or the other, involved in New Bremen's Skywatch operation. Betty and Sissy were observers, Niles tried to be helpful in any way he could, Cliff's wife brought out lemonade and cookies, and Cliff gave us our marching orders as he waved a clipboard holding sheets covered with places to record various pieces of information about the intruding aircraft.

"Read and memorize these manuals," he commanded while pointing to a thin book containing drawings of Russian aircraft. "Learn to record your sightings in the log clipboard." And, while holding out a black telephone handset, he added, "Learn to report your findings on the special telephone!"

He also laid out the schedules we were to follow. "Two people for each two-hour shift. Work it out for yourselves."

"Yes, sir!" we replied. Then he gave us little lapel pins that included the Civil Air Patrol's emblem. We were working for the US Air Force and defending the country against those sneaky Russians! Every evening before going to bed, I removed that pin from the shirt I had been wearing that day and had it ready to pin on the next day's shirt. I was never going to be without it!

But since the limited sky views in Cliff's backyard weren't leading to much in the way of things to report, we—Betty, Sissy, Pat, Tim, cousins Paul and Bill, and others—spent more time in that temporary "observation point" tent innocently learning more about boys and girls than we did Russian bombers. There were long periods of time needing to be somehow occupied between the occasional Russian bomber overflights in the skies of New Bremen. Spin the bottle—we were twelve and thirteen at the time—became one way of passing some of those long hours.

Boredom leads to finding ways to avoid it.

We needed a real observation post with good, all-compass-points views. And that's where the New Bremen Opera House came into the picture. While we were guarding the country from the backyard tent, some of the town's men built a for-real observation hut on the roof of the opera house. It was a little platform—approximately eight feet by eight feet—on the roof. We reached it by going up the broad stairway to the second floor, which in those days was a large dance hall with a small stage at the back.

To reach the observation hut, we needed to go into the men's coatroom, enter a small closet, and climb up what was essentially a ladder attached to the wall with bolted-on rungs. By climbing that ladder, we could finally go out onto the roof and walk across a kind of walkway leading to the observation hut. Chairs had been added around the sides of the observation platform, so we didn't have to stand or sit on the floor for the entire two-hour shift. All four sides were enclosed by waist-high railings with a widened top surface on one side, providing a flat place for logging our sightings on the form attached to a clipboard. The railings also gave us a steadying location to stabilize our binoculars when getting close-up views of passing airplanes—and probably to keep us from walking all around on the roof, as well.

Of course, there couldn't be any vision-limiting roof. No roof meant no observing in stormy weather; we'd just have to risk sneak attacks during the rain. The possibility of lightning and thunderstorms while on the roof was also a sobering factor.

I don't remember any of the girls from the tent observation days staying with the program when we moved it to the opera house roof. It was a little off-putting to get out there, for one thing, and I imagine their moms had something to do with it too, since most of the time we boys were—or wanted to be—available was primarily in the evenings, after dark and after the swimming pool had closed for the day. New Bremen's moms trusted us boys with their daughters—up to a point—but up on that opera house roof after dark was probably beyond that point.

Up on the roof, you could see all over downtown and several residential streets in all directions. What a cool place to be on warm summer nights; I could never wait for my shift up there to begin!

On the observation platform were the report clipboards and *the* telephone. *The* telephone was an exotic and even intimidating device: no dialing was needed. All you would do to report an aircraft sighting was pick it up. As soon as you picked it up and put it to your ear, you would hear:

"Colonel Wilson here. Please give your report, New Bremen!"

That was really a strange and impressive thing: a twelve- or thirteen-year-old kid picks up a telephone and hears this stern, important-sounding voice asking for a report. It made me feel really important. I always had visions of talking to a man with medals all over his chest who was sitting in a situation room somewhere—probably down at Wright-Patterson—with charts on the walls with little airplanes being moved around on them by lower-level airmen as the reports were phoned in.

But we never had very much to report. New Bremen was not on any flight paths as far as I could tell. There was the occasional multiengine plane flying by off in the distance, but there were never any going by overhead, so we never had any real idea of what we were seeing. We could usually tell if it was a single-, twin-, or a multiple-engine plane from the sound, but we never saw any that were close enough to tell if it was an American or Russian craft. I think we could figure out if it was a Piper Cub or maybe a Cessna, since there were occasionally some of those around. But they didn't sound at all like a warbird; there is no mistaking the way a mighty fighter or bomber sounds compared to a puny, four-cylinder personal aircraft. But to be on the safe side, we reported those, as well.

"Single-engine, unknown aircraft flying at low altitude toward the southwest; time, 8:39 p.m., July 19, 1952," we reported.

"Thank you, New Bremen. Over and out," came the reply from the man with all the medals.

Better yet, though, were the UFOs we saw nearly every night; watch the dark skies long enough and hard enough, and you were bound to see something strange … strange lights off in the distance moving silently through the night—but no sounds! Our UFOs were mostly points of light, slowly moving around in the night sky, looking possibly like serious earthling observations were being made from those silent intruding craft. Occasionally, we saw streaking objects going so fast that there was no time to call them to the attention of our observation shift partners.

"What could that have been?" my frequent observation partner, Cousin Bill, and I asked each other. "Don't know, but we'd better report it. Maybe the Russians have something new."

Most of the airplanes in those days had piston engines and propellers, and they were far from silent. Of course, we didn't know about environmental effects, such as thermoclines and how temperature layers can reflect or channel sound in ways that can redirect or even conceal it. We didn't know about the effects of wind direction on sound, either. They just had to be UFOs with strange, new, silent propulsion systems! After all, we were hearing reports of UFO sightings all the time, and we had been keeping up on all of the latest sci-fi movies from Hollywood. And anyone in the know who followed the UFO phenomena knew about Project Blue Book, the air force effort to investigate and report on all the UFO sightings. But the air force wasn't talking about it. Their refusal to release any information or even acknowledge its existence was all the proof anyone—well, I, anyway—needed to know of the actual reality of extraterrestrials, or worse yet, fantastic new Russian aircraft skittering all over our skies.

"Major Downey here. Please give your report, New Bremen," a voice said over that special telephone.

"UFO sighted west of New Bremen on northeasterly course, engine configuration unknown because of no sounds; time 10:49 p.m., August 3, 1952," I reported.

"What do you mean, UFO?" he demanded.

"We can't hear any engines, and it is moving in starts and stops," I said meekly.

"What do you mean, starts and stops?" asked the major.

"Well, it goes fast for a while, then slows down, and then speeds back up, even faster than before." The words sounded a little strange even to us as they came out of my mouth.

"Thank you, New Bremen. Over and out," the major said.

We thought he should have shown a little more interest in what we were reporting. I'm not saying we wanted to be seeing and reporting UFOs, but we felt we had to report everything we were seeing and hearing—or thought we were seeing and hearing. And reporting UFO sightings had to be more important than reporting Piper Cubs, didn't it?

Our teenage imaginations were going full bore.

Summer went on without any of us seeing much in the way of flights of bombers sneaking in from the north, which we knew was a good thing—but it sure could be boring at times, without even a Piper Cub or UFO to report. So when it came time for the Woodmen's Festival, we found a little temporary relief from our boredom.

The Woodmen's Festival was mainly, at that time, a street carnival that was held right below the opera house on the town's main and widest street. The carny workers were swarthy, sweaty-looking men who seemed as if they were from other places far from Ohio or even other than the USA. We had no idea of what most foreigners looked like, since the only people around New Bremen were all of German descent and looked like ourselves. There weren't any blue-eyed, light-skinned, German-descendant-looking carny workers. They had dark complexions, dark-colored eyes—and lots of tattoos. Some of them even wore earrings! We wondered if they were from one of those eastern states, like New Jersey or maybe Pennsylvania. But we didn't know for sure; we'd never met anyone from New Jersey.

Mothers kept their daughters close by their sides at all times during that week. You could never tell about the carny workers.

But they went about their business setting up all kinds of thrill rides and entertainment booths just below and in front of our observation post. There were no problems, and when showtime began, the men were clean and nicely dressed, working their shows or thrill rides, and no one had a second thought about it any longer—except New Bremen's mothers.

With all the noise and lights, not to mention the distraction of seeing it all just under our post, we weren't reporting much in the way of sneaky, intruding Russian bombers or observation aircraft or even UFOs for a full week, so we alternated the time on our shifts—one watching our friends down below lining up to ride the Caterpillar or the Bullet or the Flying Scooters, with the other watching the skies.

But we didn't leave our post. We were dedicated to staying up there just in case fifty or so Russian bombers flew in low overhead, avoiding Wright-Pat's long-range radar and taking advantage of all the distractions at New Bremen's Woodmen's Festival to sneak past the New Bremen Civil Air Patrol Ground Observation Corps Operation Skywatch observation post.

Our unwavering focus on doing our duty, however, made me almost miss the famous event when my cousin Tommy had his incident with the Flying Scooter.

A Flying Scooter was a motorcycle sidecar-looking thing with a large, vertical fin mounted at the front of the scooter and a pivot allowing it to be rotated left and right by a handhold slot at the back of the fin, just within easy reach of one of the passengers. The scooters were suspended on long chains from large arms rising from the central engine mechanism. When the engine began rotating the arms, the scooters began to travel around the perimeter of the ride, and because of the centrifugal force, they also began to swing up higher and higher as the speed increased. Moving the fin—airfoil—left or right allowed one of the passengers to steer the scooter in toward the central mechanism that was rotating the entire ride or out toward the extreme perimeter, higher and higher depending on how the fin was positioned.

It happened one night when I was on watch, but I wasn't exactly sure of what had taken place, and I didn't know Tommy was the pilot of that scooter. I had been dutifully watching the skies at the time—with one eye—but watching the action down in the carnival scene with the other when it happened. Because of the distance to the scooter ride and the evening lighting, I only knew that something unusual had happened. The operator quickly shut down the scooters and wildly gestured, shaking his fist at someone—a teenage boy—and stamping his feet.

Tommy, I learned, had managed to fly his scooter out to an unexpected distance and height by first cutting his scooter in very close to the central engine and strut mechanism and then back out so that when centrifugal force took his scooter out as far and as high as the chains could extend, he glanced off the Amstutz Egg Hatchery's second-story brick wall.

The scooter suffered some bent sheet metal, but the egg hatchery was undamaged, although some eggs may have been lost.

I would have gladly let a Cessna or two, or even a pack of UFOs, slip by to have watched that event. But, after all, I was watching the skies and obeying the call of duty. Tommy never mentioned exactly how his conversation with the ride's operator went that night as the man unlocked the scooter's safety door and "helped" him from the seat. But it probably went something like this:

"What the hell do you think you're doing, kid?" the operator demanded, jabbing his finger in Tommy's face.

"Nothing. I was just thinking I'd have a little extra fun," Tommy replied with a shrug. Knowing Tommy as I did, he probably would have added, "By the way, you need to move the ride out toward the middle of the street another three feet."

The ride was then shut down and relocated farther into the road so that no wild kid would manage to do that again. Banning Tommy for the duration of the festival might also have been considered.

After the festival ended, things went back to the by then humdrum of mysterious UFO sightings—which we realized we were probably never going to be able to understand—and far off, multiengine aircraft that we couldn't see. We reported everything we did see and some things we only heard too, but little else happened. It was all getting to be a little bit boring. We had signed up for action, and we weren't getting any. So, like any twelve- or thirteen-year-old kids, we needed to find new things to maintain our interest while waiting for the Russian attacks.

Well, Howell's IGA was just down the street, and they normally left their large stacks of watermelons out overnight. Such was the security of life in the '50s in a small town like New Bremen that store managers felt comfortable leaving goods out on the sidewalk overnight. We didn't take many, and they only cost twenty-five cents each if you bought one, so how bad was it to help ourselves to one every now and then when in the service of our country? We did feel bad about the watermelon rinds smashed on the sidewalk and street below, though, and we swore we'd never do it again—*every time.* And I did walk on the other side of the street whenever I saw schoolmate Dick Howell, the son of the IGA market's owner, Freeze Howell, coming my way on a sidewalk.

We also found that hiding behind the front wall by the edge of the roof provided a great position for launching water balloons late at night toward semitrailer trucks passing by. We had convinced ourselves that it was good training for launching Molotov cocktails in the preparation for the possible upcoming Russian invasions, which seemed to be more and more likely, according to the daily news reports.

"General Dempsey here. New Bremen, what is your report?" the voice would have said.

"Russian tanks heading south on Ohio State Route 66 at State Route 274. We're attacking with Molotov cocktails," I imagined. "*New Bremen, over and out. Pray for us.*"

But our failing to thoroughly pick up all water balloon attack fragments from the street and sidewalk below led to some suspicion on the Skywatch coordinator's part, what with all the red, green, yellow, and various other colored pieces of thin rubber lying around down there.

"Bobby, you and Bill were on watch last night until ten. Do you know anything about all these pieces of balloons lying all around down there?" Cliff asked.

"N-n-no, sir," I answered.

"And someone has been throwing watermelon rinds down here too!"

"We'll keep our eyes open for whoever it is and let you know, sir," I promised.

And so we had to leave our guerilla training unfinished after only a couple of weeks of our resistance-heroes-in-training exercise. Someone else would have to stop the Red Army's tanks when they drove through New Bremen.

We went back to concentrating on watching the skies again, hoping but failing to find excitement there. As fall approached, we began to realize that New Bremen was probably not going to be action central for the Cold War turned hot, if there was going to be any escalation that year. And soon it became too cold to stay up on the unsheltered observation post as the summer turned into fall and school duties fell back onto our shoulders. The grand defense of the country would have to be put off until better weather and the end of the school year next spring. The Russians weren't going to attack us over the winter, anyway, were they?

I guess the DEW Line finally must have been completed by the next year, though, because the call for volunteers never went out again.

Well, whatever; they didn't call me.

The Carbide Cannon Incident

Johnny's in the basement, mixing up the medicine.
—Bob Dylan, "Subterranean Homesick Blues"

Four restless and excitement-hungry fourteen-year-old kids were feeling bored. It was the middle of another summer between school years in our small Ohio farm community, stiflingly hot and not much going on. We were too young to drive, there were no older friends with wheels around, and most kids with connections had summer jobs to earn spending money. We were just four bored kids and their bikes.

The Fourth of July had come and gone, and all allowance and paper-route money had all been spent on firecrackers, rockets, and torpedoes the previous week. The excitement—what little there was—of the Fourth was history. Mainly, our days consisted of going to the municipal swimming pool—again—and checking out the girls. For the most part, it was a futile exercise; we were too skinny, too gawky, carless, penniless, and clueless anyway. Well, except for Ray. Ray was our coolest classmate—he had a ducktail haircut! That was very radical; the only ducktail haircut we had ever seen before that was worn by James Dean in *Rebel Without a Cause.* But that was Ray—he always marched to a different drummer than the rest of our class.

The four of us were really from different New Bremen social circles, meaning that our parents did not know the other kids' parents well and so didn't socialize. Our primary common bond was that we had all been classmates since first grade. For the few short weeks of that summer, however, we were bonded not only by our boredom but also by our personalities and some common interests. Ray, Ted, and I shared a passion for building balsa wood and paper model airplanes. At Ray's home, there was a barn that included a little walled-off workshop on the north side, separate from the bigger open areas, that was a perfect hideaway for building model airplanes and just hanging out. It was the meeting place of our airplane cult. There was always the wonderful—to us—smell of airplane glue and paint—or dope, as it was called then. *Dope* actually was a good name for it; after an hour or two of gluing or painting planes, hallucinations were possible. I guess we were ahead of our time.

Barns were a wonderful aspect of life for a kid in probably any town in the Midwest, and in New Bremen, most homes had a barn out back. The barns served primarily as garages in the '50s—that is, for the parents. But for the kids, barns were everything—places to play with friends, hide out from the adults, build things like '50s-style skateboards (metal-wheeled, clamp-on roller skates nailed to 2×4s), soapbox racers, and model airplanes, painting our bikes, and so on. The world was at your fingertips if you just had a barn in the backyard.

Barns were also the place where great plots and adventures were hatched. We planned hikes, bike rides, watermelon heists, and all kinds of summer events in the wonderful secrecy of the barn.

Unfortunately, the Gilberg family didn't have a damned barn. All my barn fun had to be found in my friends' barns. Maybe that's why I always wanted a barn—and still do.

There were two things I always felt I missed out on as a kid. We didn't have a barn, and I never had a sister. One result was that I always felt like I never really quite got to know what living around a girl was like until I got married. It's tough adjusting to that experience after you are already in your midtwenties. I always figured that I would have been a better-adjusted guy if my parents had just had a barn and a daughter. On the other hand, I did have my own bedroom, with a large walk-in closet hideout, and two pretty good brothers.

Anyway, it was in Ted's barn (the barns really didn't belong to the parents; they belonged to the kids who happened to be living in the parental house) where the great carbide cannon incident came to life. And it was there, just by the cherry tree, midway between Ted's barn and the family home, where it ended and the legend was born.

The Participants

Poor Ted! It was never clear to me afterward how he got mixed up with us that summer. Ted was one of the straightest guys and best students in our high school class. His grades were always up there in the top five or six of the twenty-six students. Ray and I were middle-of-the-pack kind of guys who weren't that serious about studying and were on our way to becoming motor heads. Eventually, we threw off all pretensions of being scholars and started hanging out with guys with driver's licenses and cars. I guess it must have been the model airplane passion that, at least temporarily, threw us together.

Ray, like me, was interested in model airplanes, cars, and most things with motors. But he was also into outdoor things—hunting, fishing, and even trapping. He was the only kid I knew who had traplines in ponds, creeks, and the canal for trapping muskrats around the outskirts of town. I had never even seen a muskrat—and still haven't. They seemed to me to be some mythical creature not seen since the early settlers had cut down most of the native trees and greatly changed the landscape. With all the fishing, hiking, and playing I had done around the ponds and streams near New Bremen, I had never seen a muskrat.

Ray also liked to "practice" at squirrel hunting—I say "practice" because no one I ever knew had successfully hunted squirrels; it is impossible to catch one off guard and be able to shoot it. So you practice, but never do really hunt them. They know you are coming before you even walk into the woods and probably even before we could get off our bicycles. But Ray hunted squirrels and trapped muskrat. No one else did these things.

And then there was Charlie. Charlie had a little less in common with the rest of us. To describe him, and putting it gently, well, it's best to just say that he wasn't the most eager student. He didn't build model airplanes, didn't chase girls, wasn't into sports, and had a very independent view of life. His opinion on studying and getting good grades was that it didn't make any difference anyway, so why bother? He didn't know if he was going to finish his twelfth year—maybe graduate and maybe not; either was okay—and then probably go to work at the Meadow Gold Creamery for the rest of his life.

Or maybe not. It just didn't make any difference to him; life didn't start for real until they let you out of high school, and then you just figured things out from there. That's when things counted; all the stuff before that was just stuff adults made kids do. At some times, I think we were all worried he might be right, but we were also afraid to believe in it. It was a big gamble.

Charlie was skinny. He looked like a candidate for the Charles Atlas ads in the back of *Popular Mechanics*. He was the kid in the ad who the bullies kicked sand on. And he slouched like no one I have ever known before or since. I think he got the look from Brando and others in *Blackboard Jungle*. We all wanted to look like the toughs from the movie, with "motorcycle boots," turned-up collars, and rolled-up jeans. But for most of us, being short, fair-skinned, blue-eyed Ohio farm boys made that improbable. Charlie perfected the look, though. It also may have been because he was fairly tall. Tall kids were unusual around New Bremen then, and being tall wasn't as cool as it is today in our sports-minded world. The slouch may have been an attempt to look like the rest of us short kids. Skateboarders today, with the backward baseball caps, sloppy, baggy, below-the-knee shorts, and hanging shirttails, have no idea of what a "cool" slouch look is. Charlie had it patented.

Charlie also smoked cigarettes long before the rest of us. He was already smoking in junior high and had a hacking cough by the time he was sixteen. But Charlie was also a fun guy with a friendly sense of humor, who was willing to go along with anything and everything the guys wanted to do. He had an impish face and sparkling eyes that told you that he was ready for a fun time at the drop of a hat. You could not dislike Charlie.

Charlie, like the rest of us, also occasionally hunted. He had an old, "been-in-the-family-a-long-time," Iver Johnson 16-gauge, single-round shotgun. The hammer was worn down by so many years of hunting that it could—and did—slip from the grip if the hunter wasn't very careful when cocking or uncocking it.

That hammer had a very heavy pull, and with the serrations mostly worn away on the part of the hammer where you placed your thumb when cocking and uncocking it, the gun bearer had to be extremely careful to make sure that he had a good grip on the hammer—and the gun pointed straight down at the ground.

Charlie nearly shot off my right leg one year while we were hunting. He had missed an opportunity to shoot at a flushed rabbit and was uncocking the gun when the hammer slipped away from his thumb. The shot blew out a twelve-inch-diameter patch of brush just in front of where I was about to place my right foot. We discussed gun handling and how to please point the g—— gun away from everyone in the hunting line in the future. I used the strongest words I knew at that point in my life, which weren't much different from the ones I'd choose today—and I'm a lot less inhibited in 2014, nearly sixty years later. We could all cuss pretty good back then, even though it was the Pleasant Fifties; but up to that point, I hadn't known I could cuss like that.

"Charlie, Jesus H. Christ! What the hell are you doing? You have to point that f—— thing at the ground in front of you whenever you mess with that hammer!" I shouted.

"Sorry," Charlie said mutedly.

"Go down to the end of the line with that g—— thing so it's not pointed at the rest of us when we're line walking," I ordered.

Charlie did as told, lit a cigarette, and—holding it between his lips, both hands on the gun—walked the line with us. There were no more misadventures, but we all nervously watched every move he made after that. We probably missed any number of rabbits that day because, out of the corners of our eyes, we were all watching every move Charlie made.

Ted never smoked. Ray and I were just starting to occasionally smoke Lucky Strikes. We rolled the cigarette package up into our T-shirt sleeves because our Levi's were too tight to allow them to fit them into the pockets without completely crunching up perfectly good cigarettes. We rode our bicycles and smoked Lucky Strikes at the same time. We thought it was cool, but we had to be careful to keep the hot ashes from flying back into our eyes. We didn't smoke around our model airplane factory, though. All that stuff was highly flammable, and we didn't want to risk losing Ray's barn.

I was the smallest kid of the bunch back then—skinny, short, bespectacled, and sporting the most common haircut in those days: a flattop where the top was cut absolutely flat and the sides shorn almost down to the scalp. Flatness was the measure of a flattop. A perfectly flat haircut was perfection. Our local barber, Ernie, had even perfected a device he used to produce the most perfect, absolutely flat and level flattop in the county. It was an adjustable stand with a swiveling arm that held an electric razor. He would set the razor at the right height for your head, make you sit perfectly still, and rotate the razor horizontally through your hair, changing the radius with each pass until the entire head of hair was a flat as a billiard table.

My ears stuck out like handles, but my haircut was *flat.*

Why the flattops were so popular back then was a good question, but we all had them. Most of us certainly didn't look that handsome with them; *jug-eared* is a pretty good description. Maybe it was because Ernie was so good at them. We thought Ernie had to be the fastest barber around; a flattop only took around fifteen minutes. My dad claimed that Ernie could cut your hair just in the time it took to walk past his shop; you didn't even have to go in and sit in the chair.

Our interests were, like most of us male kids back then, whatever was in the latest issue of *Popular Science* or *Popular Mechanics.* They were always discussing things like how to build a sailboat out of a rowboat and a parachute, or cars that could fly, or jet-powered model airplanes or cars. We could dream, even if we didn't have any of the skills, parts, or money to do most of that stuff. But we could tinker away in our barns or our dads' garages. At that age, with a barn or a garage or maybe even a basement, our dads' tools and scrap wood, metal pieces, or water pipe, a kid could visualize making anything. We all liked tinkering with stuff.

#

So there you have the cast: a very good student and the school's … ah … well … most disinterested student, with Ray and me somewhere in between. A dedicated nonsmoker, Ted, a dedicated long-term smoking addict, Charlie, and two who smoked but only away from classes and home, pushing their *cool* look. Three of us were into building model airplanes, and one had no visible interests of any kind, other than having a good time—Charlie. That long, so-far-boring summer, we were desperately in need of something exciting that we could do together.

A Carbide What?

Then we heard about carbide cannons. It seems that all the older generation knew about carbide cannons but had never mentioned them before. One evening when my dad and an uncle were reminiscing about their old days around New Bremen, they talked about having carbide cannons when they were kids. But none of our younger generation knew of anyone having one anymore. They seemed to be like all those other old, bygone things parents talked about in the evenings when they reminisced with friends—cool-sounding things that no one had seen in years, like high-wheeler bicycles and the like.

"Dad, just what is a carbide cannon, anyway?" I asked.

"Well, it's just a little thing that looks like a cannon that uses carbide instead of gunpowder," he said.

"Why?"

"Well, it's safer," he replied.

"How so?"

"Just because," he said, starting to look a little irritated.

"Oh, okay, I see." I didn't question *just because*. "And does that mean we could have one?"

"Maybe, but I don't know where you'd find one. I haven't seen one of them in lots of years," he mused.

Typical, wasn't it? Something a fourteen-year-old kid could probably have a lot of fun with but no one bothered to keep. I guess that was long before keeping and collecting old stuff got popular. Everything and anything that fell into disuse or became damaged either went into the basement to rust and rot or into the attic to gather dust and get crushed under more and more stuff as the years went by. Finally, then, when the homeowners became too old to stay in their houses any longer or passed away, the stuff got carted out into the yard and auctioned off. These were old-time auctions with real auctioneers in straw hats and suspenders, who chewed tobacco, spitting into a spittoon or on the lawn whenever the bidding got hot and they needed to articulate their auctioneer chatter faster. The auctioneer held up each piece in turn and started the bidding with an arbitrary price, or a price that his experience told him was the right price to start with, and then he'd go into the auctioneer's routine. I had visions of how the last carbide cannon in the county was sold at one of those auctions:

"I've got a nice carbide cannon here. Let's start the bidding for this nearly new toy cannon at seventy-five cents," said the sweating, red-faced auctioneer. "Who'll give me seventy-five cents for this marvelous toy cannon? Sebentyfive, sebentyfive, sebentyfive, abbadddaabbbbaa, bababdabbaseventyfive, abbabbaabbbba, sebentyfive, babbbab—you, sir? Sebentyfive it is. I have sebentyfive cents. Now who'll give me one dollar for this here perfect little cannon?" said the auctioneer, wiping tobacco juice from the corner of his mouth with the back of his hand. "You can call the family to supper with this toy cannon! Who'll give me a dollar for this toy cannon? One dollar, one dollar, one dollar, babbabbabba, dabbaddabba, babbbabbbabaaaab, one dollar?" he yelled, wiping the back of his hot, wrinkled, red neck with a blue-and-white handkerchief. "Come on, people, this here's the best toy cannon in Auglaize County. Even Judge Hautenbergerstein told me it's the best—one dollar, folks—babbbabbadabbbaaddaba—abbadabbbabbba—how about you, sir? I have a one-dollar bid from the gentleman in the back for this perfect toy cannon!

"Listen, farmers, you can use this here cannon to scare the crows and starlings out of yer fields with just a shot or two. I have a dollar. Who'll give me a dollar twenty-five? I need a dollar twenty-five—need a dollar and a quarter—a buck twenty-five—who's got a buck and a quarter?"

And on and on for my toy cannon, I imagined, with the bidding inching higher by a nickel or sometimes a dime and the auctioneer waving his hammer in one hand and his tobacco-stained handkerchief in the other. The hotter the bidding got, the darker the handkerchief became. A trickle of tobacco juice always seemed to escape the corner of his mouth and drip partway down his chin until the handkerchief would make a fast swipe and quickly be back, waving around in the air, the fast move almost invisible to most auction watchers.

"Going once, going twice … gone, to the bidder with the John Deere hat and red bandanna in the back for one dollar and seventy-five cents!" he said as he unbuttoned his long-sleeved white shirt one more button—revealing even more gray chest hairs—and readjusting his suspenders while hiking up his sagging baggy trousers. Then he lifted his straw hat a few inches off his balding head to let some heat out.

That's probably how the last carbide cannon in Auglaize County got away from us—sold to someone who probably then forgot he had it. And as we were soon to decide, we just had to have one.

But we kids didn't know a thing about carbide cannons other than what we'd heard from the older generation.

They sounded really neat. Little, shiny, brass miniature cannons that actually might be able to shoot things like marbles. Apparently, they were used at sporting events as starting guns—but without projectiles—because they made such a loud bang. And they were very popular toys at Fourth of July time during our dads' and uncles' childhoods just after the turn of the twentieth century and on into the first few decades. But later on, carbide cannons were replaced by handheld pistols firing blank ammunition, which is probably why they were no longer around during the '50s.

How the subject of carbide cannons first came up is a little fuzzy now, but it probably came up while sitting outside on one of those hot July evenings when it was too warm to be in the house and everyone stayed outside around the smudge pots until it cooled off enough to go in to bed.

Smudge pots were essential appliances for survival in the Midwest in the '50s. They were just large-size coffee cans filled with dirt, and we poured enough kerosene into the can to fully saturate the enclosed soil. The pots, when lit, would slowly burn and give off an oily, smelly smoke that was supposed to ward off mosquitoes.

Enough smudge pots and you could keep the mosquitoes at bay clear over to Lock Two!

Lock Two was the little town of no more than twenty houses built at the site of the second lock on the Miami and Erie Canal going north from New Bremen. The towns are roughly one mile apart and at that time held a very stagnant section of the canal between them. It was a mosquito haven. The area produced a huge number of mosquitoes—probably enough mosquitoes to populate the entire state of Ohio, given the right wind conditions. The smudge pots were undoubtedly overmatched by the canal's booming mosquito production, but they at least worked long enough for a few hours in the backyard.

Usually, we had the benefit of the summertime fogging truck to keep the mosquitoes down, but in the several weeks between the fog truck's rampage through town, we had to do something when the mosquitoes counterattacked, hence the smudge pots. These fog trucks were pickup trucks outfitted with some kind of machine mounted in the truck's bed that emitted a fog of a DDT-based gas. It had a kind of grinding sound that all of us kids recognized at the first hint of its arrival. We'd hear it clear across town in the late-evening hours—which were chosen, I guess, because it was assumed that the citizens were all in bed and not wandering around and so were not likely to be exposed to the gassing of the town. But any late bar patrons—New Bremen didn't have any town drunks—wandering home at these times were on their own. Of course, we had no idea at that time that there was DDT in the gas, but we probably wouldn't have cared, anyway.

Funny how there was never any advance notice of this attack on the mosquito population or any mention of staying indoors or warnings to use respirators—or notices to the elderly, the infants, the infirm, or those with breathing issues to stay in the house and to try not to breathe. But it was the '50s, and there was no EPA in those days. We just all trusted the government and industry and didn't question authority. It would be another ten years before Bob Dylan warned us about being careful in whom we trusted.

The truck just appeared late at night—around nine or ten—and started gassing the streets, alleys, parking lots, and our section of Ohio State Route 66. Our curiosity was stronger than our judgment at that time in our lives. We'd jump on our bicycles, no matter what the time, and ride to find the truck. We just had to find it and then ride behind it, breathing in the fumes—gases—just to see what it was all about. The driver never seemed to mind—or care about any possible harmful effects, for that matter. He didn't try to warn us away; maybe he didn't like kids.

We kids didn't know exactly what the gas was; all we knew was that it was bad for mosquitoes, but we somehow assumed that it was okay for us to breathe. They wouldn't spray it all over town if it wasn't safe, would they? What logic convinced us of that rationale still escapes me.

What the heck—getting a little cough was an okay trade-off for not getting malaria, right?

So when we sat in our backyards relying on smudge pots to hold off the mosquitoes during those long, hot nights, waiting for the house to cool down, those kerosene fumes could go to work on us. There had to be some hallucinogenic effect—probably at least as much as riding behind the fog trucks. Sitting out there late into the night in the summertime, listening to the adults talk, breathing in the kerosene fumes, we could imagine and dream almost anything.

Anything—like having a carbide cannon. If only we could get our hands on a carbide cannon, our summer would be complete.

But we had no idea of how to find one, since this was before the Internet, eBay, and Google. In those days, if they didn't carry it at Abbott's Hobby Shop or the five-and-dime store, our best shot at finding stuff was in *Popular Mechanics* or *Popular Science* or sometimes *True* magazine—back there in the pages with all those little ads for radio-controlled airplanes, the Rosicrucians, rare postage stamps, acne creams, Charles Atlas, and other neat stuff.

The problem was that if you found something you wanted, you had to order it through the US Postal Service, and that meant that you had to go to the post office, get a money order, and include it in the envelope along with your letter asking some anonymous person in some particular company, "Please accept my order for an XYZ Widget," signed Bobby Gilberg.

Back then, something you found and ordered in May was lucky to be delivered that same summer. You spent the days waiting breathlessly for your letter to be received and processed and the product trucked back to your house. Even worse, it was likely that your mom would find it in the mail before you did. And, of course, that was downright dangerous or embarrassing, depending on what you had ordered. The odds were pretty high that it would be confiscated before you even knew it had arrived. I could have been out playing softball or at the swimming pool or on an all-day bike adventure when it arrived, and, of course, then I would find myself standing there explaining why I needed a such and such.

No, ordering a carbide cannon wasn't an option. We were going to have to make our own.

The Plan

Since we were all handy with our dads' tools and stray pieces of water pipe, discarded bits of wood, nails, screws, and stuff, it seemed that we could build our own cannon using just our imaginations and whatever we could find lying around our houses.

It may have been Ted's idea and design—since he grew up to be a mechanical engineer—but it seemed to all of us that some water pipe and fittings would be all that was needed. We could start simple, with no wheels or polished brass in the beginning, perfect the design, and maybe then get fancier as we became better cannoneers. We quickly agreed on the design: a twelve-inch piece of three-quarter-inch threaded water pipe with a tiny hole drilled near one end for lighting the charge and a pipe cap for the cannon back. We could add a fancy gun carriage with axles and wheels later, when we were ready to show off our ingenuity and mechanical skills.

With the design mastered, the key thing then was to get the project going. We could get the hardware right out of our barns and basements, which was the easy part. The next fundamental and bigger question was where to get the carbide.

All it took was a little asking around, and we found that we might be able to get the carbide at the New Bremen Machine and Tool Shop, owned by Norbert (Norb) Roettger.

We went there the next day, four kids and their bicycles, meekly walking into a machine shop where grown men were working with lathes and mills.

"Mr. Roettger, we'd like to buy some carbide, please," Ray said.

"Why do you kids want carbide?" Norb asked, skepticism showing all over his face.

"We're gonna make a carbide cannon," Ray answered.

"Okay, and how much carbide do you want for your cannon?" Norb wanted to know, showing more interest.

"How much can we get for two dollars?" I asked. We had each chipped in fifty cents.

"Five pounds."

We all looked at each other wondering if it would be enough, when Ray said, "Sounds okay to us."

Norb disappeared into a back room and within a few minutes returned, carrying a large cardboard box. "Kids, if there is one thing you need to do, it's make sure you keep it dry. That's why I packed it in a plastic bag before putting it in the box," he said.

We all looked at each other. "Sure, whatever."

We didn't know it, but carbide—when mixed with water—becomes acetylene gas, used by machine shops for cutting and welding torches. All we knew was that carbide was needed for carbide cannons.

And we had no idea how much carbide a carbide cannon used per charge, but five pounds sounded like enough to do whatever we needed. We scooted out of there like a pack of thieves. We had our carbide, and we had a design for the cannon. We had the rest of the summer, and we finally had excitement we craved. It was going to be a very successful summer, after all.

The Cannon

The cannon was a flop. We couldn't get it to fire. It just fizzled and fizzled. No bang! No marble projectiles rocketing across the barn and disintegrating into shrapnel against the walls. Nothing—just foamy stuff running out of the business end of the cannon. And worse, we couldn't figure out what was going wrong.

There was no way we could make the cannon work. We put some water down the pipe, added some carbide, and before we could get "Fire in the hole!" things had just fizzled out the end of the barrel. We had no clue about how real carbide cannons worked.

Since studying up on the matter, it is clear that inside these simple-looking toys was some pretty serious engineering at work. It turns out that we'd used way too much carbide and water. Later on, having done a little reading about it, I learned that a typical charge of carbide per shot in the smaller cannons amounts to about 0.0025 ounces per shot—about as much as you can put on the end of you little fingernail. And the better cannons had an internal mechanism that fed just the right amount of carbide powder and water into a separate firing chamber. We didn't have any special chamber or loading mechanism. We were using gobs of the stuff; we were shoveling it in there by the teaspoon. We wanted a big bang, and we had five pounds of the stuff to light off. We were trying to go big time, fast.

We had bought enough carbide to fire our water pipe cannon *ten thousand times* or more—in other words, probably enough to level the town, or at least enough to drive all the swallows, crows, robins, and other bird life over to nearby Kettlersville for the rest of the summer.

But our cannon miserably only dribbled everything out the front of the barrel. Our enthusiasm for cannons was beginning to suffer. Clearly, we didn't know what we were up against. Our model for how this thing should work had been like gunpowder cannons: the cannoneers loaded everything in from the front, jumped out of the way, and lit it off at the touch hole.

Ha, in our dreams!

What Else Can You Do with Five Pounds of Carbide?

It was getting to be late in the morning, and after spending too many frustrating hours being continually defeated by this thing, we were ready for something else. The "something else" was another fascinating-sounding use for carbide that our dads and uncles told us they had in their "good old days." We were getting a little dubious by then.

Supposedly, the other great thing you could do with carbide was blow up trash cans. Now this didn't sound quite as neat as a cannon, but it did have some appeal. Allegedly, the thing you were really going to do was blow the lids off trash cans to unimaginable heights.

Our fathers were using numbers like one hundred feet. All you had to do was place an "amount" (funny how no one ever knew exact measurements) of carbide in the bottom of an empty trash can, add "an amount" of water, slam the lid on, and stand back.

And, yes, we wanted to make sure that the can had been emptied and was clean before adding the carbide and water. In this case, there was no need to light the gas; just the sudden expansion of the gas was supposed to be enough to blow the lid into Shelby County.

So we would do the trash-can thing and salvage the summer—and find a great purpose for the nearly still full, five-pound box of carbide. We had to have something special to remember over the coming winter, and that large box was starting to become something of a dark cloud. I mean, what do you do with enough carbide to level the town? Where can you safely store it? What happens if it accidentally gets wet down there in the basement of your parents' house or back in the leaky barn where we tried to hide it from prying parental eyes?

In those days, our garbage cans held thirty-five gallons and were made of galvanized metal—not tin, mind you; we're talking sheet metal. They were indestructible and lasted forever. They didn't rust, they didn't get holes poked in them, and they didn't crack after standing in the sun for twenty or thirty years. But they did get bent up. They were all bent and beat up from tens of years of being bounced in and out of Harold Ahlers's garbage truck. None of New Bremen's garbage cans were round anymore. They were all either sort of elliptical or some form of a polygon, and none of them had matching lids. The elliptical can had a polygon lid; the polygon can with five sides had a polygon lid with six sides, and so on.

What that meant to us cannoneers was that the damned things didn't seal! We put the carbide in, we put some water in, and the thing would just sit there and fizzle. Just like the water pipe cannon did.

We began to understand that there was a level of precision needed in this armament manufacturing business that might just be beyond our capabilities. This may have been our first encounter with concepts like "qualifications" and "background" and "skill sets." Ugh, we just wanted to do it!

Maybe Charlie was selling education a little short?

After trying the trash-can rocketry thing a few more times, we could see that it wasn't going to take us into the world of excitement that we had been visualizing. We were never going to impress any of our friends with our trash-can rockets when all we could manage was some fizzle dripping over the can's sides. Something had to be done—and fast—to salvage our dream.

The Depth-Charge Experiment

I may be the one who came up with this idea—after all, the canal was my favorite playground—and I have to admit that I had a passion for playing with firecrackers. Tossing firecrackers into the canal had always been fascinating for me, and it was a perfectly normal way to play with fireworks for many of us kids growing up around the canal in those days. We had all been to some WWII movies showing destroyers depth-charging German submarines. We pretended that we were American sailors blowing up German subs by tossing firecrackers into the canal. And while we didn't kill any enemies or civilians, we did traumatize a few carp and catfish. Cherry bombs worked the best; they had waterproof fuses that would not go out underwater. How neat was that?

Well, anyway, whoever thought of it over our lunch of Eskimo Pies hit it on the nose. A little carbide and water placed in a Mason jar was a thing of beauty. And we had finally gotten the "amount" thing right; we realized that using just the smallest amount needed gave us the best results. It allowed us time to get that Mason jar lid screwed on tight before the thing blew up in our hands. A lesson in "just in time" manufacturing. It's still a wonder to me that none of us got fragged in that episode.

But the Mason jar bomb was, to us, perfection. It was just the right size to handle and throw, the lid screwed on nicely to produce a gas-tight seal—and Ted's mom had a whole case of them on the back porch.

But the Early Release 1.0 devices just floated on top of the water until they blew up. This was not a good idea since the glass shards covered the distance to the canal bank faster than we could run.

"Jesus Christ, Charlie, throw that thing out farther!" Ray screamed—a little late, just before it exploded as it hit the water.

"This could be a little tricky!" Ted worriedly yelled.

"We need to make these things sink!" Charlie offered.

"Let's put rocks in the jar before we put the carbide and water in," I said as the engineer in me woke up.

And Ray added, "Then throw the damn thing before it explodes!"

So the new design (Release 1.1) included rocks in the jar. We depth-charged the canal from the top of the locks until we ran out of Mason jars. Since we had spent all our money at the Norb's machine shop buying the carbide, we were too broke to buy more Mason jars, and we didn't really want to steal more from Ted's mother, who was in the process of canning fruit.

So, having mastered the art of depth charges and leaving the canal pretty much the worse for wear, what with all the groggy fish dizzily swimming around at the surface, we at last felt that we had gotten good value out of our carbide investment. Oh yes, and since people did occasionally swim in the canal, our consciences left us feeling a little guilty about all that broken glass in the muddy canal bottom, and we decided to end the project on a positive note. And since the top of the locks was mid-downtown and not exactly a secluded place to be perfecting our depth-charge devices, we knew we had been pushing our luck with the town chief of police: a gruff but kindly and elderly Ichabod Crane–looking man named Molly Wehrman. But kids played around up there routinely, and it seemed no one had been paying us any attention, probably figuring that we were just doing the usual kid things—like skipping rocks and throwing at anything that moved around in the water. We looked as innocent as we could, skipping away from the canal's locks like a band of kids leaving Sunday school before Molly or any other adults showed up.

The Cistern, the Ultimate Challenge

It was getting to be late in the afternoon, and we had been at our carbide projects since our early morning visit to the machine shop where we had purchased the now boring powder. We were beginning to tire of too much science with too meager results. But we had finally begun to understand the complexity of working with volatile gases and by then had had some limited success, even though we didn't have a spiffy cannon we could demonstrate for people. We still had most of that big box of carbide left.

And, speaking honestly, we were anxious to be off on to some new adventures the next day involving flaming model airplanes. No use repeating stuff we had already "mastered," we figured.

So, what to do with the roughly four pounds of carbide that no one really wanted to take home and sneak under his bed or hide somewhere that an adult might find it? Making explanations about that is tricky—you just dig deeper and deeper.

After having left the canal in smoking ruins and being back at Ted's barn late that same afternoon, we were laughing over the day's adventures. Charlie was having a cigarette, and the rest of us were watching him smoke while we puzzled over what to do next. Even then, teenagers had an insatiable need for "what's next?"

"So, what do we do now with all this stuff?" Ted asked no one in particular.

No one wanted to keep the carbide; we were beginning to realize that it represented some danger, and it would be too hard to explain to any parent.

"I don't know. I don't want to keep riding around with it in my bike basket," I said.

"I'm not gonna take it home and hide it in my barn," Ray insisted.

"Me either!" Ted added.

We were sitting, leaning against the barn's side, looking toward Ted's house when, seemingly, we all noticed the lid covering the cistern at the same time.

Aha, the cistern! We all looked at each other and grinned.

Cisterns were cement chambers in the ground for storing water from the houses' rain gutters. After some settling time, the water was then used for nonpotable household purposes. By the 1950s, with city water available nearly everywhere in New Bremen, most cisterns had fallen into disuse, but in many cases, the cisterns were still in place, covered by those giant cement lids weighing hundreds of pounds. The lid usually had a small hole in the center that had allowed the placement of a cast-iron hand pump. However, in those days, most cisterns no longer had hand pumps installed, since the water was no longer being used for household purposes, so the cisterns still sat there in the ground, marked by their huge cement lids, drawing the fascination of any inquiring kid's mind. And even without the rain gutters feeding water into the cisterns, they usually had small amounts of water in them from normal rainfall and seepage.

Maybe this was the opportunity to use the remaining carbide in one last big gusher of acetylene gas! Although we didn't think of it as acetylene gas at the time. Since we had never managed to ignite the stuff after a whole day of trying, I think we all thought of it as "fizzy stuff" that expanded quickly, like compressed air.

"Let's dump it in the cistern!" Charlie said.

"How about that?" I asked everyone but no one in particular.

"Why not?" Ray replied.

Ted, who might have wanted to slow things down a little, just shrugged.

All we had to do was pour the remaining carbide powder down the center hole in the cistern lid and see what happened. We would probably get a great gush of fizzy stuff that would then fizzle out after a short while, and we would have safely dispensed with the rest of the carbide. Neat—a final cool use of the rest of the now tiresome box of powder.

Charlie's Moment of Immortality

Without thinking about it more than a nanosecond, one of us—which one is still a secret—then said, "I'll do it." He grabbed the box and casually dumped it all through the hole in the big cement cover.

There was no discussion of potential upsides and downsides, what-ifs, or possible environmental effects. *Splash.* Down it went.

We didn't discuss the possibility that there might be frogs and insects down there or that it might be the home of furry animals or that the resultant fizzy stuff might be a cloud of poisonous gas that could end up shortening the lives of the farmers downwind in Kettlersville or Botkins. We were creatures of instinct; and our instincts were telling us that something awesome could happen, and we naturally had to see what it would be.

So down it went.

It took a few minutes for the pressure to build up. It was sort of quiet at first with a gentle but then growing hissing sound that built and built until it began to make the transition to more of a roaring sound. We heard a dull kind of roar that sort of hummed, as well. Not a frightening sound, but a sound that let us know something serious was really going on down there. A visible jet of something whooshed from the center hole of the cistern cover. It was a kind of clear or translucent yet somehow visible jet that we knew was there because it distorted the appearance of things behind it. The jet made everything on the other side, including Ted's house, look all wavy and strange, like objects in the mirrors at the fun house over at Russells Point Amusement Park. That, too, probably should have been enough to let us know that something extreme was going on down there.

But it wasn't all that exciting after the first minute or two; who would want to just sit there watching that wavy plume of what we were now beginning to understand was a gas shoot out of there for an unknown amount of time? We were getting bored.

So Charlie said, "I'll see if I can light it with a match!"

We all thought, *Why not? Let's see what happens.*

The first match went out, extinguished by the force of the jet. No, it didn't occur to any of us to say, "Maybe we should think about this first." We all wanted to know what was going to happen if we (Charlie) lit it. Something about inquiring teenage minds, I guess.

So Charlie struck another match and held it in the classic Bogart fashion—all cupped in his hands, close up to his chest.

"I'll get it this time," he promised.

Then he crawled out onto the lid and, with his face nearly over the hole but slightly back from the jet stream, pushed the lit match out into the unknown, with both hands still protecting it.

Whoosh! Kaboom! Crash!

The force of the explosion lifted the heavy concrete cover into the air to a height of several feet—with Charlie at first still sprawled across it. But then he came off, sort of levitated on his back, and sailed backward away from the cistern. Charlie landed at the foot of the cherry tree about the same time the cistern lid came back to earth. We had seen a red flame shoot out of the center hole of the cistern cover that rose to a height of the second story of the house. There it had spread into a large ball of smoke and flame, with sparks emitting from the dark, roiling cloud.

Just like that, it was over. Charlie was lying at the foot of the cherry tree, dazed but conscious. The lid had been fractured into six or eight large, pie-shaped wedges of eight-inch-thick concrete that were now lying more or less back in place around the cistern. Charlie moaned, looking very dizzy and in need of medical attention. We were all dumbstruck. We hadn't imagined the destructive power that we had been playing with all day and carrying around in my bicycle basket.

We all looked at each other in disbelief. Before any of us could move, Ted's dad, who worked the third shift and had been sleeping, came stumbling groggily out of the back porch door in his underwear, his thinning hair standing straight up.

"Jesus Christ! What the hell are you kids doing?" he demanded.

"Nothin', just playing with some firecrackers," Ted said. "We threw 'em down the cistern."

The rest of us nodded in agreement, as though it was a perfectly normal thing to do.

He didn't notice the fractured cistern lid. And, thankfully, he didn't notice that Charlie, lying under the cherry tree, no longer had any eyebrows or eyelashes—or, for that matter, hair at the top of his forehead.

The important thing at that point, other than avoiding explaining any of this to any adults, was to get Charlie to Doc Fledderjohann's office as quickly as possible. Charlie was coming out of shock and beginning to feel a little singed. He didn't remember much and seemed fairly calm about the whole thing. We loaded him on the back of Ted's Schwinn—a cruiser model with a tank horn, headlight, chrome front-wheel springs, and a chrome backseat carrier.

As luck would have it, when we got to the doc's office, there were no other patients, and we were able to see him immediately. We walked into the waiting room, shuffling, staring at our shoes, wondering exactly how we would explain it to Doc.

"Let's just tell him what happened so he knows how to treat Charlie," Ted said.

"Okay, you tell him, then," Ray replied.

"Good idea," I added.

Charlie said, "But we have to ask him to please don't tell my mom and dad."

We had to take the doc into our confidence that day so that Charlie could get proper treatment. We didn't want him treated for sunburn or poison ivy with the wrong medication. But with Charlie's missing eyebrows and eyelashes, it didn't seem we had to worry about that.

Doc Fledderjohann was every kid's best friend—a kindly old gentleman who we always felt comfortable telling what was wrong—for example, how one of us *had gotten that stick imbedded in our knee that somehow we could never quite tell our moms about.* So we told Doc what he needed to know, and he took care of the rest. He had one of those old country doctor offices with shelves and cabinets full of dark-brown bottles with all sorts of elixirs and chemicals that nearly always could cure whatever needed curing. (I still would like to have a bottle of his cough medicine now and then, but it would probably land me in jail. It had the most amazing ability to make me feel good—right away—no matter how bad the cold.)

Doc put some salve on Charlie's face, told us that he had first-degree burns over much of his face and some second-degree burns on his forehead and hands but that there was no serious injury. He mixed some ointments in a small brown bottle for Charlie and sent us on our way, muttering something about *Kids will be kids … it'll be a wonder if they survive it!*

No questions and no charges, either. Truly a wonderful man and doctor. Try that today with all of our waivers and disclosures and preauthorizations, insurance forms, co-pays, and parental permissions!

There were no major repercussions from the carbide cannon incident. Charlie's burns weren't all that serious, though he did look weird the rest of the summer. And his parents were very forgiving, liberal people. Well, as far as we knew, anyway. He never told the rest of us about that first conversation with them, and we did see him around later on that summer.

I think they also believed that old mantra: *Kids will be kids; what can you do?*

I never mentioned the episode to my parents and was only going to answer questions if specifically asked about it. Luckily, they didn't find out about it—or at least about my involvement in the affair—but I did try to avoid conversations with them as much as possible for several days.

I think most of the people who knew of the event really couldn't imagine exactly what had happened and what it was we were playing with. And I know that had any parents been there to see the explosion that day, we would not have seen the outside of the house the rest of that summer. But there were no TV reporters with satellite feeds or cell-phone-camera news junkies or newshound print reporters racing around to record every tiny event, in every tiny town, in every corner of the state in those days. Even our little newspaper, the *New Bremen Sun*, didn't carry anything about the event. What would certainly have been reported nationally over and over again 24-7 today publicly disappeared within a few days back in 1955.

But the story did, quietly and slowly, spread around our class and immediate circle of friends over the following months. It eventually became a class legend such that many years later, people who had not even been close to Ted's house that day told the story as though they had been there and knew exactly how it had all happened. The story is still a favorite at class reunions, well into the twenty-first century.

Polio

Doctors have come from distant cities just to see me …
—Natalie Merchant, "Wonder"

Doc Fledderjohann and Doc Rabe, our two small-town country doctors, were the first line of defense against all the common diseases in the '50s. Both men worked alone, without nurses or office staff. They answered their own telephones and made their own appointments, including house calls. If the caller sounded too sick, Doc Fledderjohann would be on his way as soon as possible—or Doc Rabe, who only made house calls, would be there as soon as he could. But we could also walk into either of their offices and wait for one of them to see us. They both had small offices with little waiting rooms in old, wooden-floored, dead-quiet buildings with solemn interiors. I remember the wooden shutters covering the windows, stained along with all the furniture in a gloomy, dark oak shade popular then. They were somber places without music and covered with drab wallpaper—no brightly painted walls and colorful wall hangings. Medicine was serious business, and sitting and waiting to see one of the docs made me feel as though the end of my world could be lurking there in that next room behind that closed door.

They carried big, wrinkled leather bags to their house calls. Inside, there were stethoscopes, thermometers, and shiny metal things that looked like funnels with bright lights inside that were used for inspecting your ears, nose, mouth, and throat—anything that needed peeking into. There were blood-pressure-measuring instruments, syringes, and various things with which to cut or prick you. There were wooden

Popsicle-like sticks for pushing things around, endless dark bottles of ointments and medicines, bandages, and tubes of salves.

We got through most of our childhood diseases by being cured with things in those bags. Except for polio.

If the doc suspected polio, you were on your way to the big hospital in Lima—fast!

#

Hardly anyone today knows or remembers what the polio epidemics of the '40s and '50s were like or meant to us. To those of us who lived with and through it, it was a real threat of coming down with a horrible disease that, in the best cases, left the victim with a deformed or withered limb, or in the worst case, dead or slowly dying in an iron lung. We knew about horrible diseases that would sometimes sweep through places in Africa or China, but this was Ohio, in the United States of America. For the first time, I began to understand, in some very limited way, how kids had to feel about serious diseases in those other places.

Our mothers and fathers were all terrified that their kids were going to come down with polio—infantile paralysis or poliomyelitis or polioencephalitis—all polio, and all were horrible. And while it seemed that mostly kids got polio, it wasn't limited to kids; anyone could get it. Some families had a mother or father suffering from polio.

During the height of the polio epidemic, reports in newspapers said that some of the bigger towns and cities around Ohio were closing their swimming pools for the summer, which, in Ohio, meant all year. Many mothers would not even let their kids go to pools that were open for the fear of contracting the dreaded disease. That, at times when the newspaper reports were truly frightening, included my mom. We'd heard all about how President Franklin Roosevelt had supposedly contracted polio by swimming in a favorite family lake on a hot summer day, catching a chill, and developing polio by the next day. Everyone knew of someone in their distant family or circle of friends who had polio. We also had seen the pictures too common in those days of polio patients lying in iron lungs, unable to breathe on their own. We went to school with kids who walked with limps—like our upperclassmen, Dave and Red—or who had withered arms from narrow escapes from polio. We saw kids stiffly trying to walk with those horrible, clamp-on leg braces sticking out from under their pants cuffs, sadness on their faces.

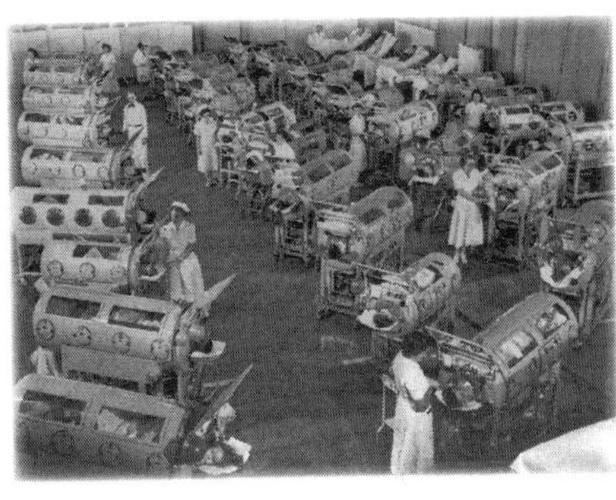

And the very name of something called an *iron lung* was enough to scare the daylights out of all of us. These things looked like some kind of medieval torture device; the afflicted person's body was inserted into and totally enclosed by the iron lung—a body-length metal cylinder—with just the head sticking out.

The sight of people lying in those chambers, staring up at a mirror suspended above their faces so they could see visitors, unable to use their arms, lying there 24-7, was beyond horrific. It made kids listen to their moms.

"Bobby, you're gonna get polio if you don't come in here and lie down in the house for a while," my mom would say.

"Okay, Mom," I always answered. *I'd do it!*

Other than the extreme terror of running into a shortage of allowance money, in the early '50s, our lives seemed to be constantly threatened by all kinds of scary stuff: atomic warfare with Russia, flying saucers, and polio. Polio seemed to me much more real than all those other horrors, though, having seen too many victims and having read too much about it by the time I was thirteen.

But there were also all kinds of other diseases then that are hardly mentioned today. We had all survived the mumps, measles, and chicken pox, which were just all part of growing up then, since we were not given vaccinations for them. Pinkeye, scarlet fever, strep throat, and an assortment of carbuncles, boils, and other nasty things that also got in the way of serious fun were routine. We did get the smallpox vaccinations where a nurse scratched our upper arms with what looked like a broken glass stick that had the vaccine on it. We got ugly scars on our arms, maybe a slight reaction, but we were safe from smallpox. Scary times, for sure.

In those days, being safe from all the nasty diseases was something we all hoped and prayed for. We knew about tuberculosis, but no one seemed to be worried about it anymore. And we had been told by our elders of some of the horrors that early residents had gone through around western Ohio, including New Bremen, such as when, in the mid-1800s, a cholera epidemic had completely wiped out a little village of several dozen families a fraction of a mile south of our town. The epidemic had ravaged New Bremen too, but the town managed to survive it.

New Amsterdam had been located on the east bank of the Miami and Erie Canal, just off the New Amsterdam Road, one-half mile south of New Bremen. It was an area I frequently walked through as a bored kid in the summertime, looking for something to do, following the canal southward. There were small piles of concrete and stone building blocks scattered around one area that I always believed must have been the only remaining traces of that little village. Sad reminders of a disaster—I couldn't begin to imagine the horror the residents experienced. Reports I had read talked about how everyone in the village became sick with cholera in a matter of days, with mothers unable to care for children, husbands unable to care for wives, livestock uncared for, until finally the entire village was dead.

Cholera and tuberculosis were no longer the major life-threatening illnesses by our time, but polio had replaced them. Polio frightened us so much that we even included a special request for protection from it in our bedtime prayers: "*And please, God, protect us from all the bad diseases—especially polio.*"

We always listened to our moms warning us about scary diseases and obeyed their rules for play and rest. We sort of ignored all their other warnings, such as "Stop playing with sticks, or you'll put your eye out," or "Stop aiming that BB gun at your brother." But we listened when it came to polio!

Until Sabin and Salk, there seemed to be nothing but folk remedies—hot compresses and bed rest and a lot of prayer—or the iron lung, which was not really a remedy but a survival technique. Because of the new vaccines—a shot for Salk's in '54 or '55 or later, a sugar cube with a few drops of liquid for the Sabin—we were able to go back to living our normal lives in our little farm town in western Ohio, going to the swimming pool when we wanted, playing baseball in the midday heat, riding our bikes wherever we wanted, and living our lives without the dread of catching polio. It was the best news since the end of the Korean War.

In the mid-1950s, New Bremen and the rest of the country were nearly through with polio. There should have been parades and public celebrations for both men in our nation's capital. There should have been a national holiday in honor of their work. But I don't think there were any celebrations like that for them; we didn't—and still don't—celebrate our science heroes as we should.

Summertime Blues

Ain't no cure for the …
—Eddie Cochran, "Summertime Blues" (E. Cochran and J. Capehart)

I thought by finally making the school basketball team the previous fall, I had found the answer to my dreams. But it had been a horrible experience. After the previous years in seventh and eighth grades and not making the junior high basketball teams, I had some serious confidence scars. I always had been one of the guys left standing in line after our coach, Pete, had made his final cuts for the team.

I still remember how his eyes would scan up and down the line of hopefuls, looking at each of us in turn, thinking each one of us over—*Is he tall enough? Is he strong enough? Is he fast enough? Can he dribble and handle the ball well enough? Can he shoot well enough? Does he play with 100 percent?* He always had his first five picks—the starters—right away; the lineup was just to pick the subs, usually five more kids. Then, after he had made his next three picks and we were down to the last two, his eyes stopped on me for a second and then moved on down to the end of the line. Then he scanned back, stopping with his eyes on the kid next to me, Jim. He nodded and said, "You."

He then scanned past me, not even stopping this time, and said to the kid next to me on the other side, Jerry, "You."

That had been how it ended for me in both those seventh and eighth grade years—left standing, humiliated and disappointed, and sneaking into the locker room to get dressed and out before the others came in. I slinked around school for the next week or two, trying not to be noticed—the kid who couldn't make the team.

But in my freshman year, a little taller and with a new coach, I believed it would be my year. I was optimistic after getting some help from my neighbor, Bill—a very good all-around athlete—and having practiced all summer at our own backyard hoop.

I made the team but didn't really "own" any position: I wasn't tall enough for the front line. With my small hands, I wasn't a great ball handler, and I was barely fast enough for the back court. The coach, when we were hopelessly ahead or hopelessly behind, would put me in at different positions to let me show what I could do. I think I accumulated all of fifteen to twenty minutes of playing time—total—at all five positions during the entire year. I could count the points I scored on one hand; they were all free throws. In the last game of the year, when we were hopelessly behind, Coach Jerry put me in at *center!* I was around five eight, and I embarrassed myself in front of the entire school population and people in the stands. The other team's center was several inches taller than I was, and everyone on both sides playing the front line outweighed me. With my bifocal glasses (I'd worn bifocals since third grade) fogged over and nearly impossible to see through, and at my 120 pounds, I was pushed and shoved around out there under the basket like a little puppy eagerly trying to play the game but getting stepped on, shoved, and elbowed out of the action. When the game ended—we lost by double digits—I was happy that it was over but very sad because I realized that basketball wasn't going to be my thing.

Because of that horrible experience, I had made up my mind to never try out for the team again, unless I magically grew six inches and added thirty pounds. I wanted to forget about the whole thing and find a way to have a good summer.

And girls were also beginning to enter my mind more frequently around then.

Life in New Bremen in the '50s for teenage kids—especially those too young to drive—revolved around two primary social seasons: the fall-through-winter high school basketball season and the summertime swimming season at the municipal pool. Both seasons carried with them the opportunity, and the need, to be adept at dealing with the opposite sex in some way. Before my experience of the previous winter, I had believed that the best way was to be a hero on the basketball team.

But I had just learned that I wasn't ever going to be that basketball hero, I was at least two years away from owing and driving a cool car, and even worse, I couldn't swim.

I didn't feel very good about my maleness around then, thinking that I should be good at something and demonstrating at least a minimal amount of athletic prowess. Playing with fireworks, one of my usual ways of escaping my boredom and finding excitement, wasn't cutting it any longer and certainly wasn't going to get me where I needed to be with any girls. On the contrary, they seemed to be put off by fireworks—another mystery about girls.

Up to that point, fireworks had always been a big thing for my friends and me. We used firecrackers of all sizes all summer long for the usual purposes of blowing tin cans sky high, setting them off inside various pipes and tubes for terrific cannon-like sounds, and just in general to surprise people—or cats and dogs—when they weren't expecting it. They were more than a one-day, single-event, Fourth of July thing for us. Firecrackers were a lifestyle.

And we had recently discovered torpedoes. Torpedoes were foil-wrapped devices about the size of a large marble that had the wonderful attribute of exploding on contact when thrown against something hard. No need to carry matches around and mess with fuses. Just throw the thing at something or near someone and watch the fun. Of course, we also needed to be ready to run, depending on what or who the target was. But we didn't use torpedoes maliciously; they were mostly used as a way of surprising friends. I carried torpedoes in my pockets at nearly all times and nearly everywhere, just in case the right opportunity came up.

But something had to change. The fireworks thing was all kid stuff, and I needed to move my life and social status up a notch. I was determined to make it happen.

#

With school finally out and going into midsummer—the Fourth of July over—the weeks and months went into the usual boring, drone-like mode. I had the summertime blues. The humidity and temperature increased on a nearly daily basis, and the only thing going on—now with the polio crisis finally over—was our daily visit to the municipal swimming pool, where we practiced our diving.

Diving, to us, meant trying to outdo each other with ever more outrageous flopping, splashing, and dumb-looking water entries. There was the frog, the cannonball, the slide, the zombie, and others, all conjured up to make the biggest possible splash directed at some target (meaning a pretty girl we wanted to impress) while looking as clownish as possible.

How that was supposed to advance our causes with the girls is now a mystery, but it seemed to make sense then.

These dives were performed off the low board, a diving board around three feet above pool level and near the ropes dividing the pool's deep end from the shallow end. This was pretty safe since no matter how badly we landed, we weren't likely to get hurt too much. And I could generally sneak dives off the low board even though I hadn't yet passed the across-and-back test that demonstrated swimming proficiency to the lifeguards. Generally speaking, the worst thing was a landing on the flat of one's back or stomach if we were trying something radical, like a flip. But real acrobatic diving, the kind that really would impress a fourteen- or fifteen-year-old girl—flips, gainers, anything calling for full body rotation—was way beyond all of us.

All of us with one exception: Dave Freimering, the kid who could do a real full gainer.

"Dave, show us the gainer!" someone would shout at him.

How could he ignore that? A chance to show off to us younger kids—he was around three years older than my group of friends—and probably impress any of the girls around who were near his age, all with one dive? He was happy to do it.

A gainer is a reverse flip where, instead of diving with one's head down first, followed by the feet coming over the back and rotating forward into a barrel-like move, it calls for the feet going out and up into the sky first followed by the head dropping backward, down below the upward-pointing feet, and the feet and legs rotating backward over the head and shoulders. The legs then come back between the diver and the diving board, rotating down for a legs-first entry.

It's complicated. The motion is all backward and uses none of the body's natural forward momentum in a dive. It is a brute-force kind of dive where one works, temporarily, against gravity, getting the feet up high and out in front of the body and above the head, when everything is really wanting to pull the head and body down first, with the legs following instead of leading.

Dave was the only guy in town, or maybe the whole county, who could do that gainer. And he did it off the high board. The high board was the only practical board to use for a gainer, since extra time and height is needed to get that backward rotation complete before hitting the water. But there was hell to pay when the dive went wrong! The impact was brutal.

Dave had been one of New Bremen's polio victims in his youth. He had a weakened right leg and walked with a limp. It seemed he also dived with a limp; his weakened leg never straightened out like the other leg did at the appropriate point in a dive; it stayed sort of bent at the knee. It was most noticed when he started his approach to a dive by, well, hopping with that bad leg the length of the board, rather than the usual skipping approach divers normally use. But that was a minor thing to us, because he could do that dive.

"Okay, jerks, watch this!" he'd shout after climbing to the top of the high board and walking out to the business end. There, he'd bounce up and down, up and down, getting the feel of the board's springs. Then he'd walk back to the end of the board where the steps ended and just stand there … waiting. I think it was all intended to increase the drama—*man versus gravity*. The effect was riveting: we all sat there, not breathing, just waiting. Then Dave would launch his full gainer.

That gainer was ugly. He flailed and waved every muscle and limb on his body to get those gravity-defying legs up and out there until he could begin dropping his head and start the backward rotation. He had a motion with his arms that seemed as if he were trying to paddle against the air. His arms were straight out from each shoulder and rotating backward; I guessed he was trying to get some grip on the air to help force his legs out and up. It was an amazing thing to watch, sort of all brute force and willpower.

But it worked. He flailed away at the air, getting his feet up in front of his head, and began to rotate backward with his head beginning to drop down behind and under. Then he'd pull his legs into a crouch somewhere directly above his head in order to speed up the rotation, and with his arms behind his back—still paddling furiously—he would pull his head out of the way, drop his legs down behind him, and begin to unravel his body for the entry.

It was a curious thing: all wild motions, ungraceful, and death defying. There was so much contortion and motion going on that it looked as if he were being attacked by demons in the air. But we really weren't bothered by how weird it looked at the time. We were all in awe of Dave. All the strange flailing and writhing around served to make it look incredibly difficult and brave.

I always wondered how it went the first time he ever tried it. How did he get up the nerve to take that leap off the high board and try a backward flip ten or twelve feet above the water? What was his first entry—or, more likely, his first water crash—like? All I could imagine was a landing where he only got three-fourths of the way around and ended up landing flat on his face and stomach.

"J-J-J-J-Jesus Christ, that hurt!" he must have said.

He probably had a cherry belly for a week. And how did he get up the nerve to try it all over again—and again—and again? Belly flop after belly flop after belly flop.

Braver than Dick Tracy! I thought.

But, after all, this was the kind of stuff that got a guy dates with the coolest girls. We couldn't question that.

None of us could do anything like that dive. We muddled around on the low board most of the time with our silly, big-splash dives, trying to look cool. But all along, we were working up the nerve to move up to the high board. We had to. By the time a guy became a sophomore, he had better be diving from the high board. It was just like anything in life; the guys a class or two ahead of us were doing the next dangerous, cool thing, and so we had to keep going on to the next level or probably never get a date with any of the cheerleaders. But for my friends who could go off the high board at that time, they just jumped off, feetfirst, holding their noses. Headfirst dives were something yet to be conquered.

The high board was a nine-foot platform that towered into the sky and could make the would-be daredevil dizzy just standing on the end of the board, looking down into that postage stamp–sized deep end of the pool. Well, admittedly, the entire pool was sort of postage stamp sized to begin with, so the effect was even greater.

Terrifying stuff—but a prerequisite to manhood and girls.

Learning to Swim

Before any of this high-board adventure, though, I had to learn to swim. No one was allowed off the high dive until he or she could demonstrate proficiency in swimming. That meant being able to swim across the width of the pool, in deep water, right under the lifeguard tower and back. The lifeguard watched the whole thing and either pronounced you a "swimmer" able to go into the deep water, beyond the ropes, or still just a water-treader.

I was a paddler-water treader-floater well past the point most guys were supposed to be able to really swim. And it was embarrassing.

"C'mon, Bobby, get in the game!" the guys said as they lined up for some follow-the-leader off the high dive or a game of tag that wandered all over the pool.

"No, I can't go over the ropes; the lifeguard will throw me out," I answered, feeling very left out of the fun. I hoped no one else, especially any nearby girls, would notice. What a miserable feeling; everyone else could go wherever they wanted and do just about anything they wanted, and later on when everyone gathered around the upper deck of the pool patio area to drink a Coke or have an ice cream bar, I had to listen to them talk about the fun they'd had.

But I couldn't play water tag if I couldn't swim. There was no way I could keep up with the action by paddling or walking around the pool with my feet on the bottom. Water tag was where the action really was with most of my male friends: Ray, Ted, Charlie, Dave, my brother Ron, or my cousins Bill, Joe, or Paul. And many of our school girl friends—not yet in the romantic sense—also played in these games. This was where we made our first *real* early contact with the opposite sex. We chased each other, dunked one another, "accidentally" brushed against one another, and, of course, finally got to find out what it was like to touch a girl's bare skin somewhere other than, say, on an arm.

A touch on a knee or lower leg, for instance, or maybe even the upper leg?

"Watch your hands, Bobby!" I was warned.

"Oops, sorry. I slipped," I lied.

This was beyond exciting, and I had to be there.

In the days of full-length skirts and slips, it was a very exotic thing just to be in the pool with girls in swimming suits, even though they were those rubbery, one-piece Jantzen things that extended from the neck down to the upper thighs. So different from today: no form-hugging Lycra fabrics, no glimpses of cleavage or bare midriffs and navels or a peek at a partly exposed cheek now and then. We only had our imaginations.

There was even a version of water tag where the girls would ride on the guys' shoulders, one leg on each side of his neck: sort of a horseback water tag. It was enough to keep me awake at night, thinking about the next time.

So that was the summer I vowed to learn to swim and hopefully even go out on a date. I never was much of a swimmer, including later in my adult life. Synchronizing my breathing and arm strokes always eluded me. I tended to breathe anytime I needed air—to the detriment of my lungs. Usually, after swimming around five strokes, I would get all out of sync, need air fast, and breathe right then. I had more of those choking, hacking episodes with water coming out of my mouth, nose, and probably ears than anyone I knew.

I was desperate for a way to pass the swimming test. It came to me one day in a practice session at the kiddies' end of the pool, down there where it is less than three feet deep. Since I knew I wasn't going to drown there, I could try almost anything. I found that if I swam as fast as I could by keeping my head low in the water and without breathing at all, I could easily get all the way across the pool and even some distance back. All I needed to do was improve my distance and speed, and I could do the full across and back lap legitimately swimming. The key thing was not to breathe the entire time.

It would work, if I could get a lifeguard to buy it. After a week or so of practice, I told the goddess lifeguard, Sissy—another of the trim, tanned, unreachable lifeguard beauties—that I was ready to do the test for the deep end of the pool. Sissy was my classmate Betty's older sister. She was probably a high school junior then; sixteen or seventeen years old, driving a car, and not about to take any flak from fourteen-year-olds. She wouldn't cut me any slack because I was her sister Betty's classmate, either. She looked at me contemptuously, probably thinking, *This twerp has spent the whole summer wallowing around the kiddies' end of the pool, and now he thinks he's ready for the deep end.*

I have to admit that I was a skinny, 120-pound, bifocal-bespectacled, fourteen-year-old and no great physical specimen. I felt beneath contempt and incredibly conspicuous standing there in my baggy swimming trunks, trying to look convincing before the goddess of swim. Sissy took no prisoners in *her* pool.

But I knew I would rather have Sissy grading my efforts than some of the other lifeguard beauties employed at the pool. For example, Judy Dietrich, already a senior, was an all-American-looking beauty, one of the town's sweethearts, and a terrific swimmer who looked like she just stepped off of an Esther Williams movie set. It was too humbling, me in my baggy swimming trunks and at least three years her junior, to just stand in front of a mature girl like that and ask her to watch me swim across the pool and back. Failure at that point would have been a near-death experience; I'm sure I wouldn't have returned to the pool the rest of the summer. At least I knew Sissy, and I thought she'd only humiliate me a little if I failed. Failing in front of Judy Dietrich would be total humiliation.

"Sissy, I'm ready to swim across and back now," I said meekly.

After thinking about it and looking me over carefully, she said, "Okay, do it right here in front of the lifeguard tower."

She blew her whistle and waved everyone away to clear a lane in front of the tower just alongside the ropes dividing the deep water from the shallow water. Hoping no one was paying any attention—in case I failed—I gulped as much air as I could hold in my lungs, planted my feet hard against the poolside, drew my feet up to my chest as close as I could, and launched myself at the far side of the pool. The first leg of the swim was easy enough, but since I couldn't do those underwater racing turns the competitive swimmers did—water always got up my nose and in my ears when I turned upside down underwater—I wasted time and breath getting myself turned around by grabbing the pool gutter and pushing myself around to head the other way. I kept my face down in the water to avoid my usual uncoordinated breathing and stroking problem and started flailing away, heading back to the starting point. As I ran out of air, I made desperate kicking motions to propel me the last few feet so I could tag the pool wall before I sucked in a big gulp of chlorinated water. My lungs felt as if they were about to explode.

When I touched the pool's wall, I lifted my head and gasped for air. I had done it! If just barely.

Sissy seemed a little astonished at this. "Why don't you breathe when you swim?"

"Since it was just a short distance, I didn't need to."

"Well, okay. It was really ugly, but I guess you pass," she said, and then she yelled, "But I want to see you breathing! So work on it!"

"I will," I promised, and then I broke into a big grin. Freedom! I was one of the big guys now! I could go anywhere in the pool and play all the water games. I could even dive off the high board—when I got the nerve. And I could join the water tag games with all the other guys—and girls! It was the confidence builder I needed; it might even lead me to that holy grail of having a date. I thought it was a huge step for me to finally take, and while it seemed a little late to my friends, they were glad to have me in the games. In helping me celebrate, they all took turns dunking me, one after the other, leaving no time for me to gulp a breath of air. Now that I was a "swimmer," I was nearly drowning.

The prospects for the rest of the summer had become a lot brighter. I wouldn't have to make excuses when water tag started or the guys wanted to play follow-the-leader diving games.

Great prospects indeed. A summer of new experiences at the pool with all the other guys and girls and then the upcoming, end-of-summer Woodmen's Festival. We all talked about getting dates to go with us to the festival and be able to go on the thrill rides with a girl rather than one of the other guys again. A girl sitting by my side, screaming and laughing—holding on to me—while I sat through the ride, being all brave and cool about it as if it's a routine thing. It sounded perfect.

The Woodmen's Festival

The climax of summer was the Woodmen's Festival, which was held in mid-August. It seemed logical that this would be held later in the year, when the temperature was back under ninety degrees and maybe when pumpkins and such were being harvested. But Defiance, Ohio, already had that one locked up with its Pumpkin Festival. Most of these festivals in the Ohio farm country are linked in some way to agricultural events, primarily the harvesting of something growing out of the ground. But New Bremen's Woodmen's Festival didn't seem to have an official farm product to celebrate. That's because the stuff growing around there wasn't exactly exciting. New Bremen's primary agricultural products were various grains. Mainly, it was corn, the starchy yellow kind grown primarily for feeding livestock, not the sweet white corn we ate all summer from our home gardens. And there was wheat, oats, hay, alfalfa, and soybeans—all pretty dull stuff. It's pretty clear why there wasn't a hay or wheat or oats festival in New Bremen. Who would even bother to go downtown or come in from Minster or Fort Laramie for a Soybeans Festival? Or imagine an Alfalfa Festival.

So New Bremen had its Woodmen's Festival, held in hot, steamy mid-August again. During the polio scares of the early to mid-1950s, it had been held a little later in the year, hoping for cooler weather and reduced chances of a polio outbreak. But by the summer of '55, now that we were all vaccinated and doing things pretty much when we wanted, the Woodmen's Festival was back at the top of our agendas.

August: ninety degrees and 90 percent relative humidity! It was a time when even in the evenings, the nighttime temperature was usually only a couple of degrees cooler than the midday heat, but the humidity had gone higher. The nighttime air had a hot, damp, sticky feeling that could only be temporarily relieved by climbing the municipal swimming pool fence for a late-night swim or taking a drive in a convertible to see the fireflies thickly swarming over our lawns and fields. But these invariably left a person feeling hotter, stickier, and more uncomfortable than before. Never having even been in a building with air-conditioning, we just lived with it.

Even with the heat, the Woodsmen's Festival was the top attraction for folks from miles around. And a ride on the Ferris wheel or the Bullet or the Octopus was a great way to cool down and even forget the heat for a while.

I had sworn (secretly, to myself) that the 1955 Woodmen's Festival would be the occasion of my first date with a girl. It had to happen that summer. I was getting older and needed to break the ice. All the other guys were either talking about doing it or actually had. What would it be like to hold hands, to walk down the midway and be seen by everyone who would now know that you were growing up and dating? And then walk her home and maybe get a kiss?

I knew who I wanted to ask to go to the festival—the choice was obvious—but I didn't yet know how to ask her.

Pat

Pat had become a good friend by this time and to this day remains a priceless, dear memory for me. She was the first girl in my childhood who actually flirted with me. At least I thought—and hoped at the then tender age of eleven or twelve years—that it was flirting. In early encounters back then, I had sometimes seen her on sidewalks near our homes when we both lived on the northern edge of town. We were roller-skating with those clamp-on skates that we put on our street shoes and fastened with a key that tightened some side clamps to our shoes' soles.

Tighten them too little and we would find ourselves skateless at some critical point when we needed all those wheels working with us. Tighten them too much and our shoes were permanently scrunched in a way that made our feet hurt forever after when wearing those shoes. And the clamps didn't work with tennis shoes and the like; they only worked with your good, lace-up Sunday shoes that had soles with edges the clamps could really get a grip on. I never had a shiny pair of Sunday shoes after I got my first set of clamp-on skates.

The first time I saw Pat was on a day we were both skating with those clamp-ons. I was just learning and stumbling really badly. The sidewalks of New Bremen were mostly made of large, rectangular slabs of sandstone rather than concrete. They were wonderfully smooth and great to skate on except for the bad habit they had of tilting up on one end because of a tree root or the ground shifting under them. So we were always either dropping off a little ramp of one or two inches, or running into an upturned edge of one or two inches. This was tricky skating, and we needed to continually watch to see how the edge of the next slab was positioned. Take an eye off the sidewalk and we could end up a crumpled heap, lying on a sandstone slab with skinned knees and elbows.

I was picking myself up off the sidewalk when Pat, with her blonde hair in pigtails and wearing shorts that showed her pretty legs, skated smoothly and expertly around the corner. She said, "Hi. Are you okay?"

I muttered something like, "Oh, sure, I just haven't got that backward move down yet."

She smiled and skated on. I thought, *Who was that cute girl?*

That was a revelation; my experience with girls up to that point had been pretty negative. Here was a girl who actually tried to be nice to me as I crouched there on the sidewalk, looking at the torn-out knees of my jeans and trying to hide my embarrassment. There were some girls around who would have just ignored or maybe even thrown insults—just for the fun of it—at a kid in that situation.

When I had been in kindergarten—in the Dayton area during World War II—one of my classmates was a girl who never failed to sock me in the eye whenever she found me in the room with the large building blocks with the alphabet letters on them. She never socked me anywhere else—only there with the big blocks. She'd just walk up to me, smile, sock me in the eye, and walk away. What was she thinking? Was it something about the big blocks? I never knew what to think about that.

And in an episode in third grade that embarrassed me for years, classmates Betty (later of the Ground Observation Corps) and her best friend, Ruth, who lived in the old lockkeeper's house along the canal and probably was twice my weight, wrestled me to the ground on the towpath by the canal locks one day. They both then sat on me while Ruth smothered me with big, sloppy kisses for what seemed like an hour, with me squirming and trying to cover my face, hoping that no one was watching. Of course, several upperclassmen—fourth graders—were on the opposite bank, laughing. They never failed to remind me of that day.

Eddy laughed and said, "Bobby, are you going to kiss Ruthie today?"

"How do you like Ruthie sitting on you? Can't you push her off?" Roger said.

"Bobby likes being kissed by Ruthie!" they would taunt.

I had to avoid those guys for months after that so I wouldn't be embarrassed in front of my schoolmates.

But the event that had made me wonder if there was ever going to be a girl in my future happened in fifth grade. I frequently sat just behind a pretty girl named Linda. We had always seemed to be on friendly terms until the day I was looking through a *National Geographic* magazine. It probably was the first time I had ever seen a *National Geographic*. Some African nation was the featured story, and it contained the usual photos of villages, huts, wildlife, and African women—naked from the waist up. It was my first experience with photographs of a woman's naked upper torso. It was 1951; *Playboy* was still a dream—two years away—in Hugh's mind.

I have no idea what possessed me, but I thought, *I'll show it to Linda.* So, leaning forward from my desk, I tapped her on the shoulder, holding the magazine where she would nearly push her face into it when she turned around.

"Linda, look at this!" I said.

She found herself staring at a very large pair of brown, naked breasts. Linda screamed as if she were being attacked. That immediately caught the teacher's attention. Mr. Pete Blanke, the basketball coach who later on would never pick me, snatched the *National Geographic* from my hands and pulled me up from my seat. I found myself stumbling down the hall to the principal's office, where I was told to write in longhand, five hundred times, *I will never show pictures of naked women to Linda again.*

I had never written anything longer than three or four sentences at that point; a paragraph was probably it, tops. It was the most agonizing thing I could have imagined, compounded by the fact that I had to do it at home. I think they wanted my parents to see me doing it so that even more punishment would rain down on me. And, to make the punishment even more embarrassing, I would have to turn the papers in to Mr. Blanke in front of the entire assembled class—all twenty sheets—while reading one of the sentences aloud to everyone.

My humiliation was complete; I couldn't talk to Linda or look into her eyes for months after that. For that matter, I avoided all the girls in my class for a while.

Did they all then think of me as *Bobby the pervert?*

So, up until that skating accident and Pat happening by, I had always felt a little abused by the girls I had encountered.

But Pat was different. As the years went on, she became one of my favorite people and a friend as close as most of the guys I hung out with. Our friendship survived countless comings and goings of other guys and girls over the years. My mother adopted her as the daughter she never had, and amazingly, even that fact never got in the way. We were still friends even after the infamous, never-again-discussed New Bremen Water Ballet Swim Team disaster in Wapakoneta, Ohio, a few years later. I had dropped her ungracefully back into the pool during the grand finale pool exit number. As always, she had handled that one good-naturedly with a smile and never berated me over it. She could turn any disaster into a funny story to be told time and again, which she always did with her ever-present mischievous smile. Pat had the best sense of humor of any girl I'd known in those years.

So when it came time to find a date for the Woodmen's Festival, it was easy—she was the obvious choice.

But, because of our friendship, I had a hard time working up to the question of a date. Somehow, for me, that had the potential to change the relationship in a big way. I had worried about her answer quite a lot. *What if she refused? How would we carry on a friendship after that? And if the date didn't go well, what kind of relationship would we have after that? What kind of unwanted pressure would I be putting on her?* There was a lot riding on this; everything had to go right.

After worrying about it for days, I finally asked the question when just the two of us were walking home from the swimming pool. "Pat, umm-a-hmmm, aahh … ummm, would you like to go to the carnival with me this Saturday night?"

"Yes," she said. As simple as that.

What had I been worried about? It was that easy—for her. Why was it so hard for me? I guess being the one doing the *asking* is a different place than for the one doing the *answering*. A realization that stayed with me the rest of my life.

#

A few things still stand out in my mind about that first date. Gathering up the nerve to ask Pat to go to the festival was the first hurdle. Getting enough money together to actually take her for a couple of carnival rides, buying some cotton candy, and trying to win a teddy bear by tossing rings at bottle necks—this would take more cash than I earned from my paper route. How was I going to do that?

I figured I would need at least five dollars for just the one night. Carnival rides were twenty-five cents each. The Ferris wheel, the Bullet, the Octopus, and the Caterpillar (an awning folded down over the ride, making it dark, scary, and romantic) would require two dollars right there, and we had been hearing that the Flying Scooters were going to be back.

That was a big deal. They had become *the* ride after that famous incident when my cousin Tommy Stovelbeck had smacked the front wall of the Amstutz Egg Hatchery, just below the second-story windows. The time when—in a perfect storm of physics, geometry, velocity, and stupidity—the little flying scooter with Tom aboard had received a terrific dent, and the Amstutz Hatchery reportedly may have lost a few cartons of newly packaged eggs.

I think most guys had dreams of finding ways to outdo even that stunt. At that time, the city elders had considered that the flying scooters allowed a little too much individual participation, and they should reevaluate the suitability of such rides for the citizens of New Bremen. So the scooters had nearly been banished; but that year, it was rumored the Woodmen were permitting the ride's return.

Since the scooters were one of my favorite rides and back in the picture, I was at $2.50 for rides and still hadn't covered food, drinks, and the teddy-bear contests. Yes, I needed more money than I made from my paper-route profits—which were always gone the same day I made my collections.

Bringing in the Hay (The Date Money)

Hay ripens in August in Ohio. Harvesting hay is a critical time for farmers. It is needed to feed livestock and is a cash crop, as well. Hay-ripening season has its risks. If there is rain on ripe hay before it is baled and barned, it can be ruined, leaving the farmer without his own feeding supply and with the need to buy hay rather than sell it for cash. Needless to say, when the hay is ripe, the farmers are in a hurry, or even panicky, to get it safely in the barn's haymow.

And when it was haying season in Ohio in the '50s, before today's modern farm machinery, town kids hid out until it was over—unless they needed five dollars.

There were no air-conditioned, fully enclosed cabin, radio-equipped combines in those days. Haying was very hot, hard work. In the 1950s, hay was harvested by an open tractor pulling a combine that cut and baled it, shooting out bales of hay that needed to be stacked securely on a wagon trailing the combine. When the wagon was full, it was hauled back to the barn to be loaded up into the haymow—lifting and lugging those hundred-pound things again. Depending on the farm, an escalator-like machine might be available to lift the hay bales up to the barn's second-floor haymow, but in many cases, the bales had to be manually lifted.

Workers rode the hay wagon in a cloud of dust, chaff, and heat, yanking the bales onto the wagon from the rear of the combine and lifting them ever higher into multileveled stacks on those bouncing, unsteady platforms. Seen from the nearby roadways, a haying operation must have looked like a cloud of dust progressing across a field, with the front tractor wheels visible in the front part of the cloud, and the stack of hay bales on the back of the wagon visible in the rear part of the cloud. Everything else was semiobscured by the traveling dust cloud. Occasionally, you would get a glimpse of the kids staggering around on the wagon, carrying bales of hay bigger than they were, through the dust. It was a kind of dust-devil apparition seen through waves of heat rising from the field between the roadway and that strange caravan. I didn't think I wanted to ever be out there, for love or money!

Until the day I realized that I needed some real cash for my date with Pat. I had been staying off the streets during the first couple of hours after breakfast when the farmers were doing their daily sweeps through town. They were trying to find boys they could hire for five dollars per day to help bale hay. The British navy's conscription sweeps through port cities I had read about in *Two Years before the Mast* always came to mind when farmers needed help with bringing in the hay. It wasn't so much that they were going to sweep me, kicking and screaming off a street corner, as it was that, until I needed the date money, there wasn't enough money they could pay me to stand on that wagon and bale hay in August. The hay bales weighed nearly as much as I did in 1955.

But I was committed to the date with Pat. There I had been, worrying about all that interpersonal relationship stuff and not thinking about the real issue I would face on that date: how to come up with those five dollars.

I stood there on the downtown corner where Ohio 274 and Ohio 66 intersect one hot August morning at around eight o'clock and waited. It didn't take more than fifteen to twenty minutes before a couple of other kids and I were climbing into the back of the farmer's prewar Buick and heading out west of town for a day on the hay wagons.

"You boys are gonna make some money today, but you're gonna earn it," he said. "Are you city boys ready to work like a farmer?"

"Yes, sir," we answered, looking doubtfully at each other.

City boys? I guess everything is relative.

There is little to add beyond saying that I needed, from that Wednesday of baling hay to the following Saturday, to get the dust and chaff out of my ears, eyes, nose, mouth, and skin for my big date. And one other thing: the farmers' wives, when seeing me at my 120 pounds and twenty-four-inch waist, typically said, "You poor thing, doesn't your mother feed you? I'll take care of you at dinner."

Farmer mothers wanted their boys fat. Actually, the word was *stout. Stoutness* seemed to be the measure of health in those days in the Midwest before anyone had ever heard about cholesterol. Big farmer kids weren't fat; they were *stout. Stoutness* was also a measure of financial well-being and status. Skinny men were suspiciously viewed as poor providers, while *stout* men must obviously have been good providers.

We ate dinner at noon, and we called the evening meal *supper.* The noon meal was the main meal of the day for most farmers. There were ten of us at the table—three of us *city boys* and seven from the farmer's family, including his wife and kids. Our meal that day consisted of roast beef, roast pork, fried chicken, mashed potatoes, white bread and butter, two or three vegetables—either fresh from the farmer's garden or canned by the farmer's wife the previous year—and the ever-present piccalilli garnish. There were sweet pickles (also called butter pickles) and wedge-shaped dill pickles, and sometimes even sauerkraut.

We're talking Germans here. *Stout* Germans.

This was accompanied by several pitchers of iced tea, milk, and coffee. Dessert was either fresh cherry pie or chiffon cake with ice cream, or maybe both.

Then we went back out into the ninety-degree, 90 percent humidity and worked for another six hours. It may have been calorie-overload-induced delirium, because I don't remember much of that afternoon other than how great it felt to finally get off that wagon, sunburned, filthy, and exhausted, finally out of the heat—but with my five dollars.

What wouldn't I do for the promise of that big date? Next time, it wouldn't include baling hay in August!

The Date

Saturday night came, and I rode my bicycle across town for my date with Pat. I left my bike at her house, and we walked downtown to the New Bremen Woodmen's Festival for the carny rides, teddy-bear games, freak shows, cotton candy, and all the excitement we wanted.

We saw all of the carnival sideshows and skill games, rode the usual rides, ate cotton candy—and burned through my hard-earned five dollars of hay money in the first hour and a half.

"Pat, I've spent all my money, and we can't ride any more rides," I had to admit.

"I've got some money. Let's go ride that thing. I've never seen it before!" she exclaimed, pointing at a Ferris wheel–looking thing across the midway.

"Do you mean it? I feel really stupid."

She smiled. "Come on. Let's have fun. That's what we're here for."

"Okay, but I owe you. I'll pay you back."

The new ride looked like a Ferris wheel with seats inside steel-mesh cages. We were strapped in with belts and shoulder bars, rather than just the lap bar that ordinary Ferris wheel seats used. The passenger cages had a brake bar near the floor that, when pressed down hard with one's foot, locked up the pivots and let the entire seat and cage assembly turn upside down as the big wheel rotated up to the top of its orbit, rather than pivoting and staying upright as regular Ferris wheel seats do.

Getting upside down was always a fascination thing with me; I never could do it with pool diving or any kind of acrobatics, so any mechanical contraption that allowed me to do it at will was kind of a miracle. I was ready for this new ride and was going to do it with everything I had—or until one of us got sick.

Using Pat's money, we boarded the ride for our last thrill of the evening before she was going to buy burgers and Cokes. We were strapped into the ride with seat belts that were so wide that they covered us from our knees to our hips. The ride attendant then rotated the padded metal bars from the upper part of the cage and locked them into position over our shoulders to keep us in place when we went upside down. He made a final check to ensure that everything was properly set and then pushed our cage away from the loading dock. We made some standard Ferris wheel–like rotations around the big ride for a few minutes, and I was then ready for the upside-down part.

"Okay, are you ready to go over?" I asked Pat.

She just looked at me and said, "What have we been waiting for?"

I should have known; Pat was always ready for fun.

"Here we go!" I said, and with my feet, I pushed hard on the locking bar near the floor, causing the cage to rotate as the big wheel took us up toward the dark sky. The cage went fully upside down at the highest point of the ride. Hanging there, upside down at the top of the ride and looking at the people waiting in line for their turn on the ride was just what I had been hoping for—the kind of experience an airplane pilot would have when flying barrel rolls or loops. I loved every second of it. But out of the corner of my eye, I noticed that something seemed to be rattling around near the cage top, which then was beneath our heads.

What was it? Or what were they?

As we started to come back down toward the bottom of the ride and the cage resumed its normal attitude, the *things* began to fall from the cage top to the cage floor near our feet and rattled around down there. Little silver balls were on the floor, just rolling and rolling around.

The silver things continued to roll and rattle around in the cage for one or two more wheel rotations. Then, as our cage rotated upside down again for the second or third time, those *things* exploded all around us. One exploded just a few inches from my left ear with a bright flash, and some fragments hit my cheek.

Pat looked at me with startled eyes, as if asking, *What was that?*

I didn't say anything and acted as surprised as she was.

Several more went off by the time we reached the bottom of the ride, where the operator had realized something unusual was going on and reached for the controls to begin shutting the big wheel down.

No one else knew what cage the explosions had come from—and I wasn't talking. I think the carnies thought they should be looking for bullet holes. Pat and I slipped away and headed for the burger stands, with Pat still eyeing me suspiciously.

"What was that?" she asked—this time in words, along with that same look, now demanding an answer.

"Oh, just some torpedoes," I answered, trying to be nonchalant.

She gave me a sidelong glance, so I told her about the torpedoes and how my friends and I carried them around at most times. The torpedoes had all fallen out of my shirt pocket and began exploding during the second or third upside-down rotation. They continued to rattle around in that steel cage until, one by one, they all exploded: at our feet, between us and the cage screen, and the one beside my face. It seemed as if they were going off everywhere.

"On a date?" she asked, incredulous.

"Well, it was *just* a slight oversight. I had *just* forgotten to remove them," I said.

Pat flashed me that mischievous little smile of hers. It said, *Okay, I get it, and it's little more than BS, and I'll never let you forget it. But it was fun.*

She understood boys better than most other girls and maybe even better than their moms. And she didn't mind having to loan me the extra money for the rest of the date, which was a good thing, because I'd rather borrow the whole $7.50 we spent that night than work on another hay wagon in Ohio during August.

I walked her home, and as we stood at the front door, Pat smiled with a look that said, *I'm ready for a kiss, if you want.*

I didn't say a thing. I was thinking, *After loaning me money, and after my torpedo-terrifying-her disaster, and after not having won a teddy bear for her, she still would give me a kiss?*

I leaned forward from where I was standing a foot or two away, put one arm around her shoulders and the other on her hip; she did the same, and our tightly closed lips met there—in midair, upper bodies apart, waists even farther apart—and it was heavenly. I felt electricity yet tenderness and friendship. It would be a good thing to do, again and again, whenever I found the opportunity—to chase away the summertime blues.

Dancing at the Opera House

Bop bop-a-lu a wop bam boom!
—Little Richard, "Tutti Frutti" (J. Penniman and D. LaBostrie)

In the mid-1950s, teenagers' dances, held on the big dance floor in the opera house, were arranged and chaperoned by Carl Watkins, our crew cut–, cardigan sweater–, and Hush Puppies–wearing history teacher and varsity basketball coach. Carl's wife, Donna, usually accompanied him. This was at the time when, for kids all across America, the pop music of the '40s and early '50s was about to be thrown under the bus and replaced by rock and roll. But the older generation, including our high school teachers, was holding on to the music of the big band era and the schmaltzy tunes of AM radio's popular music of the times.

We kids were just getting into the new music at those teenagers' dances. Since we knew little else, we adapted the swing dance styles of the '40s and '50s to our rock-and-roll dancing. It was the kind of dancing where the boy and girl always stayed in contact, with at least one hand held in the other's hand through all the twirls, spins, and slides and with the guy giving the girl a big dip at the end. But a new style of dancing was appearing on TV shows that was without all the contact; the boy and girl were out on the dance floor together and may not have any contact throughout the entire dance. Dancing without touching—it seemed like a strange concept. It was mostly a whole lotta shakin' goin' on and spinning and jumping, with the couple usually—but not always—facing each other. Then, at the end of the dance, they had a quick embrace with a little dip in conclusion and walked off the dance floor. It did seem to be an easier way to dance, since there was no need to worry about coordinating moves or crashing into each other if the two hadn't danced together frequently. But it didn't have the intimacy of the older swing dancing. I liked both styles; each one suited a different kind of music.

Little Richard's music called for the new style. I'll never forget the look on Carl's face as he watched us dancing to "Tutti Frutti" when Little Richard first broke onto the popular music scene. Carl, standing near the snack counter and shaking his head, muttered to his pretty wife, "That is about the most frantic, fanatic, crazy thing I've ever seen; they look like they're having epileptic fits out there! And the same can be said for that music, if that's what you want to call it!"

She replied, "Why don't they want to play the 'Tennessee Waltz'? They could dance to that, and it would be so much nicer."

And I knew they also probably were thinking, *What happened to Perry Como and Guy Lombardo? And where are Dinah Shore and Patti Page? Why not "Moonlight in Vermont" or "How Much Is That Doggie in the Window?"*

We weren't thinking about them anymore; it was Bill Haley and the Comets, Elvis, and Little Richard. We didn't want to waltz or slow dance; we wanted to rock and roll!

The teenagers' dances at the old opera house are where most of us learned to dance. Dancing had been a scary thing at that point in our lives—for me, anyway. All the girls sat at tables on one side of the dance floor, and all the boys sat on the other side. Crossing that floor was a long, long walk.

Seeing the girls watching me after getting up the courage to make that crossing was both exciting and terrifying. Some girls looked directly at me, while others sort of watched out of the corners of their eyes. I believed there was special meaning in the various looks that needed to be heeded. They meant different things.

She's watching me sideways. I think that look means, "I hope he's not going to ask me—maybe it's time to head for the restroom."

If I detected that look before halfway across, I'd try to make a turn to head toward a different table so that it wouldn't be noticed that I'd been put off with just a look.

She's looking right at me; *I hope that means, "Hi, Bob. Are you going to ask me to dance?" Keep going, Bob!*

She's giving me that direct look with a hard stare. It probably means, "Don't ask me to dance; I'm waiting for Ray, so don't bother!" That look demanded that same midfloor correction.

It was Russian roulette! It seemed a backup plan needed to be ready for all possibilities.

But it wasn't only the girls and how they were watching that ran through my mind as I approached the targeted table. All the boys behind me watched, as well, to see who I was going to ask to dance—and to see what happened.

I was always thinking, *If the girl I have my heart set on refuses, then what do I do? Ask the girl sitting in the next chair—and make her feel like the second choice?*

"Hi, Jeanine, want to … no? Okay, sorry … How would you like to dance, Joan? Oh, that last fast dance has you all tired? Okay, I know. 'Rip It Up' is really fast, isn't it? Maybe later?"

That left both of us feeling humiliated—she for being a second choice and me for being turned down *twice.*

The paradox was this: save the second girl from that humiliation and take that long walk back across the room after the first refusal, feeling completely deflated myself, or take a chance and ask her? If I decided not to ask a second girl, all the guys back on the other side would be waiting for me, smirking and snickering.

"Look, she must have said no."

"He's coming back, the jerk."

"Let's razz his ass!"

Or should I hope lightning wouldn't strike twice and ask the second girl? But what if she said no?

"Look, she must have said no too."

"What a loser!"

"He can't get any girl to dance with him; let's *really* razz his ass!"

Somehow I always felt that it was better to be the humiliated one rather than to be the one humiliating the girl, so I promised myself I'd never try the second-choice thing. But secretly, I hoped that if I did get turned down, one of the other girls at the same table would say, "Hi, Bob. I'll dance with you!"

There were New Bremen girls who would do that.

Or maybe I had it all wrong. Maybe my second choice would have been pleased to be asked to dance anyway. But I never figured out just how a girl was going to handle things like that. They were always something of a mystery to me; one night, it would be okay, and the next, I'd be emasculated with just one withering look.

But usually, the girls in New Bremen were too polite to turn a guy down; they happily said yes—even if it meant getting bruised ankles, since I was a pretty bad dancer. Maybe that's why they all wore those thick, white bobby socks.

The solution to all our dancing difficulties, especially the "asking" part, was the Stroll. The Stroll was the hot dance in the mid-1950s because there was no asking required. All the girls lined up a few feet away from the boys, who also had lined up, facing them. The first couple on one end "strolled" down the lane between the boys and girls to the Diamonds' "The Stroll," doing all the fancy steps and moves they could conjure, returning to the end of the line to wait their turn again. They were then, in turn, followed by the next couple, and the next, and on and on. What a concept! I got to dance with nearly all the girls without any pressure, and I could do any crazy step I wanted without taking any criticism, since that was what was expected. The coolest moves would be talked about for days afterward.

Once we mastered group dances like the Stroll and the Hucklebuck—another group kind of dance—the ice seemed to be broken, and it became much easier to ask girls to actually dance one-on-one. We even did our parents' dances—the foxtrot and the two-step, and we tried a few waltzes—but we mostly did rock-and-roll dances.

The teenagers' dances were the first times we—well, I, anyway—put an arm around a girl's waist and held her close—cheek to soft cheek, her smiling face, the scent of her perfume, her arm around my back—and looked into each other's eyes in a way that was different from in the classrooms and hallways. Somehow, being close like that changed all the chemistry. *What a great feeling.* I was hooked and never looked back. Getting to know girls as someone other than a classmate was becoming magical!

Dead Man's Curve

Won't come back from …
—Jan and Dean, "Dead Man's Curve" (B. Wilson,
J. Berry, A. Kornfeld, and R. Christian)

There are Dead Man's Curves everywhere in the United States, and there really was a Dead Man's Curve near New Bremen. It had been called that since before I was born, and I only ever knew it as Dead Man's Curve. It was there long before the "Dead Man's Curve" song by Jan and Dean became popular in the early '60s. I'm not sure why ours was originally called that, but some old friends were certain it got the name after a man supposedly was killed there before our generation was around. But after a sad day in 1955, there definitely was a reason for it.

When I began driving a little more than a year later in 1956, Dead Man's Curve was always an enigma for me. It was a scary place because of its name and the things that had happened there, but I loved driving through it. It had the same kind of moth-to-flame attraction as I imagined the great racetrack curves had, like turn one at Indianapolis—both challenging and terrifying.

The curve was banked like a real racetrack. It curved almost ninety degrees and had a decreasing radius. For a first-timer, it could be deceptive; he might think it was easy going in and then realize it was serious stuff and have to reduce speed—preferably without braking—and point the car deeper in. And it seemed to narrow by several feet as the driver approached the middle of the turn, demanding even more attention. After the apex, as the radius increased, he could begin to drift out toward the exit. It felt like the real thing, just like I'd seen at the racetracks around western Ohio and nearby Indiana. Dead Man's Curve was then followed, when northbound, by an S curve that added even more interest.

I looked for roads with curves like these whenever I was out driving. And after finding one, I'd go back, again and again, just for the fun of making the curve and feeling the side forces pressing me against the driver's side door or, after I finally installed seat belts, the g-forces against the belts. I made believe that I was a race driver, and I loved it.

There was another nearby curve that also became one of my favorites, just along the German Protestant Cemetery, northbound on the New Knoxville Road. This was a different kind of curve, with a sweeping, near-constant radius to the right that I could confidently enter at whatever speed I felt would get me through and just keep the steering angle and throttle position nearly constant all the way around. That curve, like Dead Man's Curve, was followed by a tricky left turn after a narrow bridge spanning the Miami and Erie Canal, with a small rise where the bridge crossed the canal. That combination of turns, the sweeping right-hander followed by the sharp left and narrow bridge, presented a challenging driving experience I always imagined to be something like the European road-racing circuits I read about in my dad's magazines—*Speed Age* and, later on, *Road and Track*. In fact, the entire road between New Bremen and New Knoxville was a fun, curvy road that became one of my favorites. It had little traffic and good visibility, since the cornfields were set a little farther back from the roadway than usual. It also had several more sweeping left- and right-handed curves, and it was a wider and smoother road than most in the area. I drove to New Knoxville even when I had no need to go to New Knoxville just to drive that road. I'd drive there, turn around, and drive back to New Bremen, and then do it all over again. Gas was twenty-five cents a gallon—and I had all the time in the world.

Curves were there to be examined and tested—finding the best entry points, apexes and exit paths, and key driving markers to be decided on and memorized, used time and time again just for the thrill to be experienced in mastering the road.

And there was also another cemetery along that road: the Willow Grove Cemetery. I didn't have some morbid fascination with highways and curves around cemeteries; it's just that that's where they happened to be. And I'd take a curvy road anywhere I could find one. I found them to be a great relief from the endless miles of farm roads laid out in squares seemingly everywhere else in the farm country of Ohio.

Western Ohio farm country roads were a checkerboard grid spaced about one mile apart; arrow straight and flat. They were surrounded by farm fields, mostly corn or hay or wheat growing high enough so that the driver had no view of anything except for distant, tall grain silos and the treetops of the small woods most farmers left standing in some corner of their property. It was boring, confining driving, with little traffic and little to see and only the occasional small town to break the monotony.

There were no Scenic Highway signs to be found around New Bremen.

I'd go out of my way to be able to drive a curvy road to my destination.

The farmers probably saw it differently, viewing straight, narrow roads as the natural order of things in farm country. *They couldn't drift a tractor around high-speed curves, so what good were curves?*

But for us motor-head kids, highways with curves presented challenges meant to be mastered. There was an S curve between New Bremen and Minster that was legendary. It had the usual road signs: Danger, Speed Limit 45 MPH, Do Not Cross Lines, and a sign with squiggly lines indicating the S curve. A few of my friends, with newer cars than the '52 Ford convertible my brother and I owned, could take that S curve at one hundred miles an hour. We even did it sometimes in a train of two or three cars, just a couple of car lengths apart. I was usually in one of those cars as a passenger—holding my breath—and loving it. Since my car wouldn't go one hundred miles an hour and was a rickety convertible with a cloth top—and my tires at their best were only fair—I had to leave the driving to the others with better cars.

Those who did drive it at one hundred miles an hour loved to talk about how it was "just a flick of the steering wheel to the left and a flick back to the right, holding your gas foot to the floor all the way." And you were through it—if you did it right.

One day, Jack, a close friend and fellow member of the Road Rebels Car Club we started a little later on in 1956, successfully drove his fast

'52 Ford Victoria hardtop with an Olds engine, through the Ss at the usual high speed. Then, three or four minutes later, when entering New Bremen at the ordinary street speed limit, he felt a bang and a total loss of steering control. With no steering and Jack frantically pushing the brake pedal nearly to the floor, the car finally slid to a stop against the curb. His steering tie-rod had broken. The shop that had installed the Olds engine in Jack's Ford hadn't gotten all the clearances right, and under certain conditions of passenger load, speed, and the height of a street or highway bump, the engine bottom could hit the tie-rod. All those conditions were present somewhere in the ride that day, and the near worst case happened. But luckily, the final break didn't occur until Jack had slowed down as they entered the city limits.

I wasn't in the car for that ride, but a couple of the other Road Rebels were along, all of whom began reconsidering their lives for a few minutes as they stood on the sidewalk, nervously trying to hold their cigarettes in quivering hands and thinking about what had just happened—and what had not just happened. New Bremen had been just three or four minutes away from possibly having to bury three of its teenagers.

Somehow, all of my immediate friends lived through those years. But not all of New Bremen's young men did.

#

Dave looked like Tab Hunter in the movie *A Summer Place*: terrific muscular physique with broad shoulders, deep chest, friendly, happy face and eyes, and the flattop we all wore in those days. I can still see him in a white T-shirt and jeans, the prototypical all-American kid, looking as if he were ready for a career as a football player or movie star. He was the only son in his family, and his father, Hal, doted on him, bursting with pride over his handsome son. Dave was known to be a fun-loving kid and was well liked all over town. He could have gotten away with anything, but his decency, and maybe the fear of his dad's well-known temper, kept him in line.

Dave and another well-known and well-liked classmate, Red, graduated together in 1954, when my friends and I were still freshmen and sophomores. Red also had the same kind of all-American football player physique as Dave, but Red was also one of New Bremen's childhood polio victims and suffered from a weak right leg as a result. He walked and ran with that limp, but it in no way held him back from doing much of what he wanted to do. He was a ferocious dodgeball player, and woe to the opponent that took one of his hard ones on the backside or chest: a guaranteed bright-red cherry for the next few days.

I had more of those marks on my back or stomach than anyone needs for a lifetime from noon-hour dodgeball games on the basketball court when either one of them was playing. When they were both playing, and since we used more than one ball at a time, it was beyond dangerous to be facing them from the other side. They sometimes would both throw at the same person at the same time. We had to try to watch one of them, but which one? Watch one, and the other would throw at you. Or they both might throw at you. And both balls might hit one of us at the same time.

They loved to welcome freshmen to high school with their high, hard ones.

"How did that feel, Bobby?" Dave said with a smirk.

I brushed it off. "What, that little thing? Didn't bother me."

"Okay, Red, let's make him feel this one."

"It hurt!" I yelled in desperation. "I don't need another one; throw at Ray!"

Red, of course, had red hair, a pinkish complexion, and lots of freckles. His given name was Tom, which didn't last long after he started grade school. I never heard him called by his birth name, and I never wanted to ask which one he preferred; just his physical size and strength, combined with his red hair, intimidated me. He, like most upperclassmen, loved stepping on and grinding the bottom of his shoe sole on the tops of the white buck shoes any naive underclassman was silly enough to wear to school. It was the privilege of upperclassmen, especially if they were big, strong guys, to stand in front of one, pretending to be listening to a conversation and stepping on your white bucks—smiling the whole time. But we'd never dare squeal on them; the repercussions in the dodgeball games were too frightening to even think of doing that. Blue suede shoes, my favorite in those days, were subject to the same "welcome to high school" treatments.

Who needed that?

But no one held it against him or the others; how could we?

The two of them could have been the anchors for a football team that might have dominated western Ohio's Class C league for all their years in school. They would have been ferocious linebackers—except that New Bremen didn't have a high school football team. Our school, with fewer than 140 students in the ninth through twelfth grades, was so small that there probably wouldn't have been enough strong, athletic boys to fill all the positions required. So their athletic careers were limited to noon-time dodgeball, since their physiques didn't fit the style of basketball played in those years where any contact was an immediate foul. And of course Red's bad leg would have been too much of a limitation for basketball.

Dave and Red were larger than life, going through school and graduating together. They were everyone's role models of what high school boys should look and be like.

#

One day in the fall of 1955, my cousin Joe was riding as a passenger as Dave made a run through Dead Man's Curve. Apparently, Dave lost control of his Chevy, rolled the car, and was catapulted through the driver's side window to his death. The actual details are unknown; Joe was always vague about it afterward. He had been pretty badly injured, but he survived and had to deal with the aftermath.

One of the stories that went around was that Dave, while admittedly a fast driver but who had never had any accidents, was moving swiftly around the curve when his shirt sleeve got tangled up with the steering knob attached to his steering wheel. In wrestling to clear the sleeve from the knob, he lost control.

Steering knobs were the answer to hard, slow steering in those days when power steering was an expensive, optional purchase. A steering knob let us crank on the wheel to get faster turning, rather than the slow, hand-over-hand turning a driver had to otherwise do.

Steering knobs were fairly common back then. We loved to use them in the wintertime after a moderate snowfall to spin the car, doing "doughnuts" on the New Bremen's streets. A steering knob helped the driver to quickly crank the wheel completely over to full left or full right lock, as needed when making the car—at low speeds—spin down the street. Tap the brakes, crank the wheel over to one side or the other, and it would spin like a top! Yes, we sometimes hit a curb now and then, and even a time or two, all of us had to get out of the high-side door so we could push the car back onto its wheels. If the snow was deep enough, there would be no damage that needed to be explained.

But the steering knobs were dangerous for other reasons. We understood that we were never to use the steering knob at highway speeds, since they reduced the driver's feel for the steering system and the road and tended to let the driver oversteer. Steering knobs were meant mainly to help in steering a car when parking or maneuvering in a parking lot. They were also prophetically called "suicide knobs." They were outlawed years later—but too late for Dave.

While the suicide knob was a feasible enough story, its origin was never traced to anyone who could know. Joe wouldn't confirm it, stating that he had been knocked out and couldn't remember what had happened. That story probably started with speculation by someone, and since it did sound plausible, it stayed around.

And there was another rumor that went around at about the same time: that Joe was actually the driver that day. But Joe wouldn't confirm that, either.

Red, Dave's classmate, died a few years later, the victim of a horrible farm equipment accident. He and his brother serviced farmers needing to have grain crushed and ground into livestock feed. Red was cleaning out the grain feed hopper and screw drive at a job site one summer day when his brother, not knowing that Red was in the machine, turned it on. Our volunteer firemen responding to the call for help needed to use cutting torches to remove Red from the machine. They were not able to talk about it for months. In a possible but speculatively related event, the fireman who did the torch work that day took his own life a few years later, supposedly after suffering from depression following his years in the Korean War—and as the rumor went, possibly his experience at Red's accident scene.

#

Prior to these incidents, I had never had to confront the death of someone I knew. My parents had shielded my brothers and me from the deaths and funerals of our grandparents, so these were my first encounters with the specter of death and the notion that young people also could die at any time. As I looked at Dave in the open-casket funeral service in my own church, I was terror stricken over how a young, strong, full-of-life person could be lying there, all waxy looking and forever gone. I never forgot standing there beside his casket at the age of fourteen, realizing for the first time that it could happen to me or a brother or another friend or classmate. I guess I thought kids only died young in the movies.

Red's funeral was a closed-casket ceremony—even sadder and scarier. The thought of being caught in that machine, with no escape possible and being slowly drawn into the grinding tool, was beyond my comprehension; my mind wouldn't let it go for years afterward. It seemed like something that could only be dreamed up for a Vincent Price movie that I was being forced to watch against my will again and again. I had nightmares about it for years.

The thought of dying young haunted me for months after each of those deaths. I would lie in bed thinking about it as I tried to go to sleep. But hearing the sounds of my heart beating in the ear pressed down against my pillow … ka-shush, ka-shush, ka-shush … *What if it stops? How many times is it going to beat before it wears out or something goes wrong?* Listening to it, I believed it could never go on and on like that for a lifetime of scores of years; nothing can last that long. I began to feel vulnerable in a way I had never thought about before. I would turn my head so I didn't have to listen to my heart … *beating* … *beating* … *beating* … and surely wearing itself out. How long would it be before I would hear a sudden change of sound, like a *stuttering* or … *nothing?*

The possibility of dying young was a new reality, and I didn't like thinking about it. Along with worrying about how long my heart could keep going, thoughts of Dave and Red frequently would creep into my mind, and it would be hours before finally finding sleep.

Afterward, in my late high school years, whenever I drove out on State Route 66, going north from New Bremen and arriving at Dead

Man's Curve, I always thought about Dave and my cousin Joe. There was an old oil well that was about one hundred feet from the road near the curve's apex, and the immediate area smelled horribly of crude oil. If anyone happened to be a passenger riding with eyes closed, or even sleeping, they always knew when they were at Dead Man's Curve because of the smell. In my mind, I can still sense that smell today: the sour odor of raw crude oil. I remember it as a smell of death, thinking, *I don't ever want to die in a place like that.*

It wasn't all that unusual to see a grain grinder parked in a farm field near Dead Man's Curve, a chilling juxtaposition of the symbols of the two men's deaths.

Dave and Red were buried in those two cemeteries on the New Knoxville Road—Dave in the New Bremen German Protestant Cemetery, just inside of the curve in the road as it makes that smooth, long turn past the cemetery, and Red in the Willow Grove Cemetery, just after that next slow, sharp left turn and bridge going northeast out of town.

I looked for new roads with new curves—without those histories—for my make-believe-racetrack driving experiences. And I began to sleep on my back—or facedown on my stomach so that I wouldn't have to listen to my own heart beating.

Hammond also reported that the school district's rapid increase in valuation the last few years has already dropped the millage on the present debt almost one mill.

tails for the new $1 million plus high school.

The next step is the completion of the specifications. When these have been checked by the board, advertising for bids will begin.

during the three days.

The restriction will be lifted, according to the board president, when new facilities are installed, together with the completion of a new well.

"Hotrod" Safe And Sane Word Way It's Done In New Bremen

By MARTHA EDMISTON
Journal Herald Staff Writer

NEW BREMEN—At the very mention of "hotrod" the average, mature motorist is prone to embark on a tirade against all young drivers.

Hotrod usually conjures up a lurid, noisy picture of squealing brakes, jump starts and drag races on public highways. But in this town a group of young citizens have given the term a different, and safe connotation.

The Road Rebels club, with about 25 active members ranging from 16 years on up, is known throughout this area as an automobile safety club.

It defines itself as:

A "hotrod" organization formed by a group of responsible automobile enthusiasts, dedicated to promote interest in the sport . . . who some day hope to unveil to the public the true meaning of the word "hotrod."

Activities Described

Their definition has been put to practice so well here parents are proud to have their sons affiliated with the club.

Three members, present at the New Bremen festival yesterday to set up a club safety display, were eager to talk about their organization.

Brothers Bob and Ronnie Gilberg and Ray Meckstroth, all seniors at New Bremen high school this coming year, described the activities like this:

"We have a $5 initiation fee, with $1 dues per month. An applicant for membership must prove himself a responsible driver, and be willing to abide by club rules."

The rules are stringent.

If a member is caught speeding or "dragging," or if he violates safe driving practices, he's socked with a $5 fine.

If a court fines him, he pays the court fine and the club fines him the same amount in its own court.

Sheriff Aids Club

In the club's own "court," the president, Harold Stauten, presides as judge, while members pass on what fine or corrective measure should be taken against this offender.

The club's other officers are Richard Plattner, vice president, Roger Hegemeir, secretary, and Don Puckett, treasurer.

According to the trio who were spokesmen for the club yesterday, the county sheriff and his deputies give assistance to the organization by reporting any violators to it.

In addition, members are on the "honor system," and in several instances have reported their own violations, with the consequent fine.

The Road Rebels club is one year old this month, and it's in the process of joining the national "hotrod" association, which includes all such clubs pledged to safety and courtesy.

Road courtesy is constant with the Rebels. Any member who finds a motorist in distress will stop and offer assistance. When it's accepted the member presents the club's card with its safety slogans and brief of the organization's aims.

The members are given a club identification plaque for their car with their initiation, and they purchase shirts and jackets with the name on them. Standard car equipment includes safety belts, road flares and will include fire extinguishers.

Identification shirts and jackets are always worn for such events as a recent "liability run" which included clubs from Wapakoneta, St. Mary's and Piqua.

Social Events Held

The liability run, the boys explained, "is to see how well you can follow directions on the road, make a certain point punctually without speeding or violating traffic rules."

The last run was to Russell's Point. The next, which the club hopes to run next month, will include other clubs.

Social events include swim parties and record hops to which girls are invited.

An incorporated club, the Rebels carry their own insurance to prevent liability for parents or members.

"We try to observe every safety practice as a club and as individual members. We think people will begin to change their minds about the name 'hot-rod' if more clubs like ours are formed," said the boys.

They Campaign For Traffic Safety

NEW BREMEN—The "Road Rebels" are rebellious only about people who fail to observe safety and courtesy on the road. Members such as Ray Meckstroth, left, Bob Gilberg, center, and his brother Ronnie, right, are pledged to safety, courtesy and responsibility to other drivers. The several dozen youths in the club hope to give the driving public a new conception of the term "hotrod." (Journal Herald staff photo)

spans.

This year's program was divided into four projects. Project No. 1 is for a new span on Middle road, east of this city, at an estimate of $13,270.26; project No. 2 is on the Glynwood road in Moulton township, west of here, at an estimate of $18,493.26.

Project No. 3 two bridges on the New Knoxville-Glynwood road in Washington township, at an estimate of $30,483.48; and project No. 4, two bridges on the Maier-Baber road in Noble township, northwest of St. Marys, at an estimate of $34,104.38.

Big Transformer Is Unloaded At Bellefontaine

BELLEFONTAINE — The first of two giant transformers for the city's power plant has arrived in Bellefontaine and is now at a temporary site on south Detroit street south of the utility plant.

The 10-ton unit was lifted and lowered to the ground by the NYC System's wreck crane. Due to arrive next week is a 50-ton transformer that will be unloaded near the same spot, and then moved to a permanent concrete base being prepared nearby.

LAURA—A food sale will be sponsored here at 10:30 a.m. tomorrow by the Laura Shining Bluebirds group.

Road Rebels: Just Because

See the way he walks down the street …
—The Crystals, "He's a Rebel" (Gene Pitney)

The farmer took another bite from his *eatin'* cigar (that's what they called cigars used as chewing tobacco) and, hooking his thumbs behind the straps of his overalls, asked me, "What are Road Rebels? Why're you boys a-doin' this?" I was always afraid someone would ask those questions. I didn't have any answers. In fact, none of us had the answers. We were not rebelling against anything; we weren't really rebellious. We were just a bunch of guys who liked cars and thought we had to do something about it—and stand out from the rest a little. After all, there were car clubs out in California shown in *Hot Rod* magazine month after month in the '50s, featuring neat hot rods and custom cars. They all had plaques hanging on the rear bumpers with names like Twisters and Dukes or Cams, and the guys all had matching jackets or shirts. They customized their cars and had drag races, social outings, and pretty girls sitting in or on their cars. So, late in 1956, we had to do it too. Just because!

And maybe it was the James Dean factor: *Rebel Without a Cause.* The movie was, as far as we were concerned, the hit of our youth years and maybe even the century. Leather jackets, ducktail haircuts, turned-up shirt and jacket collars, a little attitude with some slouch, cool cars, and those California girls.

It was enough to get our teenage blood boiling and make us all want to have a little bit of it in New Bremen. Why not? After all, we had a local racetrack where Indy stars ran their short-track cars three or four times a year. The New Bremen Speedway was then owned and operated by Jack's father. Jack was a good friend and a member of the Road Rebels, so we all felt pretty connected with big-time racing. We went to all the tracks around our corner of Ohio and Indiana to see the famous drivers of our era—Troy Ruttman, A. J. Foyt, Pat O'Connor, Parnelli Jones, Bobby Unser, Johnny Rutherford, and many more—drive those terrifying short tracks, including at our hometown speedway. While we didn't have a drag strip or dry lake beds for racing like they did in California, we had the New Bremen Speedway, so we had some bona fides too.

But we really didn't have the West Coast kind of hot rods. There wasn't a shop within fifty miles of New Bremen that could chop a top or channel a body or build a full-race flathead engine. Never mind, though; we could put on fender skirts, lowering blocks, and dual exhausts and have the hood and trunk "shaved" (the hood and trunk ornaments were removed and the sheet metal smoothed by leading).

Enough of this kind of custom "lite" treatment; now we're talking, we figured.

All we needed were enough guys, some shirts, bumper plaques, and a club name, and we were in business.

Thanks to Harold, we did it. Harold had the vision for the club and got us all together, presenting the idea and urging us all to join. And, to a man—or boy—we did. With an enthusiastic bunch of guys committed to the idea, the next challenge was a club name. That could have been a real problem; clubs can fall apart before they get started as a result of arguing and disagreement over something like a name. We couldn't steal names from the California clubs; we wanted to be original and had to have something that made a statement—a statement saying, *We're cool, and we're not gonna let you forget it.*

But we had to be different too; there would not be anything wimpy or white shoes about us, so names like Friendly Riders, Fun Runners, or Good Driving Guys would not get any votes. The name had to convey the notion that we had fast cars and were very hip, and, most importantly, were also very independent—in spite of the fact that all of us still lived at home with Mom and Dad. "Road Rebels" seemed to capture all of that: independent, doin' our own thing, and hip to the California-scene-in-Ohio. And, mainly, we didn't think anyone else was using the name. It was all ours.

New Bremen was going to have a car club! *Just because.*

So that was the answer to the farmer's questions: *just because.* That was good enough. We didn't need to explain ourselves; we were doing it for ourselves! It would make us cool and different from all the other teenagers in New Bremen and the surrounding towns. We were going to show the town that we could be organized and do something important. Rather than just being a bunch of lazy teens, hanging out, smoking cigarettes, endlessly driving around town in noisy cars and annoying everyone, we would shape up, look professional (whatever that meant), and try to do some good.

We also had a notion of trying to help stranded motorists who had broken down on the highways or who needed to be rescued from snowdrifts, and, in general, actually be all-around good guys. It probably also meant that we wanted to get attention. And we would organize various car-oriented events, such as road rallies, car shows, maybe even dances—the possibilities were endless.

Listen, Mr. Farmer man. If you can't dig it, I can't explain it to you. And please don't spit down by my shoes!

We had bumper plaques made up that had "Road Rebels" in bold letters arced across the top of the plaque and crossed checkered flags below. They had polished, aluminum-gray lettering on a black background. We had matching jackets in gray with white lettering and red-and-blue flags; we used the color scheme from the Civil War's

Confederacy. Why we did that is still a good question. No one seems to remember.

We also had white shirts with a similar color scheme. We had the rebel thing down, even if we didn't live down south in rebel country. Ironically, we also had "Safety Club" embroidered on the left sleeves of the shirts. We didn't know exactly what we meant by that, either—we did have some ideas about being advocates for safe driving, but they were fairly vague. I guess we might have thought it would improve our image and give us some needed respect: cool guys, cool cars, safe drivers …

[illegible]AD REBELS — Harold Stam[illegible] third from left, president [illegible] the Road Rebels of New Bre[illegible] and three members of the group examine recently - purchased identification jackets for the club, which stresses safety and courtesy on the highway at all times. Included from left to [illegible] are Ray Meckstroth, Bob [illegible] berg, Stammen and Ron Gilbe[illegible]

"Hotrod" A Safe And Sane Word; The Way It's Done In New Bremen

[illegible]W BREMEN — This enter[illegible] Auglaize county commun[illegible] [illegible] went to the speed age [illegible] a nearby speedway — and is [illegible] than optimistic about keep[illegible] it there. [illegible] it still must concern it[illegible] with transient travel through [illegible]

An idea of the strictness of this so - called 'hotrod' fraternity can be gathered from the fact that in order to get into the organization, the prospective members must pass certain tests.

If satisfactory to all concerned, the candidate then is acquainted [illegible]

presenting a card, describing the organization's safety slogan and a brief of its ultimate aims.

The members are given a club identification plate for their cars with their initiation (costing [illegible]) and they purchase shirts and jackets with the club name [illegible]

We had thought about it enough to have calling cards made up that everyone was to carry at all times, announcing:

YOU HAVE BEEN ASSISTED BY A MEMBER OF
THE ROAD REBELS CAR CLUB

These were to be handed out whenever possible; I think we visualized ourselves as occasional white knights of the road, cruising around and helping anyone broken down with a flat tire, hot radiator, empty gas tank, and the like. And it would be especially good if the broken-down car had a teenage girl or two involved. We would create a positive image for all car guys, something I guess we thought was badly needed. I have a box of those cards now, sitting on my office credenza—still full.

But how cool was all that? We had monthly meetings, driving rallies, a car show, and later on even a race car. And, since all clubs had to have a home base, we hung out at the Hollingsworth Hotel Bar and Grille. It had a back room, called the annex, where we held our meetings. And conveniently, the barroom and restaurant where we could drink beer—even when some of us were still underage—was just through a nearby door. We talked cars, smoked, drank beer, argued about cars (usually Fords versus Chevys), and discussed the latest racing news. While old men sat at card tables out in the barroom playing euchre or pinochle or sheepshead, slapping down their trump cards noisily, we young kids planned Rod Runs and big events in the back room—including a Road Rebels' rod and custom car show.

The car show would be our biggest, most ambitious venture. We had to find and rent a venue large enough to attractively display the fifty or more cars we hoped to have entered, we had to attract car owners from throughout the area, and we had to promote and advertise the event.

Harold, again, was the force behind this, and he, more than anyone else, pulled it off. He contacted other car clubs to promote owner participation, found a way to get the show announced on nearby radio stations, and organized all the details—and, along with myself and a couple of other guys, found the venue: the Green Acres Ballroom. We spread the word about the show all around town, nailed posters to telephone and power poles, and got some ink in the area newspapers. We optimistically named it the "Tri-State Rod and Custom Car Show" sponsored by the Road Rebels Car Club of New Bremen, Ohio.

The Tri-State Rod and Custom Car Show

The Green Acres Ballroom was located in the countryside out west of Celina, one of the nearby small cities. Of the many dance ballrooms around the area in that time, only one, the Edgewater, still exists now, and is a re-creation of the original one. These ballrooms, with their grand crystal chandeliers, huge dance floors, and wide windows or shutters to let in the summertime evening breezes, had been all the rage during our parents' younger years of the '30s and '40s. But most had fallen on hard times with the advent of music everywhere: your car, your bedroom, or in your hand with the new transistor radios. Then we had 45-, 78-, and 33-rpm phonographs at home, the *Hit Parade*, and *Sing*

Along with Mitch (Miller) on TV, and most importantly, rock-and-roll music coming on.

The big bands were disappearing, and the ballrooms were losing their traditional customers, who were getting along in years and losing their interest in dancing. Rock-and-roll garage bands were yet to come, so there was little music to fill the ballrooms with dancers in those days.

So because of the changes going on in the entertainment world and the changing interests in music, some of the ballrooms were readily available for events like the car shows we wanted to have. We chose the Green Acres Ballroom because the owner seemed really interested in what we wanted to do, the price was right, and it was the most centrally located ballroom in the tristate area that we hoped to attract cars from: Indiana, Michigan, and Ohio. And the owner didn't seem to mind that hot rods with engine oil leaks, leaking brake fluid, and radiators leaking coolant would be staged all around that precious hardwood dance floor—or maybe he didn't know that that's what hot rods do.

#

With the car show all set, it was showtime at Green Acres. Riding over to the ballroom on opening night was an experience I'll never forget. Jack's dad, Frank, had managed to get the famous Elmer George to be our technical judge. Frank must have used some pull that he had in the motor-racing world to accomplish this, because Elmer was the United States Auto Club—the sanctioning body for the Indy 500—National Sprint Car driving champion at the time.

And I sat in the backseat of the car the famous Elmer George was being driven to the show in! I could barely breathe and couldn't bring myself to say a word.

He was one tough-looking guy, with scars and marks on his face that I could only imagine came from some kind of horrible racing crashes on his way up to the big time. And big time it was. He was currently the chauffeur of the HOW Specials, the team of cars owned by Mary Hulman, daughter of the Indianapolis Speedway owner Tony Hulman. She had a championship car for both the paved and dirt mile tracks, a sprint car for the half-mile short tracks, and even a midget car for the shorter tracks for Elmer to drive. They were all painted with the same black-and-white color scheme and had the same number on the hood and tail: 21. They were all named "HOW Special," HOW standing for the team's major participants, Hulman, Ober, and Wolcott, all well-known people involved in the racing scene around Indianapolis.

Being in the car with Elmer George that day brought back the memory of being a thirteen- or fourteen-year-old kid and seeing Mary Hulman at Dayton Speedway a few years earlier. On that Sunday, she was debuting her new car and racing team—and this was maybe the first or second big-time auto race I had seen.

Here was this new, terrific-looking, unpainted, bare-metal race car, with a new, upcoming driver—Jerry Hoyt—Mary had picked to drive in the initial race at Dayton. Jerry and the new car didn't win that day but qualified well and brought the new car home in the middle of the pack. It looked like a promising start for Mary and her new team. After the feature race ended, we did our usual walk through the pit area to look at the cars and racing people. As we approached the pit area for that new number 21 car, I couldn't believe my eyes!

There was the young—around twenty or twenty-one years old—beautiful, blonde Mary Hulman in tight-fitting black slacks and black blouse, drinking a can of beer, smoking a cigarette, and leaning against the pit wall by the car, laughing and talking to Hoyt and the car's mechanical crew. After a race, a racing car is usually a hot, dirty, smelly, used-up-looking thing, and the driver doesn't look much better: face covered with oil and dirt, clothing the same, and a kind of far-off, *just-looked-eternity-up-close-and-personal* stare in his eyes. Seeing a pretty, wealthy, free-spirited girl from the elite world of racing hanging around, drinking a beer and laughing with these rough, tough, brave men blew me away. I was so taken with the whole scene that I fell in love with everything and everyone that day: Mary, race cars, race drivers, and racetracks—all of it.

The thrill of it all made me want to be a race driver as soon as I could. But, luckily for me at that time, that would have been at least five more years. Five years is a long while, and a lot of things can happen in that amount of time; there is much to be learned. And life and time has a way of making a person think things over. Hoyt was killed in a bad accident a year or two later, ending a promising career. That news, and seeing too many really ugly racing accidents over the next few years, made me think differently about all that. Spectating was going to be just fine.

But I've never forgotten the young, carefree-appearing Mary Hulman. Every time I've watched the Indy 500 on TV in recent years, with Mary shouting, "Gentlemen, start your engines!" I think about that day at the Dayton Speedway almost sixty years ago.

I realized back then and there that I needed to be at some racetrack somewhere—on any given Sunday—rather than in church—doing car things with car guys.

#

So a few years later, at the time of our car show, Elmer George was driving Mary's HOW team cars, and I was in the back seat, riding with him on the way to our show. Professional baseball, football, or basketball players wouldn't have thrilled me as much as being in the same car with this brave man who drove Indy and dirt-track racing cars on tracks all around the country. Race car drivers were my heroes.

Some of the other Road Rebels and I were to escort Elmer around the rows of cars as he inspected them and delivered his judgments on their technical merits. Elmer didn't like anything he saw that day; I don't think any of them passed his technical inspection.

"That front end on this roadster will break right off when he hits a bad enough bump."

"Those brakes will never stop this car from 125 miles an hour."

"These welds aren't deep enough; something is going to break at a bad time."

"These tires are junk; so are those wheels!"

"Those safety belts won't hold a flea!"

It was all good input, but there were no safety awards in those days. It was all about looks: styling, paint, interior, chrome, and engines. Whichever cars took first, second, and third places are details now lost in time; but the awards were not based on technical merits or engineering. It was all about *show and go*, not suitability for running around racetracks at one hundred miles per hour. Few of those kinds of show cars really ever saw much street action and certainly no track action.

None of the winners were Road Rebel cars. It wouldn't have been right for the host car club to have one of the winners. And we really didn't have "show" cars in our club, anyway. We had nice-looking "drivers," with paint nicks, filthy underbodies, and dirty engine compartments. We were drivers who enjoyed cool cars but couldn't afford "trailer queens." We had to drive our cars to school or work.

We continued to watch Elmer drive around the Midwest and at Indy for several more years. He was temporarily kicked out of USAC for a major dustup with the race officials at the Langhorne Speedway in Pennsylvania sometime later. After being reinstated, Elmer wasn't finishing up front any longer and by then had married Mary Hulman. Who needs to keep risking his life in dirt-track race cars after marrying into that kind of wealth?

Elmer survived his racing days but ended up being shot to death in 1978 by a horse trainer working on the Hulman horse farm. According to newspaper reports at the time, the two had a difference of opinion and—both having guns—had fired multiple times at each other.

Dirt-car race drivers were a tough bunch.

The Road Rebels Go Racing

In the last year or so of the club's existence, the Road Rebels went racing. Hobby Stock cars were a cheap form of racing that almost anyone could get into back then. It fit our budget, which was whatever got thrown into the pot. So we went for it without any racing experience and with what probably would have instead been beer money. The rules were simple: six-cylinder engines only, no engine modifications, and stock suspensions. Few safety rules to worry about: no roll bars, fire extinguishers, specific tires, and so on were requirements. The driver needed a safety belt and helmet and was good to go. I'm not sure the organizers at the tracks even checked to see if the drivers had highway driver's licenses.

Our car was a '50 Ford two-door coupe with a flathead, two-hundred-cubic-inch, six-cylinder engine, one-barrel carburetor, and a three-on-the-tree transmission. To get it ready for racing, we stripped the car down to nothing but the engine, bare body, and the frame. We spent several evenings at Don and Betty's place, drinking beer and ripping out upholstery, flooring, side and rear glass, radio, heater, passenger seats—anything that added weight and didn't need to be there to make the car go. A huge pile of junk waited for Harold Ahlers's garbage truck after those evenings.

On the positive side, we found and installed some truck tires because we had heard that they were better for racing. We also bought and installed a lap-type seat belt from JC Whitney—where we bought most of our car stuff—and borrowed a club member's motorcycle helmet. We had finished our car "building and preparation" and were set to go racing. These cars, including ours, probably didn't have more than eighty horsepower; the goal was cheap, safe, fun racing. We could do that; we really didn't know *what* we were doing, but the Road Rebels were going racing.

However, we didn't know who would actually drive it. For sure, we weren't fighting among ourselves about it. I think we all visualized ourselves as gentlemen race car owners rather than the Elmer George type.

Hobby Stock car racing was always part of a large day or evening racing program that included very serious race cars: Super Modifieds.

Super Modifieds were about the hairiest form of racing going on anywhere. And New Bremen Speedway was one of the key tracks in the Midwest's "Super" racing scene. These cars had serious horsepower, highly modified suspensions, and radically cut-down bodies. They were scary fast, and in some cases—maybe most cases—scary to look at too. Chrysler Hemis and Buick Nailheads were the hot-ticket engines for many cars. But the newer, lighter small-block Ford and Chevy engines were starting to become popular. All of these high-horsepower engines stuffed into twenty- to thirty-year-old Ford, Plymouth, and Chevy bodies—some with the ugliest sheet metal cutting and welding you ever want to see—brought people to the Ohio and Indiana tracks by the thousands.

And since our Hobby Stocks raced as warm-up acts for the Supers, there were drivers everywhere; the only question was how to get one of them into the Road Rebels' car?

I don't know who did it or how it got done, but we managed to get one of the better Super drivers to run our car. I've always guessed that Jack's dad pulled in another favor for us: Stan Bowman was our driver.

Stan was hot and going places. A Kentuckian with a Super Modified named the Ridge Runner—or something like that—Stan was a new face in Ohio racing who was giving the regulars a run for their money. But he was late showing up as we wheeled the Road Rebels' car into the starting area. We were all looking around for our driver and nervously watching each other but avoiding direct eye contact at the same time. *What if he didn't show up?*

Don't look at me, I was thinking.

"Okay, chickenshits, I'll drive it," Dick bravely volunteered.

"Man, way to go," we said with limited enthusiasm.

He actually had warmed the car up earlier and so climbed into the driver's seat, nervously getting ready to race if needed—he had never raced before—when Stan finally showed up. Dick was out of that car as if it had an ejection seat; he was the happiest man at the track that night, probably even happier than the night's big-purse, Super Modified feature winner.

Stan drove the wheels off our little Sportsman Stock that first night, winning our first race in it. Starting positions had been determined by lottery drawing, and we hadn't had any luck with that. Stan started the race somewhere in the middle of the pack and then began working his way to the front. He passed cars on the inside groove, he passed them on the outside groove—sometimes he even passed them in the straightaways.

We looked at each other, wondering where Stan had found the extra power we didn't think the car had. He passed the leading car on the next-to-last lap. We jumped and danced around, spilling beer on each other, yelling our lungs out.

"Jesus H. Christ, he won!"

"Holy shit, *we* won!"

"Can you believe it?"

"Let's head for the finish line!"

"Bob, bring along a beer for Stan!"

"Yeah, man!"

We hadn't won because we had the fastest car, since it was pretty ordinary and didn't have any secret speed tricks; we won completely because of Stan's driving skill. The key to driving those underpowered "race" cars was momentum. Don't lose the momentum. The driver had to keep his speed up because the cars didn't have enough power for any real acceleration. Slip and slide around too much and those cars would lose forward momentum and could not accelerate fast enough to recover lost speed and track position. So the key was being smooth and maintaining speed without sawing on the steering wheel. Stan was a master of smooth. The Road Rebels Special, with Stan driving, maintained its line all around the track, not bobbling and weaving—and won the race! It was beyond our wildest hopes.

It also turned out to be the high point of the Road Rebels auto racing adventure. Stan wouldn't be available to us after that, so after that first night, we ran where we probably belonged: midpack. But it was a great experience and worth all the effort and spare change we had to put into it.

Not Fade Away

By the end of that summer of '59, Buddy Holly had been gone for several months, and I was still having a hard time accepting it. The last song his band played that February night in Clear Lake, Iowa—"Not Fade Away," one of my favorites—still resonated in my mind. My life in those times was about to fade away and become something far different. Things were changing, and I had decided that it was time to move into another phase in my life. I started to lose track of most of the guys in the Road Rebels. I never saw our race car again, although I later learned that it had been nearly destroyed in a racing accident and badly burned. The driver was not injured, but the Road Rebels had decided that the car was beyond repair and scrapped it.

The road rallies, the car show, the race car, all our projects began to come to an end sometime after that year of racing. The Road Rebels Car Club of New Bremen, Ohio, after its hopeful beginnings in late 1956, began to fade away sometime in the following year of 1960.

It had been a pretty good effort for a bunch of kids looking for excitement in our little farm town in western Ohio, all because of … well, *just because.*

The Little Race Car on the Corner

Wipe the windows, check the tires, check the oil, dollar gas …
—Chuck Berry, "Too Much Monkey Business"

It used to sit out there on the corner where State Route 66 made a sharp left turn to the west before curving northward out of town and on past the local racetrack. Whenever a big race was held at the New Bremen Speedway, that little race car sat out there on a small patch of grass on that sharp corner, under the huge pine tree, out in front of the gas pumps of the Lone Pine gas station. The car was parked there to attract race fans in for a fill-up or refreshments on their way to or from the racing. It was one of those things that could just grab a twelve-year-old kid so much that he couldn't think about anything but having one of his own. It was beautiful, with chrome spoke wheels and a chrome exhaust pipe running the entire length of the car from the engine past the rear wheels. The car's body was painted an eye-catching metallic bronze color that sparkled in that small patch of deep-green grass. Except for its size, it looked like the real thing.

It is hard to say how much extra business it actually brought into the Lone Pine, since if a driver really didn't need gas, how often would he stop just because a pretty little car was parked out front? At least it let passersby know that the gas station manager's heart was in the right place. And if anyone did need gas the next time, it had to be something he surely would remember.

After a few years, the car no longer sat in its customary place on those Sundays, and it retreated into the back of my memories. After all, I had a driver's license and, in partnership with my older brother, owned a real car. And once owning something like a 1949 black Ford two-door coupe (okay, standard model with six-cylinder engine), a teenager is a little too cool to be thinking about things like miniature race cars. His head is full of things like chrome shift knobs, rear-seat speakers, whitewall tires, and fender skirts. That was serious stuff, only for older boys. But driving our car around required money for such things as gas, insurance, and tires—all things that required that I find a way to make some money.

The Lone Pine, Fred, and Me

Fred, who owned and ran the Lone Pine gas station, was rumored to be looking for a part-time worker (meaning a high school kid who'd work for fifty cents an hour). I went to see him about it one day after school.

"Hi, Mr. Wellemeyer. I'm Bob Gilberg," I said. "I'd like to ask about the job I heard you have open."

"I know who you are; you buy gas here now and then," he said. "How old are you now?"

"Sixteen, since last October."

"I need someone in here from seven o'clock to eight o'clock in the morning to work at the pumps while I open the station," Fred said.

"Then I need you here from four o'clock to six o'clock in the afternoon while I have supper at home."

"I can do that."

"I also need you here all day Saturday from seven to six to help with all the back-room work and to work the pumps when I'm tied up in the back. I also want you to be available occasionally on Sunday afternoons."

I was already counting up the hours and multiplying by those fifty cents: I could be making twelve to fifteen dollars a week, depending on how many hours he needed me on Sundays.

"I'll take it, if you offer it to me!" I exclaimed.

Fred looked at me from head to toe; I felt as if he were trying to decide if I was really old enough and strong enough. He said, "I need you to be here on this schedule no matter what—bad weather, your friends going to do something fun, if you have a cold—anything. If you're not here, I can't get other things done, and I miss my supper at home with my family."

I gulped, realizing that this was serious stuff, and I bravely said, "I can do it."

"Okay, you start tomorrow."

This was my first experience as a paid employee of a businessman. Yes, I had the usual paper route in my bike-riding years and some occasional day jobs in the summer when the farmers came into town sweeping kids off the streets to help combine hay or whatever long grass they were in a panic to get baled up and in the barn before the next rainstorm hit. But this was a real job where I had to show up on time and be diligent about my assignments.

I needed some breaking in and was a bit small in those days for some of the heavy chores. But I think Fred weighed the pros and cons of everything and was pretty clever. While there may have been other guys around who had actually worked in gas stations before, I think the thing that sold him on me was that I lived with my parents in a house we rented right behind the Lone Pine.

That meant I couldn't easily hide when things got too busy on a Sunday afternoon or if it was a slow day and Fred wanted the afternoon off. All he had to do was look to see if our '49 Ford was in our driveway, and he would know if there was a good chance that I was home. Or he could just call Mom and tell her that he needed me. But I didn't mind, since I always needed money.

Over the next two years or so, Fred and I got used to one another, and I got a good handle on what was needed and how to do it. I worked on winter days with bad head colds when it was so cold outside that the windshield I was trying to wash for a customer would freeze into a sheet of ice before I could dry it. I worked on holidays when Fred wanted a complete day to spend with his family; I worked when I would rather have been with my friends, and on busy days, I worked from seven in the morning to nine in the evening. I felt kind of grown up and heroic about being able to do that in all kinds of Ohio weather. Never mind that Fred did it seven days a week, twelve hours a day.

It worked out well for both of us. He got time off with his family, and I got money for my teenage life. My friends would usually come by in the evenings to fill up, have a Coke, smoke (we all smoked as soon as we could), and shoot BS. We talked about cars, girls, and rock and roll—nothing new there. The job and the Lone Pine became an important part of my social life for most of my high school years.

My education as a skilled gas station attendant was a little bumpy, though. There really were some rough spots when Fred had to have the patience of Job with me. In the spring of the year of the little race car incident, my career nearly ended on a wet, rainy morning before I left for school.

Hal Hott's Buick: A Brush with Eternity

That morning, Hal Hott, a regular customer who lived just down the street, had coasted his beautiful, red-and-white 1950 Buick Roadmaster (two-door hardtop, straight-8 with overhead valves, three portholes on each side of the hood, and stick shift) into the station with a dead engine. He left it there before I arrived. My initial assignment was to help Fred get the Buick running by towing it with the Lone Pine's utility vehicle, a '48 Chevy with vacuum shift.

"Bobby, help me get the towrope hooked up to the Buick, and then you get in the Chevy and tow me until we get it started," Fred said.

"Which way are we going?" I asked.

Pointing west, he said, "In that direction, and make sure you give it plenty of gas. That Buick is a heavy car."

"I know. Let's go."

We tied a long, heavy rope from the Chevy's rear frame to the Buick's front frame. I was to gently take up the slack in the rope until there was tension and then gas the Chevy to get the Buick rolling, whereupon Fred would let out the clutch and, hopefully, the Buick would start running. Then Fred would drive it into the Lone Pine's open garage area and start trying to figure out what was wrong.

Simple—gas stations did this all the time. Fred had a big wooden push-board mounted on the Chevy's front bumper—to avoid damaging cars being pushed—but sometimes we pulled cars with a rope instead. It can work just as well as pushing, sometimes even better if the car to be started doesn't have a strong rear bumper or if the taillights are in a vulnerable position. But towing is trickier, since once the towed car starts, both vehicles have to be brought to a halt smoothly so that the towrope can be released. For example, if the towing car stops too fast, the towed car could hit the towing car. And there are some other details to keep in mind, such as being careful to avoid snapping the towrope by not carefully taking up slack first, making sure that the towrope isn't going to bend sheet metal, and so on.

It's also important to maintain eye contact between the two cars' drivers to keep things coordinated.

That morning, things got complicated because it was cold and raining. And the cantankerous vacuum shift in the Chevy, which never worked well, did not seem to be working at all. The Chevy's vacuum shift had the odd characteristic that first and third gears seemed to be in the same place, so shifting always took special care. But I had driven it enough that I usually didn't have any problem with it. We roped the cars together on the street in front of the Lone Pine. I had the windshield wipers running, and I also had the radio on because Little Richard was singing "Long Tall Sally" on WING radio from Dayton. Oh, and I also had the driver's side window rolled up.

Long tall Sally, she built pretty good. It was up loud.

After taking up the towrope slack, I couldn't get the Chevy to move that Buick! I let the clutch out and gassed it, but nothing moved, and the Chevy stalled. I tried it several times before realizing that, because of that stupid malfunctioning vacuum shift, I had the car in third gear instead of first gear.

When I finally did put the shift lever into first gear and gassed it hard, off we went. I was feeling really good about having figured out what the problem was and that finally we would get that Buick going. The only problem was, as I looked out the side window, I could see that Fred was running alongside my accelerating Chevy. He was yelling at me to roll the driver's side window down!

What was he doing out there? Who was in the Buick?

When I finally had figured out the gearshift and was ready to get things going, I hadn't taken one last look to see what was happening behind me.

It's the eye contact, stupid!

There was no one in the Buick, but I was moving smartly along with it in tow—heading west out of town—with no driver in it!

Knee-jerk reaction took over. I hit the brakes. The Chevy stopped. The Buick didn't.

It came tearing alongside of the Chevy until the rope tightened up again, but with the Buick about to pass the Chevy. The towrope was between the cars, stretched from the front end of the Buick—as it passed me—to the rear end of my Chevy. In other words, the driverless Buick was about to begin towing the Chevy. As the slack ran out of the rope with a huge jerk, both cars did a fast half spin, coming to a halt with both cars sideways in the road, the Buick a little ahead of the Chevy.

Fred was right in between the two cars when they had come alongside each other and then spun around. Somehow, defying all laws of the universe, he wasn't touched by either of the spinning cars or the straining towrope. But he looked as if he had just seen Creation up close and personal.

Parts of his face—mouth, cheeks, and nose—were ghostly pale, and other parts—neck, forehead, and ears—were beet red! I don't know how a person can be simultaneously white as a sheet from fear and yet look crimson and apoplectic from rage. But Fred managed it. Maybe he was alternating between the two, sort of flashing white then red, white then red again, and so on. I didn't really know, because I couldn't exactly look him in the face. I don't remember all of my reaction, but I rolled down the window, turned down the radio, and said something like, "Gee, Fred, the Chevy's not running so well this morning and kept wanting to stall, so I had to gas it pretty hard. By the way, what were you doing out of the car?"

Fred had known I had the Chevy in third instead of first and had been trying to get my attention by yelling through his open window and the window he imagined I had open in the Chevy. But with me rocking out in the Chevy with my windows up, I couldn't hear a thing. He thought when he saw me mashing around with the Chevy's transmission shifter that he would have time to come up and make me understand what I was doing wrong. But I had found first gear before he could reach through the window—and strangle me.

A long time passed before I regained Fred's confidence. We had other "training" adventures, but none as big as the great Buick tow. I had done all the usual raw recruit screwups: drained transmission fluids instead of engine oil while performing an oil change; opened overheated radiators without letting things cool down first and flooding the engine compartment with the surging radiator fluid; punctured inner tubes with the tire irons while attempting to fix flat tires (*But I did patch that nail hole. Why is it still hissing?*), and more.

A Buick Full of Nuns

The worst of all of these other more or less minor incidents occurred on the day a Buick, driven by the priest of New Bremen's small Catholic church, came into the gas pump area blowing the car horn and stopping just in front of the office door. I was handling the gas customers that day while Fred worked on a tune-up in the back. I stepped out into the pump area and politely said, "Hi, what can I do for you?" (We didn't know "How may I help you?" back then.)

The priest said, "The temperature gauge is in the red area. Will you please look at the engine?"

"Sure. Happy to," I said, looking warily at all of those nuns in the car. Nuns always seemed to frighten me a little, seeing those stern faces and ceaselessly watching eyes and having heard enough about rulers slapping fingers and heads. They never seemed to smile, but that may have been my own imagination—not being a Catholic, I didn't really know.

Against all of Fred's past stern warnings about this situation, I forgot everything he'd ever said. Maybe it was being confronted with a carful of nuns and a priest that boggled my mind. I wanted to be polite and as helpful as possible, and wanting to try to solve their problem as fast as I could so that they weren't blocking the gas pump lane, I opened the hood and with a standard gas station rag in my hand, placed that hand on the radiator cap, and started to twist it off. A hot radiator in a car with the temperature gauge showing over two hundred degrees Fahrenheit is a bomb waiting to go off in the face of anyone stupid enough to remove the cap. As I began to carefully twist the cap to the first stop position, trying to slowly let the pressure out of the radiator, suddenly the cap blew off, and boiling-hot radiator fluid spouted up like a geyser over my right hand and into my face. I was stunned by the force of the scalding water and was in instant, burning pain.

The nuns all scrambled out of the car along with the priest and began pouring cold water from the windshield washing bucket over my arm and hand and trying to rinse my face with a clean station rag.

"Bobby, what the h … heck happened?" Fred yelled from the back room, changing his language at the last minute when he saw all the black dresses and the black, buttoned shirt.

I needed to get to a doctor fast, but Fred couldn't leave the station, and the priest's Buick was inoperable. So Fred called my home. Mom took me to Doc Fledderjohann's office, where he smeared salve over my hand and face, wrapped and bandaged everything up, and declared that I had dodged a bullet: none of the hot fluid had gone into my eyes or nasal passages, and the rag in my right hand had absorbed most of the hot water. I had second-degree burns on my upper face and all over my right hand up to the wrist. The skin between my fingers was the worst, since the water and the soaked rag got trapped in there and stayed long enough to produce the worst burns.

With my right hand wrapped in a bandage and held in a sling to minimize pain, I was on limited duty at the station for several weeks after that and only able to pump gas left-handed and answer the telephone. Fred felt very bad about the accident, but we both knew he had warned me about how to handle that situation: "Open the hood, and make them wait in the car until the gauge is reading a low temperature."

But I had always felt sort of inadequate telling a customer to do that while I just sat in the office waiting, since I had no idea of what to talk to a bunch of nuns and a priest about to pass an hour or more.

"Seen any good movies lately?" probably wasn't a good idea.

"Have you heard Elvis's newest?" wasn't going to be any better.

So I thought I needed to try to do something right away; four nuns and a priest hanging around the station while I listened to Little Richard singing "Good Golly Miss Molly" (*She sure like to ball*), and Chuck Berry singing "Sweet Little Sixteen" (*She's sporting high-heel shoes*)?

I think I'll try to carefully let the pressure out of that radiator …

#

But those incidents all paled in comparison to the Buick-towing incident; they only cost Fred money or inconvenienced things in one way or the other. But the Buick-towing incident could have cost him his life! And for me, Buicks were fast becoming a paranoia thing.

But slowly, over time, we got past those incidents and, on balance, I think I was useful to him. That is, until the night of the little race car incident.

The Little Race Car

That little race car had been on Dad's mind. And since I was working at the Lone Pine, where it used to be seen sitting out front on race days, he was going to use my connection there with Fred to find out what had happened to it. Dad had seen it when it was first built and shown at the big races at our New Bremen Speedway in the 1930s and had never forgotten it. He always said that it was the prettiest miniature race car anyone in Auglaize County, and probably western Ohio, had ever seen.

By miniature, I don't mean to imply that it was a tiny thing that was only a model. This little car was big enough that a kid of around ten years or so could actually get in and drive. And it didn't have any lawn mower engine in it for power; it had a for-real motorcycle engine that produced serious horsepower that made for a faster-than-expected ride.

It had been built by a local company, Wehrman's Machine Shop, with great skill and precision. The car was modeled after the short-track car driven frequently in those days by Mauri Rose, who later became a three-time Indy 500 winner. A picture of the car alongside the real thing—with Mauri Rose himself in the cockpit on the front straight at the New Bremen Speedway with a young Johnny Wissman in the little car's cockpit—had been shown around town for many years. We all had heard about how Lucky Johnny got to drive demonstration laps at the speedway in the car at all the big races back in that era.

My dad knew that either Fred or Fred's wife owned it, and he was determined to find out what Fred was doing with it. One night, my dad had come into the station to gas up his Ford and BS a little with my usual group of friends, who were there waiting for me to get off work. Fred was back from his evening dinner and getting ready to close.

"Where is that car, Fred? What have you done with it? Why don't you have it around here any longer?" he asked in his usual repeat-the-question-several-different-ways style.

Fred gave some vague, off-putting answer. "Don't have room for it anymore … too much bother," or something to that effect.

My dad went on reminiscing about it for a while, going on about how he remembered Johnny Wissman running the pretty thing around the track. He named drivers I had never heard of, drivers I *had* heard of who went on to great careers, and the old days at the speedway with great fondness. After all, New Bremen was a pretty small spot at the intersection of Ohio Route 66 and Route 274, and it hadn't seen too many moments of fame in its years. The speedway had given it most of them.

The fact that the town did have a speedway with a history of great drivers and great races was something to be proud of. But it was also infamous as the track the drivers burned to the ground on that day back in the '30s when the starter's stand, the refreshment stands, the toilet buildings, the admission booths and gates—anything burnable—went up in flames. Living in a small midwestern town next to nowhere, we were happy to have any claim to fame, I guess.

I think all the talk of those days and the pretty little race car rekindled some interest in Fred that night, because the next Saturday, he told me to bring my dad over to the station, and he would show us the car. That Saturday, we went into the barn-garage behind his house, which was across the street from the Lone Pine.

Behind a pile of discarded stuff from the Lone Pine and Fred's house and old Hudson car stuff (Fred loved Hudsons) sat the pretty little thing. Under all the dust and grime, we could still see the chrome spoke wheels and chrome exhaust pipe. It had a chrome radiator shell at the front end of a beautifully fabricated sheet-steel metal body painted in that metallic bronze color. Even though I was a fairly mature kid of sixteen, the car still knocked me out. The workmanship was beautiful. It had knobby, dirt-track-style tires that looked like the real things. The whole car looked exactly like a real car, but in one-third scale. Fred showed us its JAP (John Alfred Prestwich—an English engineer) motorcycle engine and the belts and pulleys of the drive system. It even had a little leather-covered seat that looked as if it had been made in an upholstery shop.

"Let's take it over to the station," Fred said.

We cleared the stuff away from the car and carefully worked it out through the barn door, along the sidewalk, and over to the Lone Pine. Since it was getting late, Fred stored the car in the garage area of the station, and Dad and I left.

A few days later, when we were closing the station for the night, the events of the little race car transpired. Dad had stopped in for gas, and a few of my friends had been hanging out with me at the station. We were all surprised to see Fred roll the race car out of the back room and under the big roof that covered the gas pump area. We all stood around admiring the car, wondering what Fred had in mind now that he had brought it out.

We soon found out.

Fred stepped on the JAP motorcycle engine's kick-starter lever a couple of times, and it fired up. Since it had nothing but a straight exhaust pipe with no muffler, it sounded wonderful. Loud and wonderful! It made a terrific ripping sound when Fred revved the motor up and down, up and down for several minutes until the engine had warmed up enough that it would idle smoothly by itself. It sat there running and looking great—and Fred said, "Get in there, Bob."

But getting in there proved to be impossible. The car had been built for boys eight to ten years old, not sixteen. I could get *on* the car, but I could not get *in* the car. Getting on the car meant sitting up on the tail with my feet down in the cockpit, resting on the seat. Holding the steering wheel meant hunching over and reaching down and forward to grab it, my hands between my ankles.

So there I sat, *on* the car, thinking, *How would I drive from up here?*

Fred said something like, "Here is the brake, and here is the clutch," and he waved at some pedals and levers down in the dark bottom of the cockpit.

I didn't even have my feet down there—they were still planted on the leather seat—when he moved something *down there* and gave the car a little push forward. It took off like a rocket, with me nearly sliding off the car's tail.

No foot on the brake pedal, because I had no clue where it was, and no foot on the gas pedal, because I didn't know where that was, either. I was mystified that the engine ran at such an advanced throttle level without any pressure on the gas pedal.

The car tore off with me barely hanging on, gathering speed. It just ran off with me, out of that pool of light at the Lone Pine and into the dark of North Main Street where the road makes a bend into the country and heads toward Lock Two. I could barely keep my balance while sitting on the tail of that little car, which was showing just how fast it could run.

New Bremen had some really lousy roads back then. We were not a wealthy community, and roads were seldom repaved just for the purpose of making them smoother. They were patched … and repatched … and repatched. Some of the roads had areas of patching that were so rough that we couldn't ride our bicycles over them without jarring our teeth; we had to take care that our tongues weren't between our teeth when going over those bumps for fear of seriously biting it. We couldn't skate across some of those streets without taking a header, either.

In other words, they were terrible; we used to joke that the cornfields surrounding New Bremen were smoother than some of our roads. And there I was heading down one of the worst streets—in the dark—sitting up high on the back of an out-of-control, miniature race car.

I quickly learned that with a little turn of the wheel, in true race car fashion, I got an immediate reaction. So to make matters worse, as I bounced around trying to find a way to maintain my balance atop the car's tail, I was also trying to find out how to steer that speeding rocket. Small turns of the steering wheel resulted in fast, cutting arcs, with the car sweeping from curb to curb and me lurching violently from side to side, all while bouncing over some of the biggest road bumps in the county. Picture a bronco rider at the rodeo.

As the little car sped toward Lock Two and beyond, it was also getting very dark, because I had gone beyond the town's homes and was passing the first of the small farms surrounding the town. No streetlights out there, not even porch lights. With the exception of the moonlight, it was going to be pitch black, and it was even blacker down there in the cockpit where the brake and gas pedals and clutch lever were supposed to be.

I began to feel panicked. The little car had no lights, of course, so no automobile drivers were ever going to see me. A country road intersection was coming up faster than I wanted to think about, and I had no idea of how to get the car to stop. It's true that at that time of the evening and that era in the '50s, there was not likely to be any traffic on those roads, since most folks were at home and either in bed or watching their new color TV sets. But one never knows, and with my luck, a horde of cars could be converging on the intersection.

I had to either find a way to stop or at least slow down enough that I could turn around and get back to the Lone Pine. Figuring out how to stop would have been preferable, but I couldn't do it. I managed to get my left foot down into the cockpit on the side where there should have been a brake pedal. That did not help my balance problem at all, since I didn't have the advantage of one foot on each side of the seat that allowed me to use one foot, then the other, to counterbalance the bumping and swerving. I was sort of leaning forward and to the left, with my left leg stretched way out to press against the brake pedal. But I couldn't get very good leverage against the brake pedal because my butt kept wanting to slide off the back of the tail if I pressed too hard. And since I couldn't find the clutch, I needed to press very hard on the brake pedal to try to slow the car because I couldn't get the engine disengaged.

Talk about catch-22!

I pressed the brake as hard as I could without sliding backward off the car, and it finally did slow down a little. I came to a place in the road where I knew it would be wider because of mailbox pull-offs and driveways, and I determined that it was now or never. I had to either turn around there at whatever speed I could get down to, or I was going to have to chance the intersection and go on—but to where? Going on might as well mean forever—or at least past the cemetery and on to New Knoxville where I was likely to get arrested at the speed trap coming into town.

So going on was not an option. I had to chance turning around, with the risk of possibly turning over in the process because I was still going fast.

When I approached the critical point of no return, I pulled the car all the way over to the right side of the road where I began to send up a shower of gravel. Then, as I arrived at the widest spot—I could only tell this because, in the moonlight, the gravel at the mailboxes stood out as a white area contrasting with the black pavement—I cranked the steering wheel over hard left and leaned as far to the left side of the car as I dared. Hoping my lowered center of gravity and offset weight would keep the car from turning over, I hung on as the little car did what a good little race car should do: skidded sharply to the left, made a 180-degree turn, and headed off the other way.

Cool! I had passed that critical maneuver. Now, all I had to do was get back to the Lone Pine without hitting something, falling off, or being hit by someone in the dark.

I found that as I reduced the pressure on the brake pedal, the car would speed right back up just as though it had an automatic transmission being held in check by the brakes. It didn't occur to me just then, because I was so busy trying to stay on board the thing, but I found out later what was going on with the car. First, the idle adjustment on the carburetor had been left in a highly advanced position where it was normally set for warming the engine. That is why it just ran away with me. Second, the car's clutch was a lever that disengaged a system of belts and pulleys that were the car's drive system. That explained why I couldn't find a clutch pedal on the floor. And finally, when I was pressing on the brakes trying to stop the car, the belts and pulleys slipped enough to slow us down.

But I didn't know that then, and frankly, I didn't have time to think about it. All I knew was that I had managed to get turned around and was heading back to safety and that friendly pool of light back at the edge of town. Of course, the problem was going to be when I got there. *How will I stop this thing?*

Just getting slowed down again wasn't going to cut it. I mean, what good would it do to get there going a little more slowly but still fast enough to just flash through the pool of light and maybe get a loud "Help!" yelled out before I disappeared into darkness going the other way?

But that concern was just academic until I got closer to the Lone Pine. I still needed to navigate the treacherous curve just at the edge of town and the sea of bumpy road patches that covered the street at that point. These were the worst bumps I was going to encounter, and I wasn't looking forward to the experience. Somehow I had made it through them on the outbound part of the ride, but I was in no shape to take them again.

I was heading back into town on my raging ride in pitch-black darkness with my butt aching from the pounding it was taking from the car's sheet-metal tail, and the worst part of the ride coming up fast. I could no longer do a fair job of keeping my balance on my precarious seat. I was ready to get off as soon as I could it get stopped.

But all I needed to do was hang on through the last, bounding curve, and I was within striking distance of safety. I was actually beginning to formulate a plan for my arrival. It had to do with a large, thick hedge between the back side of the Lone Pine property line and my folks' rented place. Maybe it could be used as a soft crash barrier that I could steer the car toward just before I jumped off to safety. I would get skinned up a little, and the car would lose a bit of paint, but everything would work out okay.

Unfortunately, I never got to try the soft crash landing. The bad bumps got me! The first ones bounced my legs up and out of the cockpit. I had no way of maintaining my balance. My legs were outside of the car kind of windmilling along as they banged down on the road's surface. And because the speed was too high for my legs to keep up by sort of hopping along with the car, they would be pulled back behind me and toward the rear wheels. My feet were getting caught under the rear wheels, which nearly pulled me off. So I was lurching wildly around with all this when even larger bumps presented themselves. These bounced the car straight up and down. My butt flew clear of the tail and banged back down again hard enough to threaten my manhood—and the final bumps were yet to come!

The end came quickly. Those last, big bumps jerked the car from side to side, and I was history. I went over the side like a rag doll after about two left-then-right twitches of the car. There was no question of trying to heroically hang on and fight my way back into the cockpit and bring the raging thing under control. It just chucked me off like a sack of potatoes, and that was that. I bounced and rolled out there in the darkness and listened to the sound of the little car as it flew on across the road without me.

It was still upright, with the engine racing madly as the wheels bounced clear of the road and back down, and then it careened straight across the sidewalk and up a small sloping lawn. I heard a loud crash and the continued sound of the engine running at full throttle. But the sound seemed to be coming from one place, not fading away as it would if the car had continued up the road—just the sound of that single-cylinder JAP motorcycle engine at full throttle blaring away, in one place, in the darkness, alongside Mrs. Schmidt's house.

Because of the darkness, I couldn't see what was happening. But I heard the sound of the guys running down the street from the Lone Pine, yelling excitedly among themselves.

"Jesus H. Christ, where is it?"

"What did it hit?"

"Where's Bobby?"

"Oh shit!"

"It's over there by the corner of the house!"

"How do you shut it off?"

"Damn thing is really loud!"

"How do you shut the damn thing off?"

"Why didn't he drive it back?"

"Who lives here? Is anyone home?"

"That lady, Mrs. Schmidt. She's coming out the door."

"She has a heart problem, but she looks okay."

"How do you *shut* this damn thing *off*?"

"Jesus, that thing is loud!"

"She's looking pretty upset. How do you shut this damn thing off?"

"Fred is gonna shit!"

"I'm gonna shit. Where's Fred?"

"He's behind us; his butt is dragging. I don't think he wants to see it."

"There's Bobby, out in the road!"

"Bobby, why did you get off of it? Look at what it hit, you jerk!"

Why did I *get off?*

Well, I was pretty bruised and scratched and had lost some serious skin on my elbows and forehead, but there was no way I was going to mention those minor wounds when I saw Fred looking at his pretty little race car. It was lying on its side. The engine had shut itself off by running out of gas as the tank emptied itself from sustained damage.

The car had hit the corner foundation stones of Mrs. Schmidt's house and become a pile of twisted metal. The front axle was badly bent, and the car had a major kink in the frame about midway between the front and rear axles. Those pretty chrome spoke front wheels looked like pretzels, and the polished chrome radiator shell had a huge V-shaped smash in it that fit very well around the corner of the house foundation.

The sheet-metal tail seemed to look okay, but that was all that we could tell in the dark with just a quick inspection.

Mrs. Schmidt's house was in good shape, with no visible damage. But a few flowers in the flower bed next to the house had been ravaged. And Mrs. Schmidt, with a heart condition for which she was under a doctor's care—other than the initial fright—was breathing more easily.

Fred was another story. He was speechless. He had loved that little car, treasuring and protecting it and, probably against all his instincts, he'd brought it out for us all to see as a favor. Now it was junk.

Fred never talked about that car again to anyone that I know of. My dad, who was known around town as an ace mechanic and able to fix anything, had offered to repair it. Fred turned him down with no explanation.

My relationship with Fred became strained. In the ensuing days and weeks, it was pretty hard to find anything to talk about because it always seemed we were talking around things and avoiding the topic. I continued to work my schedule, and Fred even continued to pay me, but things were definitely different between us. I knew that he knew it really wasn't my fault and that he probably blamed himself—and probably my dad, as well. At sixteen years of age, it was far too complex for me to try to talk to him about it.

But it didn't get in the way of Fred's looking after my best interests.

In Spite of Everything

A few months later, I pulled the '52 Ford convertible—the one my brother Ron and I had been able to buy because of the better wages we were both earning—into the Lone Pine with my heart pounding fiercely. I had been nearly frightened off the road by my own car. While returning from Minster, the car had started wobbling and shaking all over the road after reaching highway speeds. I had to slow down and pull over to stop the shaking. It wasn't clear what had caused it, so I drove very slowly, keeping it under the speed where the shaking started, back into New Bremen and the Lone Pine. I described the incident to Fred, who wanted to look it over immediately. Since I didn't have time to stay with him, he loaned me the infamous Chevy utility car while he took the Ford into the back room.

When I returned later, Fred was standing in the office, waiting for me with a seriously irritated look on his face. When I asked what was going on, he just walked me into the back room and said, "Look at these junk tires you had on your car!"

"Oh?" I said. *We just bought the car a few months ago. How could they be junk?*

Fred had removed them from the car and said that the shaking was caused by two of the tires, which were worn to the point that there was no rubber in places, with only the internal cords and fabric showing. They were not too many miles from blowing out. The wear was so bad that the tires had lost their shape and turned into something other than nice round tires. They no longer had the perfect circularity needed on automobiles. The lumpy tires, along with old shock absorbers that no longer absorbed shocks, had caused the shaking.

Fred had taken in some used tires from a customer who had purchased new tires earlier that day. Normally, Fred would have been able to sell those tires since they were good enough for several thousand additional miles. He had mounted them on my wheels, at no charge, because he was concerned about my safety. He was irritated that I hadn't been paying attention to the health of my car while driving it as though everything were perfect.

And he was really hacked off because he knew that I had just spent all my extra money buying and installing rear-seat speakers in that car. He didn't have to say a word; his expression told me everything I needed to know: *Speakers when you needed new tires? What were you thinking? You dumb ass!*

We also ordered a new set of shock absorbers within the next fifteen minutes—the cost would be withheld from my next paycheck.

A few months later, I was offered a better-paying after-school job at a local manufacturing company with the possibility that I might be able to become an apprentice draftsman and start developing a career skill. So I took that job and left Fred to find a replacement, but I continued to help him whenever needed and whenever any of his other helpers needed time off. The good thing was that eventually his pain over the little race car affair, while never going completely away, diminished to the point that things became mostly normal between us again. It got to be one of those things that was always there, and we both knew it was always going to be there, but we could deal with it and even begin to enjoy one another again. After all, with all those mishaps between us, we would always be able to look back and have a good laugh.

And we did have those laughs—through my college years when I would just go in to visit or help him out and beyond when I began my career as an engineer in Dayton. He was fascinated by the Alfa Romeo Giulietta roadster I'd bought in my final year at Ohio State when I drove it in to visit with him: double overhead cams, all-aluminum engine, transmission, differential, and brake drums, with four on the floor. He loved the styling and technical innovation in that car, and we talked cars for hours and hours.

Eventually, I lost track of Fred and the little race car when, after a few years in Dayton, my new wife and I headed for California. But I had learned a lot while working for him from these different events back in those days; bad things can happen if you're not paying attention every minute. Danger doesn't take time off, and it is best to not forget that. But, as it turns out, I did forget it—and in the not-too-distant future.

#

So the little race car disappeared again. This time forever, as far as anyone knows. I heard a rumor that the car had been sold to a farmer east of town who had intended to repair it. But, as the rumor went, the farmer lost interest, and the car was supposedly thrown out with the trash.

But maybe that is all it was, a rumor. Maybe someday, a young boy in New Bremen will find that pretty little car hidden away in a barn, covered with dust and junk. And maybe that young boy will get his dad to bring it home and repair it so it can again sit out on some prominent corner under a big shade tree on nice days, pleasing passersby and inspiring other young boys yet again.

Hopefully, though, if and when that happens, and they do start its engine—as they surely must—it will be in the daytime and in a very big, smooth parking lot.

You're Going to Lose That Girl

You're going to lose that girl …
—The Beatles (Lennon & McCartney)

He was standing there telling me that *he* wanted me out in the parking lot, ready to fight. I was in my bowling shoes, limping around behind the seating area of New Bremen's bowling lanes. I had a bloody bruise on my left ankle that had the same thread pattern as my cotton argyle socks. I had just thrown a gutter ball, leaving the nine and ten pins standing there … laughing at me, it seemed. The bowling ball had hit my left ankle as I released it too close to my sliding left foot; I missed my spare with the ensuing gutter ball, lost the beer frame, and nearly had passed out from the pain. And this guy had come into the Ray-Ann Lanes to pick a fight with me. I was still seeing stars spinning around in my head and was more than a little woozy from my clash with the bowling ball.

"I don't fight, don't know how to fight, and you can call me all the names you want and pound away, but I'm not fighting," I said.

It was true; I didn't know how to fight, had never been in a fight, and really didn't want to get into a fight. Fights were something I had always avoided, being through most of my school years one of the skinniest and smallest boys for my age. *He* was bigger and older than I was, had recently returned from a stint in the marine corps, probably really knew about fighting (that's what they taught marines, after all), and would probably kill me.

He scowled at me with a fierce look that said, *You coward*, displaying his incredulousness. I guess he expected me to take the challenge like any other marine or townie he might have had a run-in with when he was still in the service. I told him again he could hit away, but I wasn't going to fight him, hoping *he* would lose interest and abandon the whole thing.

What was it all about? I wondered.

Turned out it was all about Joanie. He had her, and I didn't. She had been the love of my young life ever since I had seen her at the swimming pool a year or so earlier, long before that bowling alley scene.

#

Joanie was a pretty, lissome girl from Minster, Ohio. Girls from Minster were sort of taboo for New Bremen guys. As nearby towns always seem to be, it was our permanent basketball rival and the town we usually had to beat to get to the district championships. They usually beat us, and we hated them for it. Then there was the religion thing between the two towns; it was not uncommon at that time for small towns in western Ohio to be all Catholic or all Protestant, having to do with where the original town settlers came from in Europe. They had carried their beliefs—and suspicions, and biases, and bad feelings from the Reformation—to Ohio where those feelings took root and seemed to thrive there too.

I always thought, *Hey, this was supposed to be the New World, wasn't it? Why did all that religious disagreement stuff have to come along?*

Boys and girls from Minster and New Bremen rarely dated, and it was even rarer for them to marry, unless it was one of New Bremen's few Catholics marrying a Minster Catholic. A Protestant kid dating a Catholic from Minster was viewed as an almost traitorous act.

But I felt kind of edgy to be doing it. Dating Joanie had added a touch of daring to my otherwise ordinary life. Above all, she was very pretty, and, to me, somewhat exotic because of the *taboo* sort of thing that went on between Minster and New Bremen, and, to a lesser degree, the basketball rivalry.

I didn't buy into the religion matter, anyway, maybe because of that freedom my grandparents had given my father, which had then been given, in turn, to me. *Choose for yourself, young man.* I could do that.

Another thing I loved about her was that it seemed as if the religion issue didn't get in the way for us. I believed she took her religion seriously, but we didn't discuss the potential complications, figuring that would be something possibly needing to be worked out down the road. That was fine with me; I knew I had some flexibility.

I had been dating Joanie on and off for several months before the bowling alley incident, but just a few weeks before that, everything had fallen apart.

#

Long before meeting Joanie, things hadn't been going well for me with the different New Bremen girls I had been dating. Some of the girls then had other boyfriends, some were even already going steady, and my close friend and occasional date, Pat, was never without one guy or another presenting himself for her affections, so it seemed she wasn't ready to settle for just one guy. It was tough competition, and I wasn't doing very well. And Pat was also virtually my sister. Because of her outgoing personality, and because she was always looking for a little space from her own mother, she was around our house frequently. She had become the daughter my mother always wanted but never had. That complicated things.

I wanted and needed—or thought I wanted and needed—a lover, not a sister. And I didn't need to date someone my own mother would be worrying over as if she were her own daughter who was out too late with me. It looked as if I could be getting it from both angles: naughty son as well as the naughty boy who kept Mom's (virtual) daughter out too late. While it's probably true that any boy's mother would worry about the girl her son was dating and keeping out too late, it seemed exponentially true in Pat's case. It had become too complicated.

I wanted that perfect girl: a *dream lover—that I could call my own*, as Bobby Darin sang.

So one summer day at the pool when I was without a close girlfriend, a group of girls I had never seen before caught my eye. Asking around, I discovered that they were from Minster. The three girls seemed to be together most of the time. I found that their names were Joanie, Barbara, and Bette. Barbara was dark haired and had a shapely, fully developed set of curves, and Bette was more the tomboy figure, with a less developed shape and sort of the kid-sister type, while Joanie was slender and girlish with brown hair.

I fell in love at first sight.

In addition, Joanie turned out to be the quiet type that suggested the more intimate relationship I was looking for, while the other girls were very outgoing and ready to joke and flirt with anyone. Since I was never the class clown or the smooth-talking type, Joanie's quiet demeanor seemed to match my personality better. And she was beautiful—Natalie Wood beautiful.

I couldn't think about any other girl from then on. Joanie began to slip into my mind in most of my waking and sleeping hours—before I ever met her. I began chasing that dream.

It had taken a long time to meet her since she was from Minster, and she wasn't in my limited social circles. But after Ray got his driver's license and a car, we began to look for ways to just "happen across" Joanie and her friends Barbara and Bette every time we got a chance. We saw Joanie and her girlfriends frequently riding around in a new pink-and-charcoal-colored Pontiac two-door hardtop being driven by an older, geeky-looking guy. Picture the character Toad in *American Graffiti*.

What were those pretty girls doing riding around all the time with that guy?

But it was clear to us that they did enjoy riding around in a cool car on warm summer evenings, just for the fun of riding. We could do that. Ray had the car, and we both had the time.

How we finally made the connection with them is a lost memory. It probably wasn't anything more complicated than saying hello at some opportune time. I'd like to think we did something really clever that impressed the girls so much that they couldn't help but notice us, but if that had happened, both Ray and I would remember it. We don't forget things like that. The important thing is that eventually it did happen, and we became frequent companions, driving around in Ray's car, going to the pool, and having other summertime fun.

The three girls all were very pretty, and like all teenage girls, they were exciting to be around: a little flirty, at times teasingly elusive, but looking for good times. Of course, they also had other friends and plenty of other guys after them, which made the chase that much more exciting.

They favored short-shorts and loose-fitting, long-sleeved, men's-style dress shirts—usually pink—for their nearly everyday wear in the summertime. There's something about a girl in a man's long-sleeved shirt, shirttail nearly fully covering her shorts—all the way down to the bottoms, so it looks as though the shirt is the only thing she's wearing. Intentional or not, it's a sexy, attention-getting look—and it never failed to get mine.

Initially, we were all just friends with no pairing up going on, but secretly, I was falling head over heels for Joanie. I didn't want to break up our fun group by starting anything with romantic overtones, but I also knew I wanted to go beyond being just friends. That changed when Ray gave Joanne, a pretty girl in the New Bremen High School class just behind us, his class ring, and they started going steady. That allowed me to ask Joanie to be my date for the coming (the following spring—several months off) junior prom. She accepted, and I was on clouds. We had several dates over the next few months, including the prom, and I felt as if everything was going pretty well—except for the fact that everyone seemed to be after her.

She was everything I had hoped for: a wonderful companion with interests similar to mine in music and movies. She was fascinated with the *Eddie Duchin Story* (Kim Novak, Tyrone Power), and I was fascinated with *The Girl Can't Help It* (Jayne Mansfield, Little Richard). Well, we both were interested in movies and music, but our common interests may have parted ways a little when it came to the finer points of the arts.

Joanie was easy to get along with, not demanding, and to my eyes, the prettiest girl in the county. And was she very affectionate. She was the first girl who had ever wrapped her arms over my shoulders, placing her hands in my hair on the back of my head, and very lightly pressed me toward her when kissing. I had never experienced a kiss as tender and yet affectionate as that. It had a touch of elegance and warmth I didn't know existed. I had always thought of kissing as a kind of forceful thing where the harder you kissed—both pressing lips together hard enough to seal a Mason jar—was how it was supposed to be done. That's what I always thought they were doing in the movies, anyway. I had a lot to learn—and I knew she could teach me. I was a teenager in love. "I want you, I need you, I-I-I love you," Elvis sang. *Tell me about it, Elvis*, I thought again and again.

But was I going to be able to hold on to her? What did I have to offer her? I didn't have anything more than a part-time job in a gas station, one-half of a car I shared with my brother, and frankly, I was still pretty skinny and wearing those bifocals. And I was always more than a little self-conscious about my family's recent difficulties. My dad had serious back problems with herniated disks that led to his inability to keep a job, since all the work he had done in his life included at least some manual labor. That led to a nervous breakdown, which led to a long period of depression, which led to the horror of electroshock treatments. Several months passed before he was able to return to productive work, but he still had the bad back. The bad back eventually required spinal surgery that was, by today's standards, very primitive. He had a huge incision requiring months for complete healing, and it still left him with a painful back for the rest of his life.

In those days, in those little towns—including surrounding towns—everyone knew everyone else's problems. The stigma of that nervous breakdown—which of course was considered a mental illness—and those drastic treatments always left me feeling as if everyone whispered about our family. I probably just imagined it, but I couldn't shake it.

Would Joanie know? What would she think? What would her parents think? Everyone seemed to treat our family and me just fine, but I always had that doubt.

In one encouraging sign, though, Joanie had come to see me at my home the first day or two after the boiling radiator fluid, Buick-full-of-nuns accident at the Lone Pine gas station. She, Barbara, and Bette were all there. My face was wrapped in bandages, and my right arm was also bandaged and in a sling. I needed the sling to keep my arm up around chest level, since dropping that arm to waist level increased the burn pains in my hand to nearly intolerable levels. Supposedly, keeping the arm up higher reduced the blood flow and reduced the pain. I had ointment smeared all over my face, which had kept me from showering and shaving my teenage facial stubble for the first two or three days, resulting in a grimy, greasy look that embarrassed me. I was happy to see Joanie and Barb and Bette, but I didn't really want them to see me looking like a refugee from a horror movie.

Coming to New Bremen to visit me at my home was a really nice gesture by Joanie and her friends, and I hoped it meant good things for us. My mom was more than impressed that such pretty, nice girls from another town had come to visit me.

Still, in spite of her visit, I never did become confident about Joanie. I always had a back-of-my-mind feeling that this wasn't for real. "The Great Pretender" (*too real is this feeling of make believe*) by the Platters kept playing over and over in my head.

Very soon after the nuns and the boiling radiator incident, I heard about another guy in the picture. *He* had come back to the area from the marines. *He* was a very good-looking guy with wavy blond hair who had been away from his hometown, New Knoxville—four miles northeast of New Bremen—for the past few years. To any teenage, junior class, high school girl, he had to look very enchanting—and worldly.

He drove a flashy, all-white, 1955 Ford Victoria convertible with a white top, white interior, and white sidewalls. He had a job, money, Hollywood good looks … and he found Joanie. His name was Bill.

I saw her riding in that convertible with him shortly afterward.

At that moment, I knew I was going to lose that girl. I would become a historical footnote in her life—and maybe not even that. And while I didn't fully know it at that point, the truth was I had already lost her. Soon after seeing them together in his convertible, word came that they were going steady.

We never had any parting conversation or sad love letters. No confrontations or angry words. Only a silly telephone call I made to her.

"Hi, Joanie, I just wanted to call to tell you that, in spite of everything, you are the most wonderful, unforgettable girl I've ever known."

Then I hung up, without giving her a chance to reply. I mean, what could she say to that? *Thank you?* I doubted that it would make her change her mind. And I didn't want to create a clumsy situation for her. After all, we weren't going steady, she didn't have my class ring, and she had never promised me anything—and certainly didn't owe me anything. I just had wanted to let her know that she had been very special to me. But secretly, I hoped she'd interrupt me and say, "Wait, Bob, you've got it all wrong."

Of course, it never happened, and I had a rough time dealing with knowing that there'd be no Joanie after that. At least she didn't say, "I'd still like to have you as a friend."

I hated that one.

Losing Joanie is what eventually led to the bowling alley affair. I had gone back to hanging out with my Road Rebel friends, which meant spending most evenings in the Hollingsworth Hotel Bar and Grille's annex, drinking too many beers, smoking too many Pall Malls, and being a little too obnoxious.

One night, we had been doing exactly that until around ten o'clock. Since it was a warm night, we went out to sit on New Bremen's Monroe Street bridge over the canal to hurl wisecracks at people—mostly acquaintances—driving by.

Bill drove by in his too-cool white '55 Ford. We yelled some stronger insults at *him* (he was from New Knoxville, after all)—probably with extra emphasis from me—forgot about him, and waited for the next victim. Most people took it for what it was: a few young twerps with more time on their hands than sense, doing stupid things. He apparently didn't see it that way.

It may be that I was the only one he recognized, or it may be that he decided that since he had won Joanie, he'd rub it in a little by singling me out from the bunch and punching me out.

He found me at that bowling alley a few nights later.

And my strategy worked; he didn't want to hit a guy who wouldn't defend himself. He growled some obscure comments and left in his white '55 Ford convertible … with the white interior … and white sidewalls.

So the whole affair, Joanie and Bill (and very soon my bowling career) all ended then and there, that night. I had lost that girl, embarrassed myself by not fighting, and realized that I was not going to be any good at bowling anytime soon—all in one flash of self-awareness. I went back to the ball rack for my turn in the tenth frame and confirmed it: I hit my ankle again.

Bowling was costing me too much money, anyway. I always lost the beer frames and had to buy rounds for the whole team. And I could never drink as much as the rest of the team; I would be on beer number three—with about three more open, getting warm and waiting for me to catch up—while the rest of the guys waited for me to screw up so I could buy yet another round. *Which they could count on!*

I thought I needed to get back to being a Road Rebel full time—and fast. Cars were something I understood much better than affairs of the heart or playing at New Bremen's most popular, ankle-busting winter pastime.

And sadly, by then, all the other girls in my life had found steady guys. I had lost them all while chasing my Joanie dream. I badly needed something to break my way—graduation was coming soon. The Skyliners' music on the radio at that time only made my sadness worse: *I-I-I don't have anything ... since I don't have you.*

The Last Road Rebel

Don't know much about history …
—Sam Cooke, "Wonderful World" (S. Cooke, H. Alpert, and L. Adler)

The Road Rebels were never going to save me from myself. They were great friends and guys I could depend on, but they all had their own self-interests that came first. When it came down to girlfriends and careers, they were going to do what was best for them. No one could argue with that. But things began to change as guys made those decisions for themselves and the club began to lose members and its attractions for some of the others as time and life caught up with us. We kept going, though, much as before, holding the usual monthly meetings and the informal, in-between meetings, talking cars, racing, and planning new projects. But I was about to find that I needed to begin making some of my own life decisions, rather than just continuing to bump along, day to day.

#

I hadn't been the best student in high school and wasn't an obvious candidate for college-level education. I would had to have done vastly better for any scholarship awards, so there wasn't going to be any financial assistance, and my family certainly didn't have the money to pay for my next level of education. It wasn't even clear that I could handle anything above twelfth-grade studies. I hadn't really tried. After all, I was a motor head and didn't care about much else.

The result of my wasted time in high school became my new reality when I decided shortly before my 1958 graduation to go with two classmates and friends, Judy and (Carbide) Ted, to check out some colleges they were considering. The only college I thought might work for me was the University of Cincinnati. Cincinnati would have been a good solution since their engineering school was a co-op deal that let a student alternate working and school time on a quarter-by-quarter basis. I thought I might be able to afford going to college this way, if I could get accepted.

Ted and Judy were accepted—they always had good grades. My letter said, in so many words, "Hello, thanks for your interest, but you are rejected."

It was a punch in the gut since it seemed to be my only option. I wasn't really surprised, but I was badly disappointed and then had one of my first serious meetings with reality. My new reality.

Following that, the local company where I had a part-time, after-school job let me know that there wouldn't be an opportunity to move into a full-time position—and they were discontinuing my part-time work, as well. I had been hoping that after graduation I would be able to move into a full-time, apprentice draftsman position.

That was punch-in-the-gut number two, both coming within a few weeks. I had hoped the draftsman position would be my best chance at a near-professional career, avoiding a lifetime spent working in a manual-labor-type job. It seems strange now, looking back, that I hoped to have a career using my brain for a living when I really hadn't tried using my brain during school. All of a sudden, I realized that working at manual labor—renting out my muscles, so to speak—wasn't the life I wanted. But that was probably what I would be doing.

What had I been thinking? I had been focused on the car-guy, good-old-boy thing for the past three or four years when I should have been thinking about developing my mind. The year 1958 also marked the beginning of one of the worst recessions of the twentieth century. Companies were laying people off far more than they were hiring. I had graduated into a bad recession with nothing to offer. I had a little woodworking shop, a little math, some chemistry and physics—none of which I had done well in—and had worked part-time in a gas station.

All that would only get me into the employment office long enough to fill out an application and then—nothing.

The understanding that the fantasy life of high school abruptly ends and you meet your future—most likely the day after graduation—had escaped me for at least my last four school years, if not all twelve.

In New Bremen, and probably all over rural Ohio in those days, going directly out of high school with no further training meant that the odds were at least 90 percent that I would be working somewhere as a shop worker. For those whose families owned farms, the odds were much the same that the kids would become farmers. But the Gilbergs weren't farmers and didn't own a farm, so it was likely going to be shop work or some type of construction job for me.

Say hello to your new, high-top Red Wing work boots.

And all of that came on top of having lost Joanie. Maybe she saw me more clearly than I had been seeing me. All the possibilities I had always assumed would be open to me during my dreamy years in high school seemed to have become impossibilities in my new, real world.

But finally, one of the two or three local manufacturing companies that were going pretty well in spite of the recession hired me as a shop helper. That meant I walked in at 7:00 a.m. and found out what I would be doing for the day or maybe the next hour or few hours. Then it was off to some other task where a warm body was needed. It might be moving equipment around the shop, as things were constantly being rearranged to increase production, or it might mean painting walls, or pushing a wheelbarrow to a new concrete floor being poured. I weighed 135 pounds; a wheelbarrow full of concrete seemed to weigh at least 300 pounds. I could already picture myself walking around with the aid of a stick in a short time—maybe even the next week.

My first assignment was deburring pinion gears for TV antenna rotator drive systems as they came off the lathes in bucket loads. They dripped with lathe oil, sloshing around in those buckets and needing to be deburred on a bench grinder fitted with a rotary wire brush instead of a grinding wheel. One by one, I slid a pinion gear onto a ten-penny nail held in my left hand, and with my right hand, I pushed it up into the rotating wire brush to knock off the burrs. I used my index finger on the right hand, with a leather sleeve on it, to rotate the pinion gear around in the spinning wire brush several times to guarantee that the burrs were removed all around the pinion. Losing all the skin on that index finger in the first five minutes was a distinct possibility I warily tried to avoid.

So there I was, starting my new career and post–high school life, sitting on a stool in front of a rotating wire brush, pushing oil-soaked, peanut-sized pinion gears into the brush that—no surprise—sucked all the oil from the pinion gear and sprayed it back off that spinning finger-eater directly onto whoever happened to be sitting on that stool. Me.

I had worn a clean work shirt and pants that first morning, hoping to make a good impression, but within fifteen minutes of sitting in front of that rotating wire brush, my shirt had a three-inch-wide streak of oil that extended from my crotch to my neck. My face was covered with oil, my glasses were covered with oil, oil dripped off of my nose, and it had pretty well oiled down my pride-and-joy flattop. I also had dozens of the little wires that had separated from the spinning brush embedded in my shirt front, including some that had penetrated my skin. I looked and felt like an oil-covered pincushion.

And I was going to have to do it all day—and the day after that, and the day after that.

I realized right then and there that this was a no-future proposition: *one dollar per hour, no benefits, and boring work that would have me babbling riddles to myself in no time.*

I thought of reconsidering that offer from my uncle Paul Gilberg, who owned a mortuary business, to send me to embalming school. But remembering how creepy it felt when my brothers and I stayed with his family in their home—above the funeral parlor—I still doubted that I was the right person for that business. I always had visions of fully embalmed corpses returning to life and coming to find me in my bedroom at 12:01 a.m. It wasn't that deburring pinion gears and taking oil baths every day looked great, but at least I wasn't going to get strangled by the walking dead.

And how do I explain to a pretty girl that I want to romance and marry that she would be married to an undertaker? I had enough problems with the opposite sex without having to deal with that too. If I ever managed to get to that serious point with some as-yet-unknown girl, I didn't think I would know how to tell her, "Not tonight, dear, I just embalmed Ralph!"

Thanks for the offer, Uncle Paul, but I think I need something involving wrenches and gasoline.

I had little choice other than to keep on keepin' on until I had a better plan. It was a beautiful summer, with warm evenings to spend doing things that let me avoid thinking about the hard choices I really needed to be thinking about. And while I knew it would change soon, most of my friends and the Road Rebels club members were still around for that summer. So I continued doing most of the same things I had done for the previous couple of years: hang out in the evenings with the guys and girls, go to the swimming pool, drive around a lot, do some water-skiing, have a few dates, and do Road Rebel things, such as going to races and working on cars. I only thought about the big issue of what to do about a real goal in life when I was at work, doing another, what seemed to me, meaningless task. Meaningful to the company certainly, but meaningless to me.

As the summer of '58 wore on, I began to feel lost; it seemed as if everyone was going away—off doing better things than I was doing as a shop roustabout. I wasn't learning to run any of the really good machine tools in the shop—and if I had been, it would have probably made me feel differently about my self-worth. Actually, that was probably a good thing; I might have just decided that things were good enough.

#

I still remember that really lonely feeling I had in the fall of '58: everyone going off in their new life directions with exciting things to do and places to go, and yet I was just driving around by myself in my '52 convertible on those warm evenings, all alone. The Skyliners were still singing "Since I Don't Have You," and the Flamingos were singing "I Only Have Eyes for You" on the car's radio. Those songs continually reminded me of the fact that all the girls I had been interested in, including the past love of my teenage life, Joanie, were gone—either to college, going steady or engaged, or already married. The music seemed to never let me alone: Little Anthony and the Imperials' "Tears on My

Pillow," the Rays' "Silhouettes on the Shade," Ricky Nelson's "Poor Little Fool"—it was getting to be too much.

I had a hard time accepting it all; there were too many examples of me meeting up with my new reality: buckets full of oily pinion gears, a disappearing circle of friends, and no potential girlfriends in sight. I was wallowing in self-pity, trying to hide it and make the best of things. Something had to change. Winter was coming.

#

Because I had so many family members and friends in my hometown, the desolation of an Ohio winter didn't fully set in until after the Thanksgiving and Christmas holidays and festivities. The eternally overcast skies of the coming January and February, the brown fields, and bare, dark skeleton trees were, for me, powerful depressants. I needed something to help me through the coming winter, and bowling wasn't it.

My high school classmate Jim, who was attending Miami (of Ohio) University, had invited me to Oxford, Ohio, to spend a weekend, attend a school basketball game, visit a few bars, and check out the college scene. I accepted and made the almost one-hundred-mile drive over a bitterly cold January weekend. The higher level of basketball played in a university of that size—compared to the level I had been used to seeing at high school games—impressed me. The college cheerleaders impressed me even more. Of course, I enjoyed the bar scenes even more still. But what really caught my attention was the excitement I found radiating off those thousands of students—all nearly my age—living in a community of young people, excited and optimistic about their lives and futures.

What a difference from the life I was living!

Driving the hundred miles back home, the differences between the scenes I had just glimpsed compared to my life glared at me more and more contemptuously with each mile. The funk I was falling into grew deeper as I passed by all the brown and gray fields surrounding the highways. And I wasn't looking forward to going back to that job on Monday morning.

But I also came away from that weekend with something new and very influential to me: jazz music. I had heard certain tunes that were very popular on the campus over and over during the weekend. One of Jim's roommates had a 78-rpm album by an artist I had never heard of before—pianist André Previn and *Secret Songs for Young Lovers*, with the hit track "Like Young." It featured jazz piano with orchestral string backing—cool jazz and symphonic sounds at the same time. I had never heard anything like it. My music diet had been one of '50s AM radio: rock and roll and rockabilly—a singer and three guys in the backup band, three chords, two minutes and thirty seconds in length, and "*baby, baby, baby*" for lyrics.

"Like Young" made me want to be sitting in some hip city bar with low lights and sexy women in form-fitting, low-cut dresses and high heels, smoking long cigarettes, sipping strong drinks from crystal cocktail glasses, and listening to music being played by men in tuxedoes.

It wasn't going to happen at the Hotel Hollingsworth Bar and Grille—that tune wasn't even listed on its Wurlitzer or probably any jukebox in all of Auglaize County.

And another jazz tune with an exotic sound and mood, "Harlem Nocturne" by the Viscounts, had also been playing again and again in the bars in Oxford. It was the *sexiest, moodiest, make-you-want-to-visit-some-city late at night and walk down damp, dimly lit streets with music drifting out of clubs with mysterious women sipping cocktails, casting knowing glances my way as I strolled by* that I could imagine. The seductive sound of that saxophone playing those haunting, new sounds captivated me. It took me away to sophisticated cities and people living the sophisticated lifestyles that I only saw on TV programs like *Mike Hammer* or *Peter Gunn*. It took me away to New York City or Chicago, and the pretty girls I knew lived there.

All this new music told me that there were newer and better things to be found out there in the world. *But how to get there?*

#

While I agonized over my situation early in the spring of 1959, I found a brief bright spot in all my gloom and hopelessness. She was Linda—not the fifth-grade classmate Linda of the *National Geographic* episode—but my old neighbor from the days when my family lived in a house at the south end of town. We had flirted a little when I lived next to her, but with my classmate and once-or-twice date Judy and longtime friend and date Pat practically living next door, things were a little too complicated to begin dating her at that time.

But now that we were living just out of town to the north, I no longer had that limitation, and Judy and Pat were going with other guys, anyway. Linda asked me to be her date for her prom, and I accepted. We had a good time, but the past prom with Joanie was still in my memory, and I couldn't stop thinking about her throughout the evening. In spite of Linda's best efforts, my mind was elsewhere.

Her best efforts included dressing very prettily in a pink prom gown, being very attentive to me all evening, and later on, her never-to-be-forgotten *full-body kisses.*

I had never experienced anything like it, and I had been trying to experience it all.

Linda kissed in full contact, with everything she had, from her ankles to her forehead pressed against mine. We were thigh to thigh, pelvis to pelvis, hip to hip, and chest to chest. It seemed as if a vacuum might form between us. Of course, this was a neat trick when she was wearing a strapless gown with layers and layers of slips, and I was in a full-dress suit with a necktie.

T-shirts and shorts would have been better. But even with all of that intervening fabric, *oh, my God, it was great.*

We dated a few more times, but in spite of Linda's wonderful attractions, the chemistry wasn't right. She had hinted about marriage on a few occasions, and while I wanted a romantic relationship with someone, that was way ahead of where I was. I couldn't imagine trying to support a wife, a place to live, a better car, and other living costs for two on that buck per hour—and no benefits.

And maybe even babies? No, no, no!

So when an older graduate with a good full-time job and paycheck appeared, she became a chapter of my history—and I breathed more easily again. She was breathtaking, though.

#

After Linda, it all seemed much worse. I was back to driving around in my convertible, looking for love in empty places and not finding it.

I was living out the ending scenes of *American Graffiti*; a movie that wouldn't be filmed until 1973. The music, fast cars, good friends, and the mysterious blonde driving around in a cool '57 Thunderbird were all drifting away at the end of their summer. And in my own end-of-summer I felt like John Milner—but without the yellow '32 Deuce coupe—standing at the airport waving good-bye to my friends. *American Graffiti* was mostly about the time when everyone—the whole scene with the friends, music, and cars—was having that great summer. But it also had that ending I could relate to all too well when seeing the movie fifteen years later. It was as if I had already lived through it. I recognized the ending before it came.

I was lost in a small town surrounded by more small towns, all of them surrounded by corn, wheat, and alfalfa fields. It only took five minutes to drive from the northern edge of town to the city limits sign at the southern edge of town, and there wasn't much of interest to a bored eighteen-year-old kid that was going to happen in those five minutes. Before I knew it, I was out among the cornfields for another five minutes before I came to the next "five-minute" town (Minster, Fort Laramie, Newport to the south, New Knoxville to the north, or Kettlersville or Botkins to the east).

I might not have had *American Graffiti*'s Wolfman Jack, but I did have Dayton's Gene "By Golly" Berry and WING radio beaming out into the cornfields on those lonely evenings and keeping me company. Gene Berry, my lonely nights' best friend. Me, my car, my radio, and Gene Berry, the star DJ at WING.

WING radio, "1410 on your radio dial," was the only bright spot in a sea of boring music. They played rock and roll as well as rhythm and blues, 24-6. On the seventh day, Sunday, all the radio stations all over Ohio switched to religious programming; some for the entire day, others just for the evening. It was enough to put me off religion. *Wasn't Sunday morning church enough? Why kill the music and preach sermons for the whole day? I'd already been to church!*

I always wondered, driving around on those Sunday nights, *what is Gene Berry doing at this moment, on a Sunday night? Probably having a lot more fun than I am.*

Spending those Sunday nights driving around in my convertible with nothing but preachers and hymns on the radio was the worst for me. I would spin the dial around on that radio madly, hoping to hear a few bars of Chuck Berry, Elvis, or Little Richard on some faraway station, maybe beaming out of Memphis or WLAC, "1510 on your AM radio," in Nashville—or anywhere. I would have even settled for a little Pat Boone, I was so desperate. I guess I could understand the radio stations not playing raunchy Little Richard and strutting Chuck Berry on Sunday nights, but I couldn't even find Julie London singing "Cry Me a River" (*I cried a river over you*) or Frank Sinatra singing "Witchcraft" (*those fingers in my hair*), either of which would have made my misery all the worse. But wanting to feel sorry for myself, those songs would have been okay too. I was deep into self-pity.

What I wouldn't have given for a pretty girl riding with me and Little Willy John's or Peggy Lee's sultry "Fever" (*fever till you sizzle, oh what a lovely way to burn*) playing on my radio.

And I always had to go back to that *job* on Monday morning. Things were getting too depressing; something really had to change.

#

It did. I met a beautiful girl from New York City.

Carol had been in New Bremen before and was returning for another visit with her cousin Jan and to stay with Doris, the sister of my high school classmate Herb, for a few weeks in that summer of 1959.

Because of the excitement and work of the Road Rebels car show and other Road Rebels projects the previous winter, I had nearly forgotten that I'd met her during that previous year-end holiday season. That Christmas, western Ohio had experienced a few unseasonable warm days that brought everyone outside to enjoy the wonderful break from the usual winter weather. It was in the seventies on Christmas Day. Driving around in my convertible with the top down, I had happened across Doris and her brother Marvin and this new girl when I cruised through the downtown area. I invited them to ride around with me for a while. They had happily accepted and rode with me for an hour or two. Carol sat in the back, so I really wasn't able to talk to her and get to know her. But as I looked at her in the rearview mirror, I was struck by how pretty she was and that she seemed to be enjoying herself immensely. The breeze was blowing her dark hair around her face, and with her beautiful smile that seemed to come so easily, it was clear that she was someone I wanted to get to know. *What a beautiful girl*, I kept thinking. *I'm going to have to follow up on this.*

We drove around town waving at everyone on the streets, feeling really good about being in my convertible with the top down on Christmas Day in Ohio. We took our time, driving slowly out into the countryside, around one of our nearby lakes, then back into town, where I dropped them off.

I had been feeling on top of the world and wanted it to go on forever. But I hadn't learned anything about Carol beyond her name, and at that point, I didn't realize that she didn't live around New Bremen. I just assumed that she was from around the area and that undoubtedly I'd see her again, since Herb's family seemed to know and associate with people from all over the county. For unknown, stupid reasons, I didn't immediately follow up on that afternoon drive. Carol returned home to New York before I had a chance to see her again, and I had returned to my shop helper job, working at any odd task needing a warm body.

When Carol returned to New Bremen later that summer, I was one year into my post–high school "career" and badly in need of a self-image boost. Herb called, inviting me out to their farm to spend some time with the family and to meet someone who had asked about me. He was vague about who it was. I was clueless but happy to find out who he was talking about. I walked into the family home's front room, and Doris smiled, saying something like, "Bob, do you remember Carol and driving us around in your convertible last Christmas?"

Carol! She gave me that make-you-want-to-kiss-her-right-now smile, and I was hooked! Again.

Our personalities and interests seemed to match, and we did a few things together over the following weeks. It surprised me, since we really had no common experiences; I was a motor head from the sticks of Ohio, and she was a beautiful girl from the biggest, most cosmopolitan city in the country. I was fascinated about getting to know someone from New York City, which seemed like—beyond on our recent senior-class trip—a place I'd never visit again and only ever read about in the newspaper or hear of on TV.

She was so much fun and not at all snobbish like we Ohio country people expected New Yorkers to be. We went to the county fair with some friends one evening, which wasn't really a date but more of a group thing, and someone—unfortunately, it wasn't me—won a teddy bear for her, making the trip a complete success. Watching her beaming with delight as it was presented to her, I realized that I was beginning to fall—hard. A few days later, I was thrilled and amazed when she agreed to go with me to see some dirt-track auto racing at our hometown speedway.

Imagine that—the pretty New York girl is going to the races with me!

When I walked into the grandstand area with her, several of my Road Rebel friends were already in their usual places at the back where they would stand throughout the racing to be nearer the beer bar. (It solved the problem of needing to step over people to get more beer every thirty minutes.) The stares coming from them, because she was so pretty—and because she was there with me—were immensely satisfying. I could feel those eyes on us. And I could see it on their faces.

"Man, who is *that?*"

"She's one great-looking chick!"

"What's she doing here with *Bob?*"

"Hi, guys. We're going to sit over here today so Carol can see things better. I'll catch you all later," I said with a big grin. No way was I going to let them near her. And I didn't introduce her to any of them.

See you, suckers.

I felt pretty good about taking this beautiful girl to a place where all my pals would see her—with me!

And I had her all to myself, since no one else knew her. *How cool was that?*

I couldn't tell if she really was interested in the racing—she appeared to be—but she asked good questions and followed everything that was happening. She was easy to talk with, had a good sense of humor, and made me feel at ease with her—all just simple things that were enough to make for a wonderful time. I didn't have to force conversation or steer it to a topic where I thought she might be more receptive. She was willing to talk about anything I brought up and never made me feel uncomfortable, which I thought was remarkable considering the social and cultural gap between us. I really couldn't articulate it in that way at that time, but I did have vague thoughts about how different our lives had to be.

Local girls I had dated on and off were in many ways much the same, and some even enjoyed the racing. But I felt more comfortable with Carol than any girl I had ever dated; it seemed to me that our chemistry was perfect. And she seemed to be paying close attention to me, more than I believed any girl ever had before. She teased me about how I sat, feet on the empty bleacher seat in front of me, elbows on my knees, forearms crossed, hands on my upper arms.

"Why are you doing that?" she asked.

"What? What am I doing?"

"Rubbing your arms like that. You keep doing it over and over."

"I don't know," I said, realizing that it was a nervous reaction to sitting there with this pretty girl I really didn't know yet, and probably being worried about the date going badly or running out of things to talk about.

Then she put her hand over mine, holding it still, and just smiled that make-you-want-to-kiss-her-now smile.

Those few times Carol and I were together were beyond my best expectations but not life changing at that point. That all happened a week or two later when I was working second shift on my "roustabout job," cleaning out a basement at the plant so that it could be painted and turned into another production line.

I was taking a break when one of the guys came down to tell me that someone was out on the sidewalk in front of the factory building asking to see me. It was Carol. She and Doris had come to find me.

"Bob, I just wanted to say good-bye before I go back to New York. We had fun together, and I do hope to see you again sometime," she said, and offered me her sweet smile.

I was floored. I was in my grubby work clothes and Red Wings, sweaty, and covered in dirt from head to foot. I felt really stupid. *Oh, God, does she have to see me this way?* There I was, working that menial, no-future job, and this beautiful New York girl was standing in front of me, saying good-bye and thanks for the fun we had together!

"Oh, are you going back already? We were just getting to know each other. I'm really sorry to hear that," I blurted out. I was amazed and pleased that she had come to see me, but I was depressed to find out that she was leaving.

"Yes, I'm going down to my aunt's house near Dayton to stay for a few days before I fly back to New York."

In a moment of inspiration that amazed me later, I asked, "How are you getting to Dayton?" And before she could answer, I said, "I'll drive you there, if you'd like."

She looked at Doris, thought for a moment, and said, "If it's okay with Doris's parents, I'd love it!"

The parents had no problem with it, and the trip was on for Friday evening. I wanted the best car I could use for the drive on that farewell evening, so I borrowed my dad's almost-new, baby-blue-and-white Ford Fairlane hardtop coupe, which was the prettiest car we'd ever had in the family. We had a wonderful, long drive talking and listening to our favorite music on the car's radio and an even better time spent parked in front of her aunt's house, talking, kissing, and—as we called it then—"necking." Necking was mostly more kissing, hugging, and breathlessness—sometimes car windows would even fog over after enough of it. I had not kissed her before that night, since I had rarely been alone with her. It wasn't something that happened because it was expected by one or the other; it was just a reflexive thing that happened when our eyes made contact at one moment, and we both knew it was the natural thing. And there was that make-you-want-to-kiss-her-right-now smile that I found so irresistible. I finally had the right opportunity; I couldn't get enough of her. I think we just melted into one another with those kisses, eager but not aggressive, tender and long lasting, loving but not sexual, eyes shut yet seeing and feeling each other. *What was it about her?*

After maybe an hour or so, she said, "You New Bremen boys are too persuasive. Would you like to meet my aunt?"

I didn't know what to say—or do. *Boys ... persuasive ... aunt?*

What did she just say? I thought about asking for clarification but decided against that. I assumed that in some unintended way, I was becoming too aggressive for her. *And what's this about New Bremen* boys*?*

I should have asked. It wouldn't be the last time I failed to understand something a girl was trying to tell me.

Instead, I said, "Oh, God, look at the time. It's one o'clock in the morning! My mom's probably sitting up waiting for me and wondering where I've crashed Dad's car. I think I'd better take you to the door; I've still got an hour's drive to get home."

She gave me a quizzical look, sighed, and said, "Okay."

As we walked to the front door, we made small talk about what we were going to be doing next. She was going back to Andrew Jackson High School in Queens, New York, to finish her senior year and then go on to a yet-to-be-decided-on college, possibly in Ohio.

I was going to be painting a factory basement!

We had a very sweet, long kiss, and she went through the front door into the house. I didn't mention meeting her aunt. My emotions and thoughts were all over the map on that long drive home: *Was I too aggressive? I don't think so. I certainly didn't want to offend her.* I believed I was being a gentleman all evening.

But I can't be sure. Maybe I should have asked? What did she mean?

Will I ever see her again? How can I see her again?

How many guys are after her at home? Dozens?

Does she have a regular guy back home? She never mentioned one, but how could she not have one?

Will I ever meet another girl like her again?

I've got to get my life into a different place!

I could never quite put my finger on what it was that made me feel so attracted to her. I knew other very pretty girls, and I also had close relationships with some of them, but Carol was very different in some way that I couldn't identify. Maybe it was that she was from New York, which itself created an exotic aura for me, or maybe it was some unknown chemistry between us. I've also thought at times that it was the extra self-confidence New Yorkers seem to have, no matter where they are or what they are doing—they're just cool. Maybe it's that New York state of mind.

I never saw or even talked to her again. There was no way with my job and on my income that I could pursue any further relationship with her, considering the possibilities that were likely going to be offered her and with her living in New York.

I deserve to be painting that basement.

I couldn't bear the thought of just selling the muscles in my back and arms and legs as my ticket to the rest of my life: one dollar per hour and no benefits, staying in that little town with only one or two places to work, and not traveling to the exciting places in the nation and world. And not meeting wonderful people from other places, like Carol.

That vision of becoming the last Road Rebel swept over me, again and again.

No, no, no! I'm not going to let it happen!

#

Even though I hadn't been deburring those oily, sloppy pinion gears for a few months—some other new kid got that slimy task—I still didn't like my job. I was moved to a business unit that contracted to the US Air Force, repairing aircraft electrical equipment. I cleaned aircraft power generators with carbon tetrachloride sprayed from a paint gun in a paint booth. I wore a respirator, but after spraying the parts, I handled them with their carbon-tetrachloride residue all day long, day after day. Cigarettes began to taste funny, and my food began to lose its taste. I wondered what that meant.

And even more of my friends began leaving town, now that the class of '59 seniors, which included many of my friends, had graduated. And more Road Rebels were getting married and going off to other things, which to me was much the same as leaving town. Once a guy gets married, something changes, and you can't talk to each other the same way anymore. You find yourself holding back, choosing different words, and you stop asking certain questions that were easy to ask when no one was married. Something changes, and friendships change along with it; a distance comes between old friends.

I didn't want to continue living at home with my parents, either, and my brother—while he was a good guy … sharing a bedroom with him? Hey, I was *eighteen*.

And I didn't want to be the last living Road Rebel. The club was getting smaller; fewer guys were showing up at meetings. Was there going to be anyone left in another year?

I had begun to have visions of myself, still single and still driving around in that convertible with the Road Rebels plaque hanging from the rear bumper, growing older and sitting in that old back room at the Hotel Hollingsworth's annex, drinking beer and talking to maybe one or two of the other guys—aging along with me—and remembering the good old days when we were still all together. And having that feeling that it all shouldn't have had to change.

Why wasn't everyone still around and doing all the things we had always been doing?

I even started having nightmares of a scene sometime in the future when, in a boarded-up and closed Hotel Hollingsworth, an exploring young kid, flashlight in hand, after descending those dark stairways into the basement where the restrooms were located, discovers a moldering, *Psycho*-like cadaver wearing a Road Rebels Car Club jacket hidden away in a locked broom closet. He had a half-smoked Pall Mall butt clenched between his grinning teeth and a Budweiser clutched in his right hand. Was I looking at my future self? I smoked Pall Malls and drank Bud at the time.

I didn't want to be the last Road Rebel—living or dead!

Back in my real world, I had to face up to my real problems. How long would I still be making that buck per hour and no benefits? In a year or two, would I have moved all the way up to maybe a buck twenty-five an hour and some vacation time, but no other benefits?

The other thing that I had started to realize from spending time with Carol was that I had no real hope of—or even reason to have thoughts of—a more permanent relationship with any girl without having some kind of rational, optimistic career plan. Who would want to get serious about a guy who doesn't know or seem to care where he's going and is making only pocket change?

I have to get out of this place!

By "place," I didn't mean the town (the town itself wasn't a bad place); it was the state I had put myself in. It was a state that was never going to take me to the places I then realized I wanted—and where

I thought I had to be—even though that thought was vague at that moment.

My "plan," such as it was, had become one of getting into college somewhere, learning a valuable skill that employers wanted, and starting a new life wherever that skill took me. I'd figure out the details as I went along. It was ad hoc, on-the-fly planning, but it was all I could think of with the limited knowledge I had at the time. Thinking about my father's difficulties in finding and keeping work, I understood that it was time to stop being the victim of circumstance, try to take the initiative, and gain control of my future.

Somehow, earlier that year, I had the foresight to begin saving as much money as I could from my shop job, and I had accepted as much part-time work as possible at the Lone Pine, helping Fred. Happily, the little race car drama was pretty well behind us at that point.

Later, to get every penny I could save, I also had decided to sell the '52 Ford convertible, which my brother Ron had thoughtfully given up his half interest in. I hated selling that car. It had been my major point of pride over the past two years. But it had to go. I would borrow my brother's or parents' cars when I could or beg rides when I needed to go somewhere by car. I could ride my bicycle everywhere else—at eighteen and almost to my nineteenth year.

I had been a proud, car-owning Road Rebel just the day before I sold that Ford to a farmer who purchased it for his son. He marveled about how clean and well cared for everything was in the interior and under the hood. I proudly told him about how frequently I'd hand waxed the body paint and had kept the chrome knobs and switches and other intricate details on the instrument panel clean and dust-free by using an old toothbrush and pipe cleaners. Inside, I ached as I bragged about how I had always maintained my car but now was only trying to get the best price—and was about to become a nineteen-year-old Road Rebel without wheels.

Are You Crazy?

But we never even know we have the key
But me, I'm already gone ...
—The Eagles, "Already Gone" (J. Tempchin and R. Strandlund)

"Are you crazy?" they shouted at me, nearly in unison.

#

Over the winter and spring months of '59, I had sent applications to a few colleges I had heard were possible places I might get accepted. But at that point, my interest in following through was more that of mild curiosity. Did I really mean to do it? Would I be accepted anywhere? Was I serious enough to leave home and jump into the unknown? My commitment to the idea had been increasing over the previous months, but those few weeks in the summer of that year when I had known Carol accelerated it. And it changed with finality after that last evening with her.

What did I have to lose?

Nothing.

My application had been accepted at Heidelberg College in Tiffin, Ohio, for the 1959/60 school year. I had also been accepted at a little-known school in northern Indiana, Tri-State College, which no one had ever heard about other than my boss at that part-time, blueprint room job I'd had when I was still in high school. It had been his school. But then, he was the guy that laid me off my job ...

Heidelberg was closely connected to my church in New Bremen, and it had been suggested by Reverend Fritz and other current New Bremen students at Heidelberg that I apply there. Whatever that connection was, it worked for me—me with my mediocre grades and my only reference probably being my preacher. So Heidelberg was the easy choice; I knew several people who attended there. Criteria simplified! I committed myself to going to Heidelberg that fall. I only had enough money for one school year, but it was a start—I'd have to figure it out one year at a time.

By the end of that summer, the word had gone around town that I was going to college, and I found myself, again and again, trying to explain to the remaining Road Rebel club members and other friends why I was going.

#

They were two of my older friends who had graduated from high school three years earlier, joined the army, and just recently completed their service. Bill and Stan were in the Lone Pine that evening to gas up their cars and BS a little while they were there, like most of my friends did in those days. They had heard about my plan to attend college that fall and believed that college was a waste of time and money. After all, look at how well things had worked out for them: two years in the army, time spent seeing some of the world—well, Alaska—and they had promising jobs in the town's largest and most successful company.

I had to keep in mind that I had always respected them, especially Bill, so it seemed I had to listen. Bill had been my neighbor for most of my grade school and junior high school years, and he generally knew everything I didn't have a clue about. He showed my brother and me how to shoot jump shots and dribble, taught us how to throw a curveball and shag grounders, and was an all-round good neighbor. Bill was patient with us; he never hesitated to show us how we were doing things wrong and was happy to repeat the training—up to a point. After that, it was "You dumb shit!" And in my case—but not my brother Ron's—he was probably right.

Standing there at the Lone Pine, he and Stan were feeling pretty satisfied with their lives. They seemed intent on convincing me that I was making a mistake.

"How much is it going to cost for each year at Heidelberg?" one of them had asked.

"Around twenty-five-hundred bucks, including tuition, room, and board, with around five dollars per week for spending money," I answered.

"So that's $10,000," Bill said.

Stan nodded and asked, "And how much are you making now that you won't make for those four years?"

I spelled it out for them. At a buck an hour, that worked out to two thousand dollars a year, assuming I took two weeks of vacation without pay, and at least that much over each of the next three years. "But if I never get a raise—which might be the case with the economy like it is—that's eight thousand total," I said.

"Okay, so you're going to just walk away from at least eighteen grand or maybe even twenty grand over the next four years, just to get a college degree—and then what?" Bill challenged. "And that's not including the *interest* you would gain if you invested the money."

"Besides, there's no guarantee you'll be able to find a job then—*even* with your college degree," Stan warned. "Then what? Are you crazy?"

Interest? I never had enough money to even fill my gas tank. It was always, "Dollar, regular gas, Fred." *What money was I was going to invest and get interest on?*

And then what?

Who knows? Maybe if I stayed in New Bremen, the company would have a bad year, and I'd get fired. Or maybe I'd break my back pushing a wheelbarrow full of concrete and never work again. All I could do was try to imagine the better things that might happen if I developed a higher level of skill than I would gain by deburring pinion gears or painting a factory basement.

My mom had been surprised when I told her about college, but she supported me. Still, she had a sad look when she said, "We're not going to be able to help you with the money, you know."

"I know, Mom, but I think I can take care of it myself with help from the government's new loan program." I was referring to the National Defense Education Act's student loan program, which the federal government had initiated after the Russians launched Sputnik. It had miraculously put the possibility of a college education within the reach of kids like me. I intended to go for it.

My dad said, "Can you really do this? Are you really going to do this?" He had that same look on his face that Mom had. *Why does Bobby think …?*

But something had changed.

I said good night to Stan and Bill and began closing the Lone Pine, where I was working part-time to help finance my first year at Heidelberg. There was no use continuing that debate; it was all what-ifs. I had decided to live with my own what-ifs rather than someone else's.

The Problem with Misty

Look at me …
—Errol Garner, "Misty"

We called it the Gray Ghost. It was a gray, 1954 Dodge Coronet that had been traveling the highways of Ohio for six salty winters before Jim bought it. So it needed a little help. Mechanically, the Gray Ghost was fine, but the six years of Ohio rain, snow, and salt had left the car a little less than bright and shiny. It had rust in all the usual places: behind the wheels in the fenders, beneath the doors in the rocker panels, and all the places water normally collects in the bodywork. In the summer of '60, between school years, Jim asked me to help him spruce the car up a little for some summertime adventures he thought we might have together.

#

I had just completed my freshman year at Heidelberg and finished transferring my credits to Ohio State for my next school year. I had discovered that I could do college-level work just fine. I had all As and Bs, except for my terrifying experience in speech class—a C grade—which was probably generous. I had stumbled through that class with about the same skill and technique that failed me with all the girls at Heidelberg, complete stage fright and self-conscious embarrassment. But in physics, I discovered that I had some instincts for science—most notably, electrical topics. This in spite of, after taking the mandatory aptitude tests the first week on campus and then meeting with my counselor, being told that the tests revealed that my highest aptitude and best career choices would be in farming or auto mechanics! *What?*

"But, I don't want to—"

"I understand, but I'm just telling you what you would be best at."

Was he telling me to go back home to that shop job and be a Road Rebel for the rest of my life? Or buy a farm? Farmers didn't hire helping hands; that's why they had kids.

Why am I here, then? I didn't come here for that!

And if I believed that and decided to follow through with that advice, were they going to refund my first semester tuition and room and board? Probably not.

To hell with the tests! The results probably have more to do with where and how I grew up than my ability to learn. It seemed to me that they should have known that and at least *mentioned it.*

Not because of the aptitude tests but because of my instinct for electrical things, I transferred to Ohio State for their electrical engineering program. I was starting to feel pretty good about getting my life pointed in a direction with a potential career path. And as a bonus, Ohio State's tuition in those years was $100 per quarter. I was beginning to see how I could actually finance my education by myself. Heidelberg's tuition was at least four times more expensive, and I had burned through my savings in my first year.

I also had learned that new graduate engineers were raking in over $5,000 per year as starting salary. *Take that, Bill and Stan!* I even dreamed that I could get a job in fabulous New York after graduation. And if I did, maybe I could see Carol, that beautiful New York girl, again but on very different terms than when I had last seen her.

#

My social life at Heidelberg had been nonexistent. I had no dates for my full freshman year, and to make matters worse, I hadn't even danced with a girl. Heidelberg certainly wasn't a party school, so the dancing opportunities were pretty limited. And when there was a dance, like the homecoming dance, I struck out completely. Part of the problem was that the music at Heidelberg wasn't what I was used to—no rock and roll being played anywhere. Heidelberg was a college with great pride in its choir and choral music programs because of its strong religious affiliations. The preferred music playing in the men's dorm at that time was modern jazz—which I liked for listening, but not dancing—and some classical music. Rock and roll was looked down on as junk music. I didn't even want to quietly play rock music on the little radio in my room for fear that an upperclassman would barge in, unplug the radio, yell at me, and pin a note on the foyer bulletin board: *Scum Gilberg listens to rock and roll!*

I didn't really know, or want to know, how to dance to all the slow, waltzy music usually playing at the school's dances. The music just didn't move me and make me want to dance. I believed a girl could easily tell, when dancing closely, if her partner didn't feel the music. *This guy's a slug.*

I was starving for a girl to twirl under my arms while rockin' out to Barrett Strong's "Money," or the Clovers' "Love Potion Number Nine." The Twilights' "Sea of Love" would have been good too, slow, sexy, and romantic. But it wasn't going to happen—to me, anyway—at Heidelberg. I missed all the hometown girls I had dated and learned to dance with. They were so easy and accommodating. "Let's dance" was all I had to say. "Sure," they always answered. I just wasn't making it with anyone at Heidelberg.

And I found that I missed my beautiful New York girlfriend, Carol, far more than I ever imagined during that first year at college. Without meeting new girls to dream about, I dreamed about the ones I knew but who unfortunately weren't near anymore. I had never danced with Carol during her short stays in New Bremen, but back in my room, I could easily dream about jitterbugging with her to some Chuck Berry or Little Richard, or slow dancing with her head on my shoulder and holding each other close while the Platters sang "Smoke Gets in Your Eyes" or while the Five Satins sang "In the Still of the Night." Heavenly dreaming. But in the end, a going-nowhere proposition.

I wouldn't let myself dream about Joanie in that same way; she was engaged to the marine and clearly out of reach.

Ironically, Carol, more than any other one person, was the reason I was in college—and she had become only a memory. It was partly that I hadn't met anyone to replace her and partly because I hadn't been able to visit her in far off New York. I didn't have a car, and it was too far to hitchhike or travel to by bus—either of which would have been too lame of a way to visit a girl I would have been wanting to romance. I couldn't do that, after all, I was—or had been—a Road Rebel. We had cool cars; we didn't ride buses! And, of course there was always the money problem: I had five dollars per week for spending money. A few beers, an occasional movie, maybe a burger after a football game, but certainly not a bus trip to New York City, meals, and dating.

With my social self-confidence at a low point and no money and no car, I decided that it was useless to try to reinsert myself into her life. Without my own wheels, there was no way I was going to be able to compete with some cool New York college frat guy that she was probably dating, and who probably drove a Corvette. I figured they all drove Corvettes in New York City …

I knew that I was quitting on myself with Carol and didn't feel good about it. But *The Graduate*, with Dustin and his Alfa Romeo, hadn't been filmed yet—and I didn't have an Alfa Romeo, anyway.

#

So I was feeling very needy when Jim proposed our Gray Ghost Summer of girls and good times. After that first year at Heidelberg, I was ready to try anything.

Other than that long-past weekend when I visited Jim at Miami U and experienced some of the things that had me on the path I was now on, we hadn't hung out together very much. That was not surprising, since he had always been more into the sports side of things and was a better student with aspirations of higher education, and I had been the motor-head, car-guy type. But during some recent parties at the home of longtime friend and date, Pat—where she had a terrific basement party room with romantic lighting and a dance floor—Jim and I had found that we had developed similar interests in new music. We were both very much into Ray Charles's and Jimmy Reed's blues sounds. Reed's "Big Boss Man," "I Found Love," and "Baby What You Want Me to Do" were our sounds. We played Jim's 78 recording of *Jimmy Reed at Carnegie Hall* at all of her parties until it had deep needle grooves nearly right through the disk and had become scratchy and staticky sounding.

It was the greatest sound for sexy, bluesy slow dancing at the time. The kind of almost-full-body-clench kind of dance where a guy might occasionally slip a leg just a little way between her legs—and she might even return the move. We couldn't get enough Jimmy Reed.

So Jim, now my closest hometown friend, needed to spiff up the car some to help us with our girl chasing. And he had a plan for all this. He could paint anything and make it look good. Jim's uncle Pete ran a summertime house-painting business when he wasn't teaching and coaching the basketball team. Jim sometimes helped him out and had even established his own sideline painting business. Whenever Jim needed a little extra spending money, he opened his TV antenna tower–painting business. These three-sided aluminum towers were up to fifty feet high, with antennas and antenna rotators mounted on the top—the same antenna rotators I had begun my post–high school life deburring pinion gears for in that buck-an-hour job. The towers needed repainting every few years. Jim fearlessly climbed to the top and painted his way down, clinging to the tower with one hand, paintbrush in the other hand, the bucket of paint hanging from his belt by a short cord, and using the horizontal struts as a ladder—no safety belt or life strap. He charged seventy-five cents per foot for this death-defying work—and promised that signal reception would not be reduced.

With Jim's knowledge of paint and painting, we were going to paint the Gray Ghost back to respectability. Not having my own wheels, I was only too happy to help. We were going to spend the summer break of 1960 going where the girls were; he had the wheels, and I had the time.

We liberally painted anything that wasn't chrome, glass, or shiny with that gray automotive primer paint. The primer was very thick, stuck to anything and everything—including rust—and nicely filled the little scratches and pockmarks. The primer also matched the Dodge's original paint pretty well—or good enough, anyway.

In my Road Rebels world, a car painted in primer was something to be reckoned with. Even if it had been painted with a brush, as in our case, a car in primer made a statement. A car in primer said that there was something going on. There was no intent to make a bright, shiny finish, because this was a car in transition to something greater—someday.

Or it could just stay that way for years, which was okay too. Primer let us get away with nearly anything, since it was understood that we were making a statement: *I'm into something here. I don't know quite what, and I need a little more money, but this is gonna be something else when I'm done.* This was Road Rebel wisdom at work.

Or it might also be a statement saying, *Stop staring, and up yours. I like my cars ugly!* Which was okay too—but not Road Rebel.

Oxford Town

We started off that summer of '60 with a less-than-shiny '54 Dodge Coronet and great expectations. Jim proposed that we get started by again going down to his school, Miami University, as an inaugural trip in the Gray Ghost.

"Gilly," Jim said, using my not-so-great-nickname at the time, "let's go down to Oxford next weekend for some fun. There's no place anywhere else in Ohio like it for cool bars, girls, and all partying, all the time. I've learned all the good places to go now, and you won't believe it. You just won't believe how many fabulous girls will be there!"

Remembering all the young people seeming to have the times of their lives that winter weekend the year before—and all those coeds—I said, "When do you want to leave?"

"Friday afternoon."

"Great. I'll be ready by four." I couldn't wait!

Viewing my own dismal state of affairs and lack of success with the female population at Heidelberg, I thought—and hoped—that he might be on to something. I was ready to try anything.

On the long drive to Oxford, Jim suggested that we pull over at a truck stop to grab a sandwich and a beer and to help us *prepare ourselves* for our arrival. He said it would be wise to be ready for all that was going to happen.

Jim came out of the men's room and handed me a round, silver dollar–sized foil container with an embossed logo—Trojan.

"You are going to need this," he said.

I swallowed hard and croaked out, "Thanks, Jim."

The feel of that shiny little disk filled me with new sensations I'd never felt before. *Terror* might have been the strongest feeling gripping me, but *wonder*, *daring*, and maybe *danger*, as well. And not being sure I had the *nerve* was a big question too. And *how* would possibly be another issue …

But I knew we were really into something! Just the feel of that little disk was excitement itself. It said, *Wild and wonderful things are about to happen; I'm going to take you places you have never been before.*

Feeling as if I were about to take the biggest step of my life up to that point, I choked back my nervousness, swallowed hard again, and thanked Jim for the good advice and all the new things he was about to unveil to me. He advised me to put the little disk in one of the inner compartments of my wallet so it would always be handy and ready for action at short notice.

I found a secret little slot that was just the right size from where it was not likely to accidentally fall out at some inopportune moment and slipped it in there, and on we went to Oxford Town, ready to rock and roll.

We spent the weekend drinking beer in empty bars—no girls in sight—talking to each other. We had conversations we could have had at home at our old Hotel Hollingsworth hangout or at Wint's Bar and Grille—or even Surf Club. There was no one in Oxford that weekend, and for the life of me, it looked as if there hadn't been anyone there for at least a month.

At the first empty bar on that late Saturday afternoon, after the second or third beer and having listened to the Everly Brothers' "Cathy's Clown," Elvis's "Are You Lonesome Tonight," and "Handyman" by Jimmy Jones, I was becoming dubious about things. I had been ready to dance with nineteen- and twenty-year-old sophomores and juniors, but there we were, just the two of us, sitting in a bar listening to crying-in-your-beer songs, like Roy Orbison's "Only the Lonely," watching the door and *a-wishin' and a-hopin'* for all those girls.

"Where is everyone?" I asked.

"They'll be showing up any time; it's early," Jim replied.

"You know, I always thought it was the really serious students who are trying to get their degrees early who stay through the summer," I said.

"No, it's the fast and hot ones who want to stay away from home and continue partying who stay," he claimed.

"Okay, that makes sense—I think. You were always the wise one," I said with resignation, thinking, *Well, he always did get better grades than I did*. So we waited.

After a while, when we realized that Mac and Joe's bar wasn't producing the action we were looking for, we moved our base camp to Al and Larry's, another empty bar—*and watched the Reds playing the Cubs on TV*. After an hour or so of that, we tried the College Inn, yet another empty bar—*and watched the Indians playing the Yankees.*

There we were, two guys singing crying-in-our-beer songs and watching televised baseball, which was by then getting very old; our *a-wishin' and a-hopin'* strategy for finding romance was not cutting it. We left after two futile days and headed the Gray Ghost home, making plans to go over to the amusement park at Indian Lake in nearby Russells Point the next weekend. We heard rumors of continuous partying and hordes of college-age girls being seen. And Chubby Checker's hit "The Twist" was the hot new dance sensation then taking the country by storm and was reportedly in vogue over there.

Maybe if we started practicing right away …

Maybe Over at Russells Point

Russells Point turned out to be much more exciting than Oxford. There actually were hordes of young people there, but the big attraction turned out to be the annual teen riots that went on, weekend after weekend, at that time. This wasn't rioting over the Vietnam War or civil rights issues or any high-purpose causes; this was before those things came to Ohio. It was just the civil unrest for the sake of civil unrest that was sweeping through young minds at the time: antiauthority, antiboredom … and probably just anti-1950s. It wasn't a Patty Page or Dinah Shore or Pat Boone world anymore, and it wasn't a Bob Dylan or

Beatles world yet either. While we couldn't really identify it, we sensed a hint of unrest in the air. We didn't know it at that point, but we really were marking time, waiting restlessly for something new to come along. In 1960, that new thing was just around the corner, and we had no idea of how it was all going to change in a few short years. Had we known, we might have tried to get it started right then—the cultural, sexual, and music revolution was about to hit us right between the eyes.

But at that time, it was just drunken kids rioting in the streets and battling the local police and firemen for the excitement in doing it—and dodging the water cannons being used against them. They actually taunted the police and firemen, daring them to bring out the water cannons. Jim and I weren't too sure of playing with police and firemen with water cannons; things were getting too serious, and kids were being arrested.

While we had seen some pretty girls doing some fabulously exaggerated versions of the Twist—in short-shorts—at a very popular bar and dance area, we decided we needed more to drink before having enough nerve to ask them to dance. Doing our stiff versions of the Twist in front of people watching the dancing needed some liquid help. Who could do that dance sober? The girls were way ahead of the boys on this, though; maybe they knew the future. Or, since the girls had been more confined in the social restrictions of the '50s, maybe they were more impatient and ready for the Twist. Whatever it was, clearly girls could do the Twist far better than any guys could, sober or even "oiled up" a little. We wanted to try, though.

But the water cannons got there first.

So the Gray Ghost, Jim, and I, with our shiny foil disks—still unopened and still in our wallets—headed back to New Bremen.

#

The Gray Ghost took us all around western Ohio that summer, but it never really got us where we wanted to be with the female population. We couldn't blame it on the car's yesteryear styling. It didn't have the massive chrome front-end styling with rear spaceship tail fins that the latest '59 and '60 Detroit models had, and it didn't have four-barrel, dual-exhaust, V8 power to make girls swoon over the brute-force acceleration.

The Gray Ghost's chrome had been applied very sparingly—we had to use some imagination—and it had an old lump of a six-cylinder engine that produced less than 100 horsepower. It wasn't going to sweep any eighteen-year-old college girl off her feet. The strategy was that we'd do that with sheer personality and charm, I guess—that and by being in the right places at the right times.

But the car did have three endearing qualities: it was reliable, got decent gas mileage, and was a very steady, predictable driver, which was what it was designed to do. We couldn't knock it off the road; it just plowed straight ahead with predictable steering and handling. Not bad qualities for a car we trusted with our lives.

#

Two years later, in November 1962, the Gray Ghost had gone to its final resting place and was no longer being flogged around Ohio's salty, bumpy farm roads and highways in search of youth happiness. Jim had gotten lucky, had a serious relationship with a pretty Miami U student from Toledo, and was no longer in the hunt. I was grinding my way through the five-year engineering program at OSU—and still looking for *that girl.*

#

Play "Misty" Again for Me

"Misty" was playing on the jukebox for probably the tenth time that night. But it was Johnny Mathis's "Misty," not Errol Garner's. No one seemed to notice. To most of us, Johnny Mathis was more familiar, anyway, since not so long before, in our high school years, we had all thrilled and made out to those gummy songs he crooned in the late '50s. Errol Garner, who actually wrote the song, was known only to those of us who were getting into modern jazz, which was a little too edgy for most folks from small Ohio farming communities like New Bremen. So it was Johnny Mathis crooning away on the jukebox. I didn't mind that it wasn't Errol Garner; the girls liked Johnny Mathis better and were happy to dance that really close way.

Pat, my cousin Paul, and four or five other friends and I were at the Surf Club, a favorite hangout for our crowd, near Grand Lake Saint Marys. Surf Club was the "in" place those days, since we were all over—or at least near—twenty-one years of age, and it had a dance floor. Twenty-one was the legal drinking age for hard liquor in Ohio, and once we were able to at least pass for twenty-one, attended college, and considered ourselves very cool, we tended to go to Surf Club on our special occasions; it was more of an upscale, hard-liquor drinks place rather than just a beer joint. The dance floor was a small, intimate place in a dark corner where we could dance really close to a smoochy tune like "Misty." That's why it was on at least its tenth play with at least another ten to twenty more to come before closing time. For me, Jimmy Reed's blues would have been better, if I couldn't have the Errol Garner version of "Misty," but we had to play whatever was on the jukebox.

The special occasion was Thanksgiving break in 1962. It was the kind of deal where we would all come back from the various colleges we were attending to compare how cool it was to be an Ohio State Buckeye, a Miami Redskin, a Kent State Golden Flash, a Heidelberg Student Prince, an Ohio University Bobcat, or Cincinnati Bearcat. We wore our school sweatshirts and talked about the football teams' records and the start of the basketball season and compared notes on history and chemistry classes. We felt very sophisticated and worldly.

Kennedy had just faced down the Russians over the Cuban Missile Crisis, but we'd hardly noticed. Sure, the papers were full of the story and the close encounter with WWIII, but that all, while scary, just seemed like overblown international politics and bluffing and posturing to most of us at twenty-one or twenty-two years old, living away from home in the company of thousands of other young adults of similar age. That's what we hoped, anyway. Besides, the Michigan game was coming up, and the Rose Bowl was on the line.

And over at the OSU basketball arena in Columbus, the fabulous combination of John Havlicek, Larry Siegfried, Bobby Knight, and Jerry Lucas was already tearing up the Big Ten opposition. University of Dayton, Cincinnati, and Ohio State were all powerhouse basketball schools in those days, and Ohio was a sports powerhouse state. We loved it!

I was on at least my fourth rum and Coke and feeling pretty good about the evening. We were all dancing, drinking, smoking, and having a great time. I had been dancing with Pat most of the night. Pat and I had known each other for years by that time; it was one of those spontaneous things when, for an evening, there is a certain connection that develops and everything seems to bring two people together in some very natural way. No forced conversations, no phony make-out talk, no awkward moments when we couldn't think of anything more to say; the evening just flowed. I wouldn't call it a romantic event that evening; we were just very close for a few hours.

Complicating things, though, was that Pat was going steady with my cousin Paul—sort of. Pat was at Ohio University in the far eastern part of the state, and Paul was still living at home and working in New Bremen. She had his ring but was said to be dating at school. At home, though, she was his steady girl—sort of.

Pat and Paul hadn't come to Surf Club together that night, since it was a very informal, last-minute thing and everyone just found their own way there. I had ridden with Paul in his almost-new 1961 Corvair.

Sometime after eleven o'clock and after one too many rum and Cokes, I knew I was too drunk and needed to get out of there before I threw up all over my brown cardigan sweater (the one my college roommate, New Jersey Al, kept telling me made me look like Mr. Peepers). Paul, who wasn't much into dancing and had been mostly sitting and talking to the others while I danced with Pat, had had more than enough to drink, as well.

We looked at each other with knowing eyes that said, *Let's get out while we can still walk.* And I also thought privately, *Before I do something unforgivable with my own cousin's girl.*

The Corvair

Ralph Nader had it only partly right when he later wrote his 1965 book: *Unsafe at Any Speed.* Especially with two drunks aboard—and one of them driving. I didn't have anything against Corvairs. Like most, if not all, of the first cars using a rear engine located behind the rear axle, Corvairs had some unique steering characteristics. The cars had very unequal weight distribution: a heavy rear end and a light front end. This, combined with its swing axle rear suspension, always resulted in a phenomenon known as initial understeer, changing to final oversteer when pushed to its handling limits. But Volkswagens, Renaults, and even Porsches were much the same, and one needed to understand how to drive them. Only Corvairs had the misfortune to be manufactured in the USA, where they were easy prey for Ralph Nader, American laws, lawyers, and courts.

So there we were, two sheets to the wind, full of merriment, headed home in the Corvair with Paul driving—and any understanding of the special driving techniques needed for heavy-in-the-back, light-in-the-front, rear-engine cars highly anesthetized in some dark corner of the brain. And I wasn't wearing a seat belt. I'm not sure the Corvair even had them. I think they were optional in those days—extra money.

In normal circumstances, my old Road Rebels driving instincts might have given me some warning of what was about to happen. Ohio farm country roads had, and still have, a few characteristics that today's National Highway Traffic Safety Administration (NHTSA) would go berserk over. They are narrow and have two- to three-foot-deep field drainage ditches along both sides—with no guardrails. They also nearly always are surrounded by cornfields planted all the way into the corners of road intersections in such a way that the driver has no clue about any possible cross traffic, and sometimes the corn obscured the traffic signs. Finally, at many intersections, the main roads tend to be elevated a little higher than the lesser intersecting road. The result is a ramp-like effect that a driver hardly notices while slowing for a stop or yield sign—but that might be noticed if the driver doesn't slow down.

This was exactly the situation at Auglaize County's Tri Township county road and Ohio Highway 219. We were on the lesser, lower country road staring at the ramp of the rapidly approaching higher state road with the Corvair's speedometer on the peg—okay, about seventy miles per hour—when, because *we didn't slow down* or come to a *stop* as we should have—the too-light nose of the Corvair suddenly pointed straight up as we launched into the starry sky. It all happened so fast that we didn't have a chance to say a word—no "Oh shit!" or "Jesus Christ!" or "Oh no!" or "Look out!" We just stared out the windshield at a very dark, midnight sky.

That was the last thing I remember until I woke up lying against a wire fence along the side of a cornfield. It was totally quiet and pitch black; I couldn't see anything.

Why am I lying here in the ditch? What happened before this?

I was with Paul in the Corvair! Where is it? Where's Paul?

God, I've got to get up and see if I can find them. What's all this wet stuff on my head and face—and now on my hands? It's in my mouth and tastes like salt. My God, it's blood!

I'm bleeding really badly. How much am I losing? I can't walk around in the dark looking for the car and Paul. I'll bleed to death. What should I do?

Think!

Wait, my cousin Ann Lynn's farmhouse is pretty close—if I'm remembering where we were in that last moment before whatever it was that happened.

Okay, walk back to that stop sign, turn right, go a little way, and on the left, that's where her house should be.

God, I hope I'm right, and the house—any house—will be there where I think it should be.

I walked, stumbling in the darkness on the side of the road, for five to ten minutes.

I'm there; that's her house! I hope to hell someone is home. I think her husband's name is Kenny; he'll probably be the one coming to the door. How will I tell him who I am or what I need? He'll probably think I'm someone who's running from the police.

I pounded on the door as hard as I could and yelled, "Ann, it's your cousin Bobby! I've been in an accident and need help badly!"

It seemed like I was waiting too long. But someone was yelling from inside the house. "I'll be there in a minute—but *who is it* pounding on the door at this time of night?"

It is Ann! She'll believe me and know who I am.

Ann Lynn

I was lucky enough to have had some incredible presence of mind considering the situation: too much rum, a bad accident, more blood on my face than I could see through—and I realized that my cousin's house was close by.

There I was, looking like a scalping victim pounding on my cousin's door at midnight, the Friday after Thanksgiving 1962. Poor Ann had come to the door, shrieked, and ran back halfway into the front room. From there, she asked me again who I was because obviously she wasn't sure she could believe I was who I said I was with all the blood coming out of my scalp and covering my face, and down the front of my coat and brown cardigan sweater. I've always tried to imagine what I looked like, standing there on the dark front porch, probably looking like an escapee from Custer's last stand—and telling her I was her cousin Bobby.

"I've been in an accident, and I've been injured. I need to get to a doctor fast."

"I'll call an ambulance right away," she said.

God, did that sound good!

After she'd made the call, Ann came out to talk to me and try to get more information. Who knows how the rest of that conversation went; it must have been a fright for her, though. The doctor later told me that when they brought me into the emergency room, my scalp was hanging down around my ears, and he said he had to reach around in there to get all the glass and dirt out.

Ann had handed me a bunch of towels, which I piled on top of my head to try to stop the bleeding. She bravely sat down on the front steps with me, and as she later told me, she held my head together, waiting with me while I hoped—and hoped—that the ambulance would arrive quickly. She asked what had happened, and I gave her as much information as I could manage. I told her about the missing Corvair and my cousin Paul. When the ambulance got there, the attendants talked about trying to find the car and the other person. I was sure I was going to bleed to death while they discussed it, not to mention spending even more time looking for Paul and loading him into the ambulance. I tried to stop myself from thinking, *Excuse me, forget him and take me to the hospital—fast!*

I couldn't help thinking that, but I also couldn't bring myself to say it. Then the paramedic saved the situation by telling the driver, "I don't think this one is going to make it if we spend time finding and loading the other one. We'd better go."

The accompanying police then went to look for Paul and the Corvair. We headed off for the hospital with me feeling badly about Paul—but better about my own prospects.

Unknown to me at the time, Ann's husband, Kenny, had jumped into his car and gone to look for Paul and the Corvair. He found Paul out of the Corvair, sitting on the roadside with a number of injuries and in need of his own ambulance. The police had requested another one, which was immediately dispatched, bringing Paul into the hospital shortly afterward. His injuries, while not life threatening, were serious, and he was taken to the big Saint Rita's Hospital in Lima for expert attention to his facial injuries. My injuries, while of no lasting damage, needed immediate attention due to major blood loss and probably would have been life ending without the terrific luck I had that night in finding my beautiful cousin Ann at home!

My New Wallet

With the accident happening in the late hours of that Friday night and no hospital visitations allowed except by immediate family members for the first day or two—and all of my college friends on their way back to their schools on Sunday—I would not see any of them again until the coming Christmas break. I felt stranded, stuck in a hospital bed when I should have been heading back to Columbus. I had been doing very well in my fall quarter classes but would miss the last three or four weeks and possibly finals. The question of how I would deal with that kept churning around and around in my mind. But I also had things of a much more immediate nature to deal with.

My mother, who had been to the hospital daily and was being as thoughtful and helpful as she possibly could be, was standing beside my bed waiting for me to open my eyes. She had asked me how I was feeling. She wanted to talk.

I had been in the hospital for three days at that point, spending a lot of my conscious time when no one else was in the room thinking about cars. Mainly, I had been thinking about and missing the old Gray Ghost. That accident would never have happened in that car, given the same circumstances. It had that heavy, cast-iron, six-banger motor up front under the hood, which resulted in heavy-in-the-front weight distribution and an almost certainly different reaction to hitting that intersection ramp. We probably would have just bounced a little and then glided on over it with a surprised look at each other, saying, "What the hell was that?"

Of course, it wasn't the Corvair's fault; it was just a matter of not remembering how light that car's front end was and not understanding how it would behave when being "ramped" like that—and the little matters of drinking too much and missing a stop sign.

Ralph Nader's complaints might be given credit in only one sense: the Corvair wasn't drunk proof. But of course, that wasn't what he was claiming.

Damn, Jim, where were you when I needed you and the Gray Ghost? That thought came to mind several times in those hospital days. The Gray Ghost didn't get us where we had dreamed, but it probably would have saved me from the more than sixty stitches needed to sew me back up, several pints of blood, a broken arm, and a complicated week of finals.

I had a pattern of sewn-up cuts on my head, starting just at the center of my front hairline, that extended back onto the top of my scalp that looked a lot like a chicken's foot, according to the ER doctor who did the repair work. The chicken's ankle was the part that started at the front hairline, right in the middle of my head, and the feet were spread up and over the top of my skull. It looked like I had been grabbed by a chicken from the front of my head. Of course, the chicken-foot pattern was accompanied by those sixty-some stitches, crossing the scalp-cuts-about-to-become-scars—at right angles, railroad tie–like—which would also leave their own little dot scars to complement the chicken's foot.

Damn! After struggling so long to learn to swim back in my early teen years, swimming in public places wasn't something I was going to be eager to do with my "Chickenstein" scalp. Mom, who had seen it a day earlier when nurses were changing the dressings on my head, had just told me that I would probably be wanting to consider hairpieces when I began to develop the standard Gilberg hairline in not too many years.

That's when I had closed my eyes and muttered, "Gee, Mom, thanks for the advice." But I was already planning my new hairdo: it was going to be *long—very long.*

Then she asked again how I was feeling, after I had just lain there, thinking of what to say. She was patiently waiting for my answer while all this had been racing around and around in my bandaged head, which was wrapped up in a mile of gauze in a way that would have worked well as headgear in the movie *Gunga Din*. My left arm was in a cast; I had discovered it was broken during my second day in the hospital when I nearly fell out of bed trying to lift myself up.

I said, "Okay, Mom, when do I get out?"

"In another day or two," she answered. Then she added, "By the way, we had to throw all your clothes away because they were too soaked with blood to be cleaned and usable again."

"I think that's really saying something in view of how they seem to be able to boil, or whatever, away all the horrid stuff that gets into hospital sheets and towels and things," I suggested.

"Well, I don't think you'd want to be wearing them after that, either."

"Does that mean my favorite brown cardigan too?"

"Yes, especially that cardigan," she said. "Besides, I always thought it made you look a little too much like that funny guy in glasses on TV—Wally, hmmmm—you know, Mr. Peepers." (That would be Mr. Rogers in today's world.)

"Oh, thanks. Have you been talking to my roommate, Al?"

She had brought along some of my just-laundered clothes from the suitcase full of grubby things I always took home from college for her to wash. And there on top of my old clothes was a new, bright-yellow cardigan.

"So who am I going to be now, Perry Como?" I asked no one in particular but thinking of what New Jersey Al would have to say about it.

I lay there quietly for a while longer, waiting to see what else she had to say.

"Here's a new wallet I bought for you. Your old one was just horrible, and I couldn't stand the thought of trying to clean it."

"Gee, Mom, thanks. You didn't have to. I could probably have managed to clean it up with some lacquer thinner and ammonia or something. Then maybe a little Pine Sol to give it a better smell," I said.

"Oh, that's okay. I wanted to get something nice for you. I was going to get one for your Christmas present, anyway, so now you can have it early."

After a moment of silence, she reached into her purse and pulled something out. "You'll have to get a new driver's license and draft card since everything in the wallet was such a mess. Except this!"

She handed me a shiny little metal foil disk embossed with one word: *Trojan!*

How do you disappear when lying in a hospital bed in one of those stupid backless gowns, hooked up to an IV, with an arm cast that seems to weigh a ton, and your head is in a three-foot-high turban? You don't. I just had to lie there in terminal embarrassment and hope that she'd move on to another subject. I wondered if I could slide my whole body up into that turban and disappear. I remember starting to mumble something like, "Oh, those. I was just carrying them for Jim because ..." And I was thinking, *Damn Jim, where the hell are you now? Maybe you'd like to explain this to Mom?*

But nothing that could possibly be believable came to mind. I just let the thought die unfinished, because whatever I said would have been unintelligible and unbelievable, anyway. And with all the revulsion I ever could have imagined pumping through my mind, I thought, *Two years carrying those stupid things, and here was my mom, handing them back to me! Two years carrying those stupid things, and there they still were—unused!*

Which was worse? Either was bad enough. But both? At the same time?

It was worse than striking out without ever swinging the bat! It was an air ball! But it was reality. My own undeniable reality. And one of those defining moments we are all supposed to remember. *I do remember.*

The only way out of that situation was to have sudden, severe pain from my injuries. "Mom, I can't talk anymore. My head is killing me, and my arm feels like it's going to break off," I muttered.

She was gracious enough to leave me to my embarrassment. Moms understand these things better than anyone. I knew, for the ninetieth time, that she was too good for me. My mother was semireligious and lived by very high moral standards, but she didn't preach to my brothers or me. Instead, she lived her life as an example for us. We knew what she expected, without the need for words.

I knew the conflict she was feeling over the Trojans; I could see it in her eyes. Yet she didn't say another thing about them; she didn't have to. But I also knew she was a practical woman who knew I was twenty-two, and she understood that young men and women at that age have to find their own way and make their own decisions in the best way they can.

She never tried to lecture me about the drinking, or driving after drinking too much—or the Trojans. She knew I would not need to be instructed about drinking and driving after that. She also knew that the Trojans were the right thing for me at that time. We didn't talk about either of these topics, because we didn't need to.

So how did I come to know all of this? She told me—years later. That was her way of letting me know that all along, she knew.

I went back to Columbus as soon as I could to try to salvage what had been a promising quarter. Paul was still in and out of hospitals, having serious dental reconstruction work that went on for months. When we all got back together at Christmas break, in spite of my arm still being in a cast and Paul still limping, we blew it off. *Kids will be kids … wonder if they'll live through it.*

Maybe, maybe not!

So that's the problem with "Misty." Since those events of 1962, whenever I hear that song, the story of Jim and the Gray Ghost, Paul and the Corvair, dancing all night with Pat, the Trojans, and Mom flash through my mind. I imagine most people have some romantic images from some long-lost love come to mind when they hear "Misty." I'd probably like that too, but I'll have to settle for these memories—which, by the way, years and years later, aren't so bad, anyway.

Tragedy

She was the high school's sweetheart. She was the entire town's sweetheart. She was also my neighbor, classmate, and occasional date in past years. She was very pretty, athletic, a lifeguard at our local swimming pool, and, in that spring of 1962, had just graduated from Miami of Ohio University. And now she was desperately crying on my shoulder.

Judy's fiancé, Larry, was dead.

As several of Judy's friends and I had sat on the front porch of her home that July afternoon, waiting for any news from the hospital about Larry's condition, she walked up the sidewalk and through the front door with the news we hoped would never come. She could barely say through her sobbing, "He's dead." Then she sat on the glider with me, leaning against my side, her head on my shoulder. She had just returned from the hospital where Larry had died only hours before. He had died from fractured vertebrae and inhaling lake water in a swimming accident. In a few weeks, they were to have been married.

I didn't know what to do; I seemed to be frozen. I didn't know how to console her.

They had been a steady couple through their last years at Miami of Ohio University and became engaged after her senior year. Larry, one year our junior, had another year to go before his graduation. And Judy, with her new teaching credentials, had obtained a teaching contract for the upcoming year in a small city near Oxford. She planned on teaching there while Larry completed his final year at Miami.

Larry was a good student, a fair athlete, and the only child of a well-liked businessman who loved sports of all kinds. He was doted on by his father and seemed to have the best of everything. While we both were junior high school students and neighbors, I had frequently been Larry's guest at his home, playing on the best home basketball court, the best badminton court, and the best backyard softball field in town. He and I continued to be good friends throughout our high school years.

He had a stylish turquoise-and-cream '57 Chevy Malibu convertible that his dad had bought for him as a high school graduation present. Larry was good-looking, well mannered, and one of the most likeable young men in town. Judy and Larry seemed to have everything going for them.

Larry and Jim—the owner of the Gray Ghost—had spent the next-to-last Sunday of Larry's life driving around in that Chevy convertible and visiting favorite spots at our two local lakes around New Bremen. They had a snack and a beer at a little beach shack at Villa Nova Beach on Grand Lake, the larger of our muddy Ohio lakes. This beach shack was just a little farther on down the "beach" road around Grand Lake from another of our favorite college years' nighttime hangouts, the Surf Club. They had then raced across the small, sandy-muddy beach and dove into the opaque lake water to freshen up some before driving back to New Bremen. Jim had finished his dive and was taking a few strokes when he heard people yelling and someone struggling in the water behind him. Larry was being pulled to the shore, unconscious. He apparently dove too steeply for the shallowness of the water and hit his head on the bottom, knocking himself out. We had all done running dives many times, but mainly at the swimming pool in New Bremen where the water depth was three feet at the shallow end of the pool, not just a foot or two as it was there at the lake beach. It was a racing dive, intended to be very shallow with minimal submergence so that the swimmer could start stroking almost immediately after contact with the water.

He was resuscitated and taken to the nearest hospital in Saint Marys where, for a while, he seemed to be recovering and even spoke with Judy. But soon after, Larry lapsed into unconsciousness and was moved to the hospital in Lima, where the most serious injuries and illnesses from the surrounding area were treated.

The entire town of New Bremen held its breath for ten days, hoping and praying for a miracle and good news but afraid of the more probable news. He had fractured vertebrae and had inhaled and filled his lungs with the filthy sediment and debris from the bottom waters of the beach. He remained in the coma and never recovered.

The death of yet another school friend—and what Judy had to be going through—shocked and depressed me. I sat there with her like a stone, thinking, *What can I say? What can I do? How do I help her? Would placing my arm around her shoulders be okay? Or would it be too presumptuous of me?* Although we were good friends, some distance had come between us through our college years and her engagement with Larry. *Should I place my hand on her arm or over her hand? What was the right thing?* Ultimately, I did nothing.

It was 1962—but socially, it was still like the '50s when people weren't as open with their emotions as we were later. We only hugged and kissed or showed emotions in private. I didn't know what would be the right thing to comfort her and was too afraid that whatever I did would be the wrong thing. In my twenty-two years of life to that point, I had never been confronted with anything like that. So I didn't do anything other than let her go on crying on my shoulder. It was pathetic of me. What kind of boneheaded stone oaf was I? I never forgave myself for not being able to make even the simplest gesture of sympathy.

I don't know if she noticed my apparent coldness or not, but somehow I guessed—and hoped—that was the last thing on her mind at that time. But I've always believed that if I could have done something that would have offered her a little comfort, it would have helped just a little. It was a small thing, I guess (and probably unnoticed by everyone there), but something that grew larger and larger to me every time I thought of her in the following years. Why couldn't I have done or said *something*?

Within a few weeks of Larry's death, Judy moved to Chicago to stay with her good friend Jeanne, who had recently joined TWA as a flight attendant. Judy couldn't bear the thought of continuing to live in New Bremen and near the cemetery where Larry was buried. Jeanne offered her a place in her apartment, encouragement, and help in finding a career and distance from the place of her great loss.

Judy returned to New Bremen for the holidays at the end of 1962. I was also in town, on Christmas break from Ohio State. I was mostly recovered from that Thanksgiving Corvair crash, with my hair thankfully regrown to the point the scars and stitches were no longer visible, although I was still wearing the cast on my arm.

I was in the mood to celebrate, not only about ridding myself of all the stitches and bandages on my scalp but more about being alive and having lived through that accident. I had even managed, with the help of my professors, to complete my final exams by taking the tests in their offices after hours. One prof had even, after reviewing my past test scores, decided that since I would probably perform on the final with the same grades I had during the quarter, I would receive an A. So he gave me the A—with no further testing! I had plenty of reasons to celebrate.

I began to wonder about asking Judy to go to the town's annual New Year's dance. The dance was always a very big event; it was *the* place to be on New Years' Eve. But it was such a terrible contrast; I had lived through my accident, and Judy's fiancé, Larry, hadn't. Would she even consider it?

Was it too soon? Was it too intrusive? Did it put pressure on a person not needing uninvited pressure? Would it even seem a little macabre and opportunistic to someone who had just suffered such a great loss?

Or would it be just the right thing to help her out of depression and get her "out" again? *All I could do was ask.*

The New Year's dance was the town's big social event of the year; what could be a better way to show that we both were conquering our setbacks and moving on? I knew it was going to be a lot easier for me than Judy, but I wanted to be there with her if at all possible.

#

I hesitated initially because I remembered how difficult it had been for me a few years before, during our high school years when I was a sophomore. Back then, I had desperately wanted to have a date with Judy, but there was this feeling of inadequacy—*not tall enough, not cool enough, not handsome enough, and more*—that had held me back. For me, she was a girl on a pedestal who only the most popular guys dated. But finally, one time when I decided I had to do it, I sat up all night, nervously thinking of how and when I was going to ask her to go out for our first date. I actually could not sleep, thinking and worrying about it. After all, she was not only my classmate who frequently sat—alphabetically—just in front of me but was also during those years my immediate neighbor. We both usually left to walk to school at nearly the same time, so the complexities seemed endless. *What if the date goes badly? What if she turns me down? How do you walk to school—at the same time—if you're not talking or are arguing over something or are embarrassed about something—ahead of her or behind her, or together—but not talking? How bad would that be?* I wondered and worried about all of these things.

And why do I always think of all the stuff that can go wrong?

I didn't know it then, but it must have been the unborn engineer in me; engineers are supposed to think of all the stuff that can go wrong and then plan or design to avoid it. While that's great engineering practice, it's a very limiting thing socially. And very hard to explain to girls, most of whom I now know usually think only of the good things that can happen.

I didn't know this then, either, but I badly needed a girl in my life to counteract my tendency to bring worst-case engineering design and thinking into everything. "Stop being so negative" was a phrase I would hear over and over again as I grew older.

I finally did overcome my fears and had asked her for the date. She accepted with no hesitation! *What had I been getting so tied up in knots about?* It seemed so easy for her and so hard for me. Clearly, I had a problem with perspective; after all, it was just a date to go to a movie, but it had seemed like a life-and-death matter for me.

I was bursting with pride the night I walked to her house and met her at the front door, and we walked downtown to the movie together. But I was as tense as a guitar string, struggling for things to talk about and trying to avoid any long periods of silence. I really wasn't the smooth type. But she seemed comfortable with everything, smiling and enjoying herself as we walked, and probably noticing how I struggled, put her hand in mine.

I hoped everyone would notice me taking Judy to the movies, buying tickets for two, and sitting up in the balcony where everyone with dates sat. For Judy, it was probably a routine date: a movie, shakes in Schwieterman's drugstore at the soda fountain, and a slow walk back to her house. For me, it was everything I had hoped for and a feeling that I had arrived at some key point in my life.

#

Remembering how well things had turned out on that date years earlier and also having overcome that girl-on-a-pedestal thing that also always seemed to be an issue for me back then, I decided to not make everything so complicated and just ask her for the New Year's date. I was thinking she would probably rather go out with someone to the dance than be home alone. So, except for my unanswerable questions about how it would relate to Larry—and knowing it possibly would be too soon for her—it was much easier. I understood that there was a high probability of a polite "no" and was ready for that answer. I also knew that she would handle it in the sweetest way possible, so there wouldn't be any hard feelings, no matter what the answer.

So I didn't sit up all night worrying about it; I just called her and asked for the date.

She accepted, and I had one of the best times of my life. She seemed free of all the bad memories and horrors of those days of the past summer. At the dance, we visited and talked with friends, laughed, danced, and stayed up through the rounds of midnight kissing and the playing of "Auld Lang Syne." I was, and I hoped she was equally, coping with our recent misfortunes. She seemed to be doing very well and enjoying herself. After the dance, we sat and talked in her living room, with her sitting across my lap, kissing long, wonderful kisses for what seemed to be hours.

But we didn't talk about the future; I didn't want to break the spell of that wonderful evening, and so we just enjoyed the moment. I think we both knew it was not the time for discussions of the future—and inside, I realized that she was probably going to be moving on—something I didn't want to hear.

After the holidays, I returned to Columbus, and Judy had returned to Chicago. I tried to maintain contact through the Ohio State winter quarter by writing her letters—something I had no skill for. I know I was overly dramatic and flowery. My roommate, Al Lipowitz (New Jersey Al), *critiqued* them by looking over my shoulder when I struggled to write something sensible. Our desks were side by side, and there were few secrets between us.

He always said, "Gilly"—that horrible name had found its way to Columbus—"you don't talk that way. Why do you write like that? Who are you trying to be?"

He hinted something about any rational girl just tossing them.

I think the few I did send were so bad that Judy probably did just throw them away; I don't remember receiving many in return. I may have thrown most of them away myself, being too embarrassed to actually mail them. But whatever, I didn't blame her; it was probably asking too much, too soon.

The last time I saw her in those years was during the following spring break from OSU. In one of my more composed letters, I had proposed driving to Chicago to see her for the weekend. She agreed and found me a bunk with one of Jeanne's male friends. We went out to dinner at a very upscale restaurant in one of Chicago's suburbs before going to see the biggest movie hit of the year, *Days of Wine and Roses* starring Lee Remick and Jack Lemmon. It was the most discussed film at the time, with a great title song by Henry Mancini and Johnny Mercer that was getting a lot of radio airplay.

Since there were no *At the Movies* film-review programs on TV in those days or similar print reviews, we tended to go to movies just on what we had informally heard from friends. We had no idea of what was coming.

The movie turned out to be a horrible downer. The couple struggled with alcoholism, and they were trying to get sober throughout the story. The movie ends with the couple's marriage falling apart and alcoholism maintaining its hold on the woman's life. While the story had nothing in common with Judy's recent tragedy, there was the one unavoidable thing: the awful sadness in both stories' endings.

Judy cried, and we left the theater as the credits started displaying on the screen. We talked very little the rest of that evening and even the next morning when I left for Ohio. Things had become sadly uncomfortable; we had few words and fewer smiles for each other. We made no plans or promises.

It wasn't me, and it wasn't *us;* I think we both knew that. It was a river of time that just needed to flow before she was over it. I knew the odds were against any long-term relationship developing, and I reconciled myself to that. I didn't want to push it if it really wasn't there, and I realized that she still needed space and time to grieve and find herself. I didn't want to reach the point where she would have to tell me to back away. Just taking it to that point would itself create hard feelings that I didn't want either of us to have.

Our lives took us in very different directions afterward. I had to get through the next year and half at Ohio State, and she had to find her new life. It would be totally consuming for each of us.

A glimpse into something beyond teenage school years' boy-girl relationships slipped unknown into my mind at some point after Chicago. It was beyond *how long and how many times can you kiss and hug a girl*, and it was beyond *I want you, I need you.* It was something about letting go when I realized that I should let go.

In those months of late 1962 and early '63, Judy, Pat, Jim, Ted, Ray, Charlie, my brothers, cousins, many other friends and Road Rebels, a married Joanie, myself—all of us—were drifting away from each other. Much like a Fourth of July pinwheel, we were the sparks flying off in all directions with different goals and new friends and loves and heading for different places. At that point in our young lives, the tendency was to run toward new things, not to look back at where we were just standing—and living. It seemed so easy to just move on. Wasn't that we were supposed—programmed—to do?

Still, it seems as if we could have tried harder to reach back to hold on to each other a little more. But, at twenty-three, who thinks about that?

Good-Bye, Columbus

Start spreading the news, I'm leaving today …
—Liza Minelli, "New York, New York" (J. Kander and F. Ebb)

The envelope had an Endicott, New York, return address, with IBM in big blue letters above. I nearly cut my hand using a kitchen knife as a letter opener. I fumbled with the enclosed letter, not bothering to completely unfold it, and only wanting to see what the opening paragraph had to say. *I couldn't believe it.* The interviewer had actually meant it: IBM was offering me a summer intern position in upstate New York at their business location in Endicott!

"Congratulations, Robert, IBM is pleased to offer you an intern position at our Endicott, NY, facility for the coming summer of 1964. Your salary will be $150 per week and include medical benefits. Please sign and return the enclosed acceptance sheet and provide your arrival date. After we have received your reply, we will be calling you to discuss the details of your travel, temporary housing, and living expenses. Include a telephone number and best times when we can contact you."

I couldn't sign and return the letter fast enough. I drove it to the post office rather than risk it getting lost in the mailman's bag or dropped on the street or some other unlikely disaster that would prevent me from taking that job. I couldn't wait to tell my housemates, Fred and Don, about it, and I proudly called my parents that evening. I was going to New York!

#

Until my last two years at OSU, I had always felt I had two homes: my apartment in Columbus and my home in New Bremen. The New Bremen address had always been my official address, home base, and place for summer jobs. I had always returned to New Bremen for the holidays and summer breaks, which allowed me to maintain old friendships. That changed abruptly in the summer of '63 when I stayed in Columbus for a better-paying summer job than I could possibly have found in New Bremen, working as an intern for the power company in Columbus. I started using some of the technical skills I had been learning at Ohio State, writing Fortran programs for power system modeling. That was followed in the spring of '64 by the summer intern job at IBM near the beautiful Finger Lakes region of upstate New York.

New Bremen would no longer be the place I listed as my home when I filled out forms and documents; I was hardly ever there and was gradually separating myself from my old home and friendships.

With the coming move to New York, I was a rolling stone, my home being wherever I happened to be staying at the moment. I'd had four mailing addresses in just the previous year: the freezing apartment Al and I had occupied through the spring quarter of '63, a friend's cabin at Buckeye Lake for that summer, an apartment in a big brick house just off campus shared with two student friends, Fred and Don, and finally, another apartment by the train switchyards the three of us moved to when the landlord needed us out of the big brick house.

And I was about to move again, this time to the job at IBM in Endicott, New York.

I had next to no belongings; the clothing I tried to keep neat I folded into one suitcase, with everything else stuffed into a duffel bag. I also had a beat-up Sears Silvertone guitar, some textbooks, and a basketball. And there was my new, most treasured possession: the 1959 Alfa Romeo roadster I had purchased from a good friend in the electrical engineering school, which he had sold to me for a very low price. He was going into a job at Cape Canaveral, working on Atlas missile launches, and had purchased a new Corvette in celebration. I had wanted that Alfa badly because of its far more advanced styling and engineering compared to the British sports cars—MGs, Austin Healys, and Triumphs—being driven around college campuses in those days. It even had roll-up windows! I thought the Alfa gave me back a little of the distinction I hadn't had in those past, carless years. Young stud with cool, red, Italian sports car headed for a summer in New York!

Everything I owned fit into the Alfa's small trunk, except the basketball, which went into the passenger seat. I had the basketball in the car with me nearly at all times back then, thanks to my friend and housemate Don Branson, a Zanesville high school all-Ohio athlete in basketball, football, and baseball. He had spent two years after high school in the Saint Louis Cardinals baseball farm system but had never gotten his big shot at the majors. He was a great athlete, equally skilled in all three sports—and also was a well-known party animal around campus. He had learned *everything* there was to learn—including partying, drinking, and more—from traveling around the minors with a bunch of other young guys living away from home and on the road for the first time. He managed to teach me enough about basketball that I could join in some of the pickup games that were always going on around OSU's outdoor courts, so I was playing at a much higher level than back in my JV days in New Bremen. I still had that high school notion of girls being impressed by basketball players with a smooth jump shot; *you never know*.

Don was a kind of big-brother figure to me—certainly not in the academic guidance sense—but more in the "ways of the world" sense that a young, black, urban man could offer. He had street smarts. I knew enough to take what I thought a naive farm town boy/engineering student should know and—hopefully—say *no, thanks* to the rest. I realized that I was flying at a pretty high altitude and into unchartered territory some of those times, but it went with the total experience and friendship. While I was very thankful about the basketball training, the *rest* was more than a serious engineering student needed to know. But Don showed me *some* of the rest, anyway—such as helping him to come up with his share of the rent money. It involved playing the innocent, mediocre pool player who suckered a greedy pool shark in for the kill, with Don, a superb pool shark himself, watching and waiting on the sidelines.

But Fred was much better at it than I was; I think my quivering pool cue and sweaty upper lip always gave it away. Don, mostly with Fred's help, always came up with his rent money.

I headed for New York, and Don headed for Chicago. I never saw him or Fred again.

#

My New York summer raced by in a blur of working at IBM, trips to the Finger Lakes, Ithaca's and Cornell's hot spots, attending racing at the world-famous Watkins Glen racetrack, a trip to the '64 World's Fair in New York City, and trips to the Adirondack Mountains areas. The entire summer was far beyond my expectations: high technology, beautiful surroundings, new people, and new experiences. I had worked with engineering interns from Big Ten schools, Cornell and other Ivy League colleges, as well as smaller, private colleges in the New York and Pennsylvania areas. They were the best of the best—and I was there with them.

IBM was a swirling mixture of new graduate hires, summer interns, and contract engineers, all on top of an already large permanent engineering staff. The place was cooking with the new System 360 rolling out, the hottest thing in the world in the computer market at the time. IBM couldn't get enough engineers. Things were so confusing, with people and projects changing and shifting, that I really didn't accomplish much for them, but I did get a feel for what things were like in the high-tech world of the '60s. I couldn't fully appreciate this yet, but my instincts told me that computers and integrated circuit technology—like I had experienced at IBM and in which they led the world—was going to be the place to be.

Even though it had been a little more than a twelve-week peek into the evolving world of computers and microelectronics, my summer internship was a huge experience for me. I had been in the labs working with real engineers and modern electronics equipment on real, state-of-the-art technical issues. I was getting a feel for what it would be like in the industry—and I started to believe that I was ready. My supervisor told me that they would have an offer ready for me when I graduated.

That was incredible news! I couldn't wait to go back to OSU for that final quarter and graduation!

Most importantly, I was feeling a lot differently about myself than I had in years—or maybe than I had ever felt. I was a completely independent person, self-sufficient, and able to make enough money, as evidenced by the salary IBM paid me, that I could see I had made the right choices. I had skills that companies were interested in, I believed I knew what I was doing, and I believed in myself. It was a long way from those oily pinion gears. And with my Alfa Romeo, I even had cool wheels again. All those impossibilities from 1958 were now being replaced by new, real possibilities.

Now, *if only* there were a girl ready to join me in my new life.

#

I headed back to OSU for the fall quarter in September 1964 and my final ten weeks of college. The quarter turned out to be uneventful, and other than my upcoming graduation, it was disappointingly routine. Most of the people I knew in Columbus had graduated the previous spring, and I felt detached from everything. I took a junky apartment on the third floor of an old house—my sixth address in the past eighteen months—that was too hot in September and too cold in December. I didn't care what it was like, since I wasn't going to be there long, and I was willing to put up with almost anything. And since, other than something disastrous occurring, whatever happened in the last quarter wouldn't affect my five-year GPA significantly, I just rode things out, not pushing myself for top grades.

My social circle had crumbled, as had my circle of engineering classmates, many of whom had stayed in summer school and graduated in August. The bar where most of my friends met—Steveo's on High Street—was full of people, as usual, but empty to me. I saw no friendly faces there, only strangers. Dianne, a beautiful girl my housemate Fred had broken off with the previous spring and who I believed was still in grad school and hoped to restart my friendship with, was nowhere to be found. There were none of the parties she used to have at her apartment—or anyone's apartment, for that matter—and no beer blasts in surrounding parks. And there weren't any of the raucous, post–football game parties with our old crowd at Steveo's or the Heidelberg South bars. It all felt dead. Even walking across campus, I missed the familiar faces of people I hadn't really known but had seen repeatedly over the years scurrying between classes. I had no interest in trying to establish a new social circle at that late point, and I attended my last OSU football games alone.

And, at seven and two, the team had a mediocre year—by Ohio State standards.

#

As I sat in the graduates' seating area of Saint John's Arena watching other engineering students receive their diplomas while waiting for my name to be called, my first year at Heidelberg and the last four years and three months at Ohio State replayed through my mind … things I knew I'd never forget …

The excitement of living away from home for the first time and meeting kids from all over Ohio and other northeastern states and learning that I could do college-level work.

Living in shabby, rent-by-the-week boardinghouses with poor heating, no cooling, and without cooking facilities during my first year in Columbus.

The apartment where New Jersey Al and I lived with water pipes that froze several times in the winter of '62 and the gas space heater that I always just knew would poison us to death in our sleep with leaking carbon monoxide.

Al and I eating our meager, home-cooked meals featuring lots of spaghetti or canned Dinty Moore beef stew.

The laughs I had with Al during our years together and his great sense of humor; his New Jersey "coolness."

Weekly trips to the coin-operated laundry with clothes that needed to be thrown out rather than rewashed.

Living with Fred and Don for most of the last two years and the parties those guys threw at the slightest suggestion.

Picking Don up at 1:00 a.m., "asleep" across three bar chairs at Steveo's, the owner impatiently waiting to close for the night.

Watching Don smoke a joint; me not knowing what it was. He just laughed at me; Don was always laughing. And pool sharking with Don when the rent was due.

Trying to come up with another good reason why Don really didn't want to borrow my Alfa Romeo. No way.

My attempts at having the fun social life unknown to engineering students by living with those two nonengineering, party-ready guys … and the GPA challenge that went with that decision.

Basketball games at Saint John's Arena and the powerful Buckeyes basketball teams of those years with five consecutive Big Ten Championships or cochampionships, one NCAA National Championship, two NCAA finals runner-ups (damn that Cincinnati!) and an overall record of 114 wins and 18 losses.

Football games at Ohio Stadium when Woody had the fabulous backs Matt Snell and Paul Warfield running—off tackle and through the line—the three yards and a cloud of dust offense. Woody even playing Snell at *defensive end. Woody* … what was there to say?

Ohio State declining the Rose Bowl invitation for the January 1, 1962, game by deciding to show an emphasis on education versus sports. *What?*

Kennedy and Khrushchev and the Cuban Missile Crisis and wondering whether or not "it" really would happen. And if it did, what would it mean to us?

Watching John Glenn and other American astronauts making the USA's first trips into space, with the national anthem playing and playing, people in public places cheering. Yet engineering school and engineering students were still *uncool.*

Feeling miserable and depressed after being told while walking between classes by a crying girl that Kennedy had been shot and might be dying.

Disbelief watching as Ruby shot Oswald on live TV.

Spending three consecutive days in front of the television at a good student-friend's house, watching everything nonstop: the Kennedy funeral procession, Jackie and the kids walking alongside the caisson, the casket, Johnson's swearing in, endless news reports, endless conspiracy theories.

Hearing Joan Baez's incredible, crystal-clear, haunting voice for the first time: "All My Sorrows" and "House of the Rising Sun" drifting down the hallway of my apartment building. Peter, Paul, and Mary, the Kingston Trio, Ian and Sylvia. Joan being labeled a "commie." Folk singers collectively being viewed suspiciously as "commies" or "pinkos."

Students beginning to protest against the war and the draft and racial discrimination and lying politicians.

Kids beginning to lose faith in the country's leaders.

Students for a Democratic Society being called "commies."

Goldwater's crazy presidential campaign, the John Birch Society, mean-spirited, racist Southern governors on TV, police dogs attacking kids, men hiding in white sheets and pointy hats. What kind of world was I heading into? (Twenty-five years later, Billy Joel captured it all with "We Didn't Start the Fire.")

Excitement and fascination with the Beatles' and Bob Dylan's first songs playing everywhere, including at Steveo's, with its Beat-era black walls and black ceilings.

Girls with long, straight hair dressed in black leotards and black turtleneck sweaters—away from home and Mom and Dad. The first miniskirts.

Seeing performers, such as Dave Brubeck and Duke Ellington and other great artists of the time, at Mershon Auditorium and other Columbus venues—performers I never would have seen back home around New Bremen. Remembering those jazz tunes from my visit to Miami University in the winter of '58 that changed my musical outlook forever.

A new model Jaguar, the XKE; I knew I had to have one.

A new car named Mustang. I knew I had to have one of those too.

Yet studying, studying, and studying—through it all.

The high level of technology I experienced at IBM during that summer job and knowing that I had to be there—in it—somewhere.

That long-ago "Are you crazy" debate with Bill and Stan, five years earlier.

If only *those* girls could see me now.

#

The dean of the engineering school handed me my diploma, and it was over. I shook hands with a few engineering school acquaintances graduating that quarter, kissed no girlfriends or female schoolmates, and went to no collegiate graduation parties. But my proud mother gave me a big hug and had tears in her eyes; my dad shook my hand and still had that look of disbelief. My younger brother, Rich, with an admiring look, shook my hand, and his girl, Bev, gave me a tender hug. The five of us went to Columbus's Varsity Club for dinner.

For me, all those years of saving every cent, studying or working every available hour, pushing myself beyond what I believed I could do just six years before, had come to an end. At times, it seemed like an endurance contest: grinding it out with the promise of a finish line and something better after it all. But it had also been exhilarating and eye opening, and there was nothing to regret. It was exciting to know that I now had something I believed could take me nearly anywhere.

But I had a slightly lonely feeling at the same time, since I would be starting my new life alone. I'd been in that place before, but this time I hoped and believed that it was going to be different.

Good-bye, Columbus.

Get a Job

Sha na na na, sha na na na na …
—The Silhouettes, "Get a Job"

After my low-key graduation, I returned to my parents' home in New Bremen for the time needed to figure out which job offer I would accept and where I would be headed after graduating. It was January—midwinter in rural Ohio—gray skies, barren trees, snow-covered fields, and not much going on. It seemed like everyone was gone again—too much like after my high school graduation in the summer of '58 and now my college graduation the previous week. And even though we had no problems between us, I knew I couldn't stay in my parents' home for more than a week or two. Not after five years on my own.

And I don't have a job again—yet. But this time, I know that won't be the case for long.

Over that last year and a half when my summer jobs were in other cities, I had been returning to New Bremen only for the traditional family gatherings of Thanksgiving and Christmas and was otherwise mostly detached from things going on back there. I had nearly lost contact with the guys in the old Road Rebels Car Club, who were mostly married by this point and no longer together as a car club. It was the same with my friends who had graduated from college the previous years and who were already in or beginning new jobs around Ohio and other states. I seldom saw any of the other friends and relatives who still lived in New Bremen. Occasionally, during my short stays during some holiday or another, I would run into a Road Rebel on the New Bremen streets, but it was as if I were running into just any of the other guys I had known during my high school years.

"Hey, Jer. How ya doin'?"

"Really good, Bob. Long time no see! Hey, I heard you finally graduated from OSU. Congratulations. Take care of yourself now."

"Sure. Bye, Jer."

The club was history; no one seemed to even mention it anymore. I didn't see anyone wearing those Road Rebel shirts or jackets or see the club plaques hanging on a rear bumper anywhere around town.

#

Graduating at the end of December, a time that was well off the main corporate recruiting schedule, had stirred within me some very mixed emotions. It had been great to finally receive that engineering degree after five years and three months of work, but the low level of corporate recruiting for the off-quarter graduates had been disappointing. There had been nothing like the frenzied, on-campus recruiting of the earlier spring quarter, for our fall graduation. Most companies planned their hiring and training programs around the spring graduates. With the exception of twenty to thirty companies that were still recruiting, we were almost ignored; some companies just put up an easel chart with corporate brochures.

But I did have several options—and I also had some of my own criteria.

I had that offer to go back to IBM, as well as a few other offers, but none of them excited me in the way I felt I needed. Most of the offers were from companies in upstate New York—Buffalo, Syracuse, and Endicott—which were nothing to sneeze at, but the winters there were bad. After enduring too many bitter winters walking between classes on Ohio State's huge campus, I wasn't looking for even worse winters.

Carol had also entered my mind during that time, because of the possibilities with the companies in New York. But those jobs were located at the far end of the state; not exactly an easy, half-day drive to the city. And more than four years had gone by since I had last heard anything about or from her. Although I was still fascinated by her memory and knew that someday, somehow, I'd look her up to tell her what she had meant to me, I couldn't really let her become a deciding factor in my job search. So I crossed New York off my list.

California interested me somewhat, but the companies hiring were primarily aircraft companies, which held no interest for me. It was all aircraft control systems, which at that time were mainly cables and pulleys, with some hydraulics, electric motors, solenoids, and switches.

The phenomenon of Silicon Valley was still a couple of years in the future.

Ford Motor Company had been on campus recruiting that fall—for trunk and door lock engineers. I swallowed my car-guy image and didn't follow up on an offer to visit Dearborn.

And—after a high school graduation celebration trip my older brother, Ron, and I had made with another Road Rebel friend in 1958 through Kentucky, Tennessee, and North Carolina—I knew the Ohio River would be my southern boundary for career opportunities. The suspicion and unfriendly looks we saw on local faces as our Ohio-licensed Ford drove through towns in those states told me all I needed to know.

So I was back in New Bremen for a few days after graduation to spend some time with my family, consider the offers I did have, and do some telephone work following up on discussions I had with other companies that had been on campus recruiting that fall.

While there, a wheel bearing on my Alfa Romeo needed replacement. Metric-sized wheel bearings weren't exactly an off-the-shelf thing in New Bremen, so I made a trip to an auto parts store in Dayton that specialized in European car parts. I also wanted to stop at the National Cash Register (NCR) headquarters while in Dayton after I read a Dayton newspaper article about NCR making a big move into computers and electronic retail terminals using integrated circuits as part of its diversification from mechanical cash registers.

I got the wheel bearing I needed and drove over to the big, campus-like NCR complex on South Main Street. Approximately twenty thousand people worked in those facilities in 1964.

I walked in—unannounced—to their R&D personnel office in Building 31 and asked for a job application. It was as if I had descended a golden, spiral stairway from new engineering graduate heaven. They had not met their needed college hiring requirements the past spring and were desperate for engineers. And there I was, walking in the front door, asking for an application form! I had a whirl of interviews and an offer sheet typed up and provided to me before I left later that day, giving me my pick of several different positions. I chose large-scale integrated circuit semiconductor component design.

Sounded like the new, new thing.

Maybe I was finally going to get my career off the ground. It was all coming together: a job in a nationally known, highly respected, Fortune 100 company; work in a technology sector my instincts told me would be *the* place to be for the future; a starting salary of $9,000 a year—with benefits; a location only fifty miles from my hometown so that I could stay in touch with family and friends—and still surrounded by all my favorite racetracks and racing haunts. It was beginning to make that $18,000 investment look pretty good.

I didn't think I could have asked for a better situation; I was elated. Finally, I knew it had been worth all the work and deprivation I'd gone through. I could only think back on all the times with my roommate Al, eating spaghetti night after night at the end of spring quarters when our money was not just running out but was already completely gone. More than once, I found myself selling textbooks for half price as soon as I finished the related finals to have enough money to buy more spaghetti and red sauce to make it through the last exams. At times, it had even come down to deciding whether to use my remaining fifty cents for laundry or two beers at Steveo's. Good-bye to all of that!

I went out to buy some new clothes.

And never again ordered red sauce.

Nikki

Little darling come with me, won't you help me share my load ...
—Van Morrison, "Bright Side of the Road"

My social life had been a black hole during my last quarter at Ohio State and continued that way for the next year and half in Dayton while I adjusted to actually working as an engineer and getting situated in the city. I had difficulty with the singles scene—there wasn't any. Dayton was a "home" person's town with very few opportunities for newly arrived, young, single people to meet. Everyone seemed to have their own circle of friends they'd known since high school or at the University of Dayton. It seemed as though no one my age needed to meet newly arrived, midtwenties people; they were content with the people they already knew.

It wasn't for lack of trying; I kept my ears open to learn about the best bars or hangouts for meeting people—hopefully girls—that were supposed to be the "in" places. As far as I could tell, there weren't any, but it may have been me more than anything. Bar talk wasn't my thing; I just could never come up with any catchy lines that were sure to get anyone interested in me. And even if I did, I never had that second, follow-up line. I was like Johnny One Note.

"Hi, good-looking. Buy you a drink?"

"I already have one, thank you; excuse me."

Or "Hello. Do you come here often?"

"No, do you? Cash me out please, bartender."

Or "Do you work at NCR? I thought I saw you in the parking lot the other day."

"NCR? You mean the 'Cash'? God, no, all those engineers!"

"But what's wrong with engineers?" I said to the back of her head.

I had always tried to stay away from discussing being an engineer with other young people not in the profession. At that time, the counterculture movement was pretty strong in the youth crowd. Many of them associated engineers with "the establishment": armament and aerospace companies and—by association—the Vietnam War. In my last years at Ohio State, it was getting so bad that I never wore my slide rule on my belt, hanging from the belt loop provided on the slide rule cases. It was a dead giveaway. *Look, he's an engineer. They are so uncool!* So, I had always tried to hide it in the pile of books I carried to class. That attitude still prevailed in the mid-1960s after I started working at NCR.

"What do I do at NCR? Well, I'm an electronics engineer there, and I'm working on—"

"But wait. Wait a minute! I have all of Bob Dylan's, Joan Baez's, and Gordon Lightfoot's albums! Do you want to come to my place and listen? Have you heard 'A Hard Rain's A-Gonna Fall'? I even have the latest Beatles LP. No?"

"Do you like Gerry Mulligan or Miles Davis? What, too weird?"

"What about Jonathan Winters? He's such a crack-up! Oh, so you think he's a little too wacky for you? How about Mort Saul? He's very sophisticated. No, not him, either? Maybe Lenny Bruce or Red Skelton?"

"So, what and who do you like? I said what and who do you like? How can I talk to you over there?"

It was probably best that I found out right away that she had no sense of good music or humor.

Now technology and all things "techy" are in. And engineers, while not exactly the model of debonairness, are at least tolerated. Geeky is even in, in some circles! And backpacks are in. Back then, we didn't have backpacks to carry laptops, iPads, iPods, smartphones—maybe to even hide a slide rule in—around to classes.

If only one of those pretty girls—and there were plenty of them around in those few Dayton hangouts or the few mixers that occasionally happened—had said, "Oh, you're an engineer. Tell me all about it. I've always wanted to meet an engineer!"

In my dreams.

One of the problems—and I was very conscious of this—was that many engineers at NCR, as was true of engineers at most other places in those days, dressed in full business suits—usually gray or blue—with white shirts and ties, and they wore white socks and brown shoes. It was a dead giveaway. White socks and brown shoes—with everything!

Marry this man, and you're going to live in the Dayton suburbs the rest of your life, raise a lot of kids, and drive around in a four-door Chevy station wagon, watch Petticoat Junction *and* The Big Valley, *and dine out at the Big Eats Cafeteria.*

How could I convince them that that wouldn't happen with me? I didn't even own a pair of brown, lace-up shoes!

I was driving around in my almost-new, primrose-yellow, 1965 Jaguar XKE Coupe, and I still had my Alfa Romeo roadster. I listened to modern jazz, rock and roll, the best folk music, and read Conrad, Steinbeck, and Hemingway, for God's sake. I was hip!

At least, I was trying to be hip. If I did manage to get to, or past, that second sentence with a pretty girl, and the word *engineer* came up, I never got to the Jaguar or Alfa Romeo or music or what I was reading—or more importantly, who I was. End of conversation.

Oh, sorry. What's your name again? Oh, yes, Bob. Bob, I just want to say hi to Greg over there.

Greg, can you give me a lift home?

They never got to know how cool I was. I just couldn't break through, even in my black Florsheim loafers and black socks. It was another one of those times in my life when *something had to change.* And it did—just at the right time—because I sure wasn't getting anywhere on my own.

#

It was so easy to fall in love.

It felt as if it happened overnight, even though it really took a few months. It started in the fall of 1966 with a blind date arranged by my business associate and friend Jim Wall, whom I'd met during my first assignment at NCR. Nikki was a beautiful girl, new to Dayton after moving there with a small company from upstate New York. Two Dayton and two New York companies were merging into one, apparently trying to become the dominant player in rare-coin catalog and auction sales. Nikki, as the bookkeeper for the larger New York firms, had to merge the books for all the companies into one set of accounting ledgers. It had buried her for the first six months she was in Dayton, and she had no social life. She wasn't meeting anyone other than the people she already knew in the coin businesses. She was no green-eyeshade mole in the accounting back room; she was an active, lively young woman who wanted a life beyond the books and was anxious to start meeting people, including guys she might date.

I was still looking for that love that had, for any number of reasons, escaped me for all that time, from high school through college and into my professional life—and now Dayton. Nikki's company had located in an office building also occupied by Jim's electronic component sales business, where she sometimes met Jim at the coffee machine. She struck up a friendship with him and started dropping hints for help with her social life.

Jim, the guy I probably identified with more than any other person I knew in my years in Dayton (he drove Corvettes and liked sailing and good music), called my office one day to ask if I would like to meet a new girl in town who was interested in meeting people—meaning guys, I hoped.

I was, and as Doris Troy sang, with *just one look*, Nikki became the second New York girl to come into my life and change everything. *Really change everything!* Jim and his wife, Sandy, organized the date. We went to see the Roy Meriwether Trio at a suburban nightclub near Wright-Patterson Air Force Base.

We were having a great time listening to Roy play his biggest numbers—"Watermelon Man" and "Drown in My Own Tears"—but with Nikki talking mostly to Sandy and me talking mostly to Jim. After around an hour and a half, Sandy apologized and announced that they had to leave early because their babysitter needed to be home by eleven o'clock that evening.

So it became one on one; time for me to find out if I could actually charm a girl with conversation and wit. Could I hold the attention of this pretty, shapely, tallish girl with her huge smile and direct, honest, look-you-right-in-the-eyes gaze?

Okay, Bob, no BS here. It won't work, so be straight now.

"So you're from New York. Where, exactly?" I asked.

"Well, I was born in Rochester, but I really grew up in Binghamton," she said.

"Binghamton!" I said with surprise. "I spent the summer of '64 in the Endicott/Binghamton area. I worked at IBM as a summer intern. Where did you live?"

"On Pierce Hill Road, just off Highway 26."

"You mean the highway down to Pennsylvania?"

"Yes."

"Can you believe it? Two other guys and I rented a place just off and below Highway 26, down by the Susquehanna River. I must have been less than a half mile from you all that time, and here we are meeting, two years later—in Dayton!" I nearly shouted.

That was it. I had made it past the first sentence, then the second, and then—we went on from there for another hour. I don't remember what Roy Meriwether played after that—this in spite of the fact that she knew I was an engineer, since Jim had given her a little background on me ahead of time when he arranged the blind date. Maybe it was because she was stranded with me, fifteen miles from her apartment. But I don't think so; we actually were enjoying each other.

We made small talk for most of that hour, but it was easy and comfortable enough that I thought there was terrific promise with her. And she had these beautiful, luscious lips I had been looking at all evening: full, eager, smiling lips framing her gleaming white teeth that all seemed to just be waiting for me, inviting me. We drove back to her apartment, just off Riverside Drive, and I walked her to her door.

"By the way, Nikki, I met a girl from Endicott that summer. You know, a friend of a friend; her name was Pat Svec. She was very pretty and seemed about your age. Did you know her?" I asked.

"Pat? Sure. We were co-city festival beauty queens our senior year."

Good God, I met the other festival queen. How is it that I didn't meet Nikki when I was there? I'm not going to let this opportunity get away.

With the first kiss, all those other girls in my past faded from memory.

This has to be the one.

We went into her apartment …

I followed up our evening by inviting Nikki to join me for breakfast the next Sunday morning. This was a really new thing for me; asking a girl for a date for breakfast, which really meant a date for the entire day—if everything worked out. It may have been a leap of confidence that we could spend a whole day together, after meeting for just a few hours one evening. But I had all my usual self-doubts.

What if we get bored with each other halfway through the coffee and fruit and never get to the eggs Benedict and pancakes?

What if we run out of things to talk about on the drive I plan to take her on in the Jag?

What if she has another date that evening?

My God, I didn't think I could deal with taking her home so she could dress for a date with another guy.

But she didn't have anything planned for the entire day and accepted. And we didn't run out of things to talk about. We found that we each loved dogs; she had a German shepherd back in New York, and I had a cocker spaniel in New Bremen—that is, our parents did. She loved cars and had a classic, turquoise-and-white '56 Thunderbird in the garage in New York that she had not brought out to Ohio yet. I had my Jag and Alfa Romeo.

She was interested in racing and had attended Formula 1 races at the famous Watkins Glen track in the Finger Lakes region, and her brother even raced stock cars on the local half-mile tracks around Binghamton. I had traveled to all the local area racetracks and the Indianapolis 500 several times and had a detailed knowledge of big-time American racing.

We had so much to talk about and share with each other.

"Let's go to my place when we get back to Dayton and listen to some albums I have," she proposed, explaining that she had *Time Out* with "Take Five" by Dave Brubeck, *Black Orpheus* by Vince Guaraldi, and newer things, including Ramsey Lewis's *The In Crowd*, some Henry Mancini and Burt Bacharach, and lots of movie scores.

"I also have Jonathan Winters and Bob Newhart comedy albums, if you like laughs," she said.

My God, I can't believe I'm hearing this. Take that, you Dayton girls who wouldn't give me the time of day. What is it with New York girls?

"Yes, yes, yes. Let's do it! And let's stop to get some pizza at Vic Cassano's place on North Main on the way."

I had to force myself to leave her apartment at the end of that day. By Christmas, four months after first meeting, we knew we wanted to be married. It wasn't a bended-knee offering of a diamond engagement ring, surprise moment. Instead, it was a moment when we were sitting in her apartment, enjoying just talking to each other and both realized we were completely in tune. I hadn't planned it ahead of time, but the thought certainly had occurred to me more than once in the preceding weeks; and it became more and more obvious to me—and probably both of us—that we really should be married.

It was as simple as me asking, "Will you marry me?"

Nikki had tears in her eyes and said, "Yes. I thought you'd never ask."

Nikki's parents were not surprised, since I had met them when we had traveled to Binghamton the past October to attend the Watkins Glen US Grand Prix race and for me to meet her family. Nikki had also met my parents in New Bremen on a few occasions in the previous months. They knew we were spending all of our free time together, since that's all we talked about.

We quickly settled the question of where and when by deciding that it would be a small, families-only wedding in my old church in New Bremen in April 1967. We were married by the same preacher who had graduated my confirmation class of my brother and me nearly fifteen years before. Neither family nor Nikki or I had the money for a big wedding, and we didn't want the hassle of preparing for that, anyway. We just wanted to get married and be together full-time as soon as possible and with the least possible distraction from our lives. We were both twenty-six, no longer kids and fast becoming adults. We didn't need a glitzy wedding.

Looking back, it seemed that there was never even any question about us getting married after the first few weeks of knowing her; I had the feeling that it was destined to happen. It had just been a matter of finally meeting her on that blind date.

Why had it been so hard, and taken so long—and then become so easy? From those teenage dances in the opera house to Heidelberg to Columbus to New York to Dayton? After fourteen years and several one-sided romances, all with wonderful girls, I found the answer to the question I had been asking myself all along: *Is it ever going to happen?*

Yes!

Buddy Holly had written and sung it with the Crickets in 1958: "It's so easy to fall in love!"

How Do You ...

If you can't explain it simply, you don't understand it well enough.
—Einstein

The more you explain it, the more I don't understand it.
—Mark Twain

Her eyes glazed over as I tried to explain, "It's all done with bright light sources and lenses and photo masks and chemicals ..." and she then reached for another glass of wine.

The question had been, "How do you stick all those little transistors on that little thingy?"

I'd had that conversation countless times before, all with the same result: a look in her or his eyes that said, *Why did I bother to ask?*

And the second question to follow was always "Why?"

"Because it's cheaper to build computers that way, and it makes them faster."

That always got the even deeper glazed stare and the look that said, *Okay, this is going nowhere. What else can I talk about to this guy I'm stuck sitting here with at this going-nowhere-party?*

Why hadn't I thought of saying, "Because it's good for mankind"? That might have been a better conversation to see how the other person viewed society and technology, but I always seemed to think of that one too late. Which was probably a good thing, *but maybe we can get into that after the fourth glass of wine, if we are still here?*

Even now, with everyone having the laptops and cell phones and "pods, pads, surfaces" common today and believing everyone has at least a rudimentary knowledge of technology and microelectronics, I still can't explain to people what I did for those thirty-five years. How do you explain to a nontechnical person that integrated circuits are designed today by engineers that—for the most part—never "see" a transistor because they are so small and that seeing one of the millions (today it's billions) on a chip isn't meaningful and that it's all done through very specialized software? How do I explain that it's a combination of physicists, chemists, materials engineers, software coders, and yes, electrical engineers who all collaborate to invent a new chip or fabrication process to make the chips? That the chips are fabricated with things called ion implanters, plasma etchers, metal evaporators, oxidation furnaces, e-beam writers, deep UV mask aligners, and so on? I can tell them this is so, but I can't explain it. I've tried, but then I get that "Why did I bother to ask?" look.

Thankfully, at last, the next question now is usually something like, "Did you see the Jon Stewart show last night?"

Aha, we can talk, after all!

#

The first eighteen years of my career had been spent in the world of designing and building microcircuits for mainframe computer companies—seven at NCR in that first, out-of-college job and the next eleven with Burroughs in their microelectronics facility in San Diego, California. And, as I tried to tell that woman—who was actually a good friend and neighbor—that night, it was all about cheaper and faster electronics. NCR and the other mainframe companies had all seen it coming; they knew they had to be able to imbed their own architectures and implementations on silicon themselves if they were going to be able to retain control over their product uniqueness and evolution. Building a computer on just a few chips—or even one chip eventually—was the Holy Grail; but it had to be their own technology rather than someone else's. Otherwise, the product cost and performance, as well as product line evolution, was going to be controlled by someone else. So they all went to great expense to build integrated circuit manufacturing facilities and hire the needed technical staffs to design the chips and run the fabrication processes. In the end game, though, it really didn't work out all that well for them. It had worked to varying degrees of success for some companies for some number of years, but as the costs of the fabrication facilities increased exponentially with the advancements in the underlying technologies, it came to the point where it became prohibitively expensive to maintain the capability for just their own limited production volumes.

And the onrushing waves of other technologies, including powerful microprocessors from Intel and Motorola, desktop and laptop computers, local and wide area networks (the Internet), open operating system standards (DOS, Windows, Unix, Apple OS), third-party software, and waves of entrepreneurs eventually sank all the mainframe and minicomputer companies. The BUNCH (Burroughs, Univac, NCR, Control Data, Honeywell) and others like DEC and Data General sank beneath the waves they either didn't see coming, didn't understand, or were powerless—being locked into their proprietary equipment and insistent customer bases—to respond to. Only IBM survived, and even then only as a much different company from the hardware and software juggernaut of its earlier existence.

In my case, though, all those years of designing and working in semiconductor fabrication operations added up to a background in demand anywhere chips were being designed and fabricated. It was a completely portable background, useful to systems companies working with silicon foundries and semiconductor component companies alike. It was almost a bulletproof résumé, unless I wanted to do something completely out of left field, such as become a software programmer (a whole different reality).

Along the way, I had worked on pioneering new computer-related products, such as one of the first bar code scanner systems back in my earliest days at NCR and one of the first commercially viable cathode ray tube, dot-matrix display systems—both of which were for NCR's new, cash register–replacing, electronic retail terminal products in the '60s. That work led to my first patents and my first completed integrated circuit designs. Later, at Burroughs, it also included leading a design team that originally invented, patented, and implemented the basic chip architecture, called the Folded Bit Line, used in most of the world's computer chip memories (DRAMs) through the '70s and into the '80s.

Newer technologies eventually obsoleted that architecture, but during its time of relevance, Burroughs licensed the design concept to many of the leading DRAM suppliers of the era.

NCR had been a great starting point. I was able to do new design work at the same time that I was living and breathing semiconductor technology, learning from the specialists the company had recruited to start their own fabrication lines. But those were also days of mystery. One day, the process would yield the expected quantity of good circuits, and the next day, the yields were zero. What was going on? In the '60s, microcircuit fabrication was still a form of alchemy not completely understood by many technologists. They all had their own theories of what worked and what didn't. Different companies were able to make things work for them that didn't work for others. We learned to devise controlled, multidimensional experiments to, as quickly as possible, try to determine what variable was out of control and what to do about it. It was an incredible learning experience in objectively analyzing data, rooting out bad theories, finding the real issues, and determining corrective actions.

Large dollar figures were always on the line, and the company's end-product shipment commitments to customers were at stake. At times, the pressure was incredible. Pressure was the one constant of life on the leading edge of electronics, and that never changed.

But my outlook on my future at NCR began to change after the first several years. NCR was basically the only high-technology game in Dayton, and the company's plans were changing. Their independent employees' union voted to bring in the United Auto Workers (UAW) union with the expectation of receiving auto worker wage scales and benefits. The other large manufacturing businesses in Dayton, Frigidaire and Delco, historically were UAW affiliates. NCR employees wanted the same kinds of compensation packages that they had read about the UAW achieving at other companies that were so widely carried in newspaper stories in those days. But they were killing the goose that laid the golden eggs.

NCR, knowing that it was going to be moving away from the skilled metalworking base needed for its cash register products and into electronics assembly of computers and transaction terminals, had other plans. Product cost pressures weren't going to support the wage and benefits scales expected in UAW plants. NCR began to start the production of the new products at new plants out of the Dayton area. When I began my first out-of-college job in Dayton, over twenty-one thousand people worked at the NCR complex; just a few thousand were still working there less than a decade later.

There was talk of moving the microelectronics operations to Colorado. Discussing this with my wife, Nikki, we decided that if we were going to be moving, we wanted to be by an ocean with beaches and warm water. We had no problems with Colorado, but after a cold, rainy, Ohio Labor Day weekend in 1971, we both decided that we'd had enough bad, weekend-spoiling weather.

"Get me to a coast—any coast—but preferably a warm one!" was her only comment. Hello, San Diego.

In the early years of the 1970s in San Diego, there was essentially no integrated circuit technology in place at any company in the area. Burroughs had acquired their facility from a Los Angeles–area company, Garrett, that had built the plant and begun staffing, but it apparently had second thoughts about going into a business so far afield from its core businesses. It was sold to Burroughs in 1971. There were two designers already on what was to be my staff, recruited by Garrett, when I joined Burroughs in the spring of 1972. They promptly both resigned and moved back to their original homes in Colorado. I was left to start building staff for the ambitious proprietary integrated circuit design program that Burroughs envisioned. So there were no designers then on staff, only a few working for other companies living in the area, and the major problem of an expensive city to relocate engineers to. With a huge recruiting effort, including hiring new electrical engineering graduates from local universities and doing the training, in three to four years, the staff had become a fully rounded design team capable of handling several complex, multiengineer projects simultaneously.

We had good reviews from our in-house Burroughs customers—a difficult task given the usual interdivisional politics. My engineering team grew to around seventy engineers and technicians by the end of the '70s.

But by the early '80s, the forces of change overtaking the entire computer marketplace were beginning to have a major impact on Burroughs, in many of the same ways as on the other mainframe companies. Burroughs tried bringing in new management from IBM at most of the top operations and technical positions in the company, merging with Sperry to increase "scale," purchasing a start-up desktop workstation company in Silicon Valley, and other strategies. But the underlying issue was that Burroughs wasn't surfing the waves, so to speak. They were mainframe people trying to scale their mainframe computer architecture down to a single chip—but with their business models still mainframe-centric. The chip wasn't the issue. The issue was in understanding the new paradigm of powerful desktop computers, open systems, and third-party software and networking technology—and no mainframes in sight. Endless reorganizations and "repurposing" of design staffs ensued, to no avail. Interdivisional rivalries and politics, at great harm to the company's future, dominated the '80s. Engineers began to lose confidence and look for new opportunities.

Managers began looking for the "savior": the guru who could solve it all with the stroke of a new design. But no new design was going to solve those deeply rooted problems. The outstanding design and technology teams I and others had with so much difficulty established over those first ten years were beginning to disintegrate. People began leaving. The technical staff of our 1970s- and early 1980s-era microelectronics operation dissolved and diffused, becoming a large part of the strong backbone of today's San Diego microelectronics expertise. San Diego's fast-developing wireless communications businesses became the beneficiaries of the Burroughs training grounds.

In 1983, I joined Linkabit in San Diego as director of very large scale integration (VLSI) design and left the mainframe computer world behind.

#

I'd started my career in the mid-1960s when twenty transistors in an integrated-circuit module was a big thing, and I finally retired from the field in 2000, shortly after one of my design teams had completed a new—first in the world—complete digital TV chip with more than a million transistors on board for the Video Cipher Division—which had, earlier in 1986, been spun out from Linkabit and sold to General Instrument. The division had battled major satellite TV signal theft and piracy problems in the late '80s. Responding to the possible company-ending crisis, I invented and patented novel semiconductor technology that ended that security problem for the company forever. The family of semiconductor chips that followed over the next several years—created by another of my design teams—has to this day never been hacked, even after nearly twenty-five years of production and several tens of millions of cable and satellite TV consumer units fielded. It's the only family of security chips in the industry that can make that claim.

That security technology saved the hard-pressed San Diego division's satellite TV business, enabling it to continue its pioneering work in digital HDTV and give the world today's five-hundred-channel satellite and cable TV systems. The San Diego business division received an Emmy Award for the antipiracy security system based on that unique, never-duplicated security chip. Surviving the piracy problem, Video Cipher continued on and received a cabinet full of Emmy Awards for digital TV, HDTV, and broadband communications to the home.

I'd found that senior management at nearly any technology company is always hungry for technical people who could bridge the gap between the company's senior managers and the usual, nerdy, somewhat introverted or shy personalities populating so much of typical technical staffs. An engineer who could easily and factually communicate with management about things like resource requirements, schedules, costs, technology, and the tradeoffs between them all—as well as deliver the goods—could go as far as he dared. I had moved up the management chain, rising eventually to becoming associate vice president of VLSI engineering at General Instrument during the company's best years. Over my thirty-five years in the field, I had met and dealt with some of the original movers and shakers in the semiconductor industry. I knew many on a first-name basis and could readily call key people all over the industry for help or support when needed.

#

I had known nothing about transistors in my high school years—only that somehow they made possible those original eight-transistor, twenty-five-dollar pocket radios that more and more people were listening to at the time. Sitting at that spinning wire brush with thousands of oily pinion gears waiting their turn, I had no idea that I'd spend thirty-five years engrossed in the technology, working with world-class computer and electronics firms and near-genius electronics engineers. It was a great ride, and I had been in it almost from the beginning.

But I still can't explain to my friends and neighbors, or even my wife, how you get all those invisible transistors on that little thingy.

In My Rearview Mirror

There are places I remember, all my life
though some have changed …
—The Beatles, "In My Life" (Lennon & McCartney)

I'll never know how close I came to not walking away from the Corvair accident or from the little race car crash or the carbide-in-the-cistern affair, too many trips through the S curves to Minster, too many trips through Dead Man's Curve, doing dumb things with fireworks and firearms, or all the childhood diseases of the '50s, any of which could have precluded all the good things that came my way.

We'll just have to leave it at that—some kids are lucky to survive their childhoods in spite of themselves; Dr. Fledderjohann had it right when he completed that old adage "Kids will be kids," with his insightful "wonder if they'll survive it."

Fifteen years after I watched the skies from that observation post above the Boesel Opera House in 1952 looking for Russian bombers and UFOs—or any excitement in the skies—I had completed my transformation. No longer a little kid playing with firecrackers and delivering newspapers, I had entered the world of engineers and scientists, computers, transistorized microelectronics, and integrated circuit design. More important than the career accomplishments and successes, I also found the love I wanted and tried to have so many times back in those early days. It seemed to be destined in that first blind date that Nikki and I would spend our lives together. And unlike those earlier concerns—buck an hour, no benefits—about providing for a good life for myself and my wife, there would never have to be any apologies for the lifestyle we were able to live.

And after another fifteen years, sitting in the annual meeting of the elite San Diego communications company Linkabit I had then just joined in the fall of 1983, I listened as the CEO listed the numbers of employees with postgraduate engineering degrees from the nation's best technology schools: MIT, Caltech, Stanford, UC Berkley, UCLA, UCSD, and more. I marveled at the fact that, with just my BSEE from Ohio State, I found myself in such company, and yet the management and technical staff treated me as a peer and valued my background, skills, and thoughts. Over the following several years, Linkabit and its engineers evolved into several spin-off companies that collectively pioneered much of the important technology that today's connected world is based on.

For me, it was a long, long way from "Hello, thanks for your application, but we feel you aren't qualified for our school, or our company, or this job."

It was a also a far different place from watching my father, bad back and unable to find jobs because of his physical limitations, fall into depression and my mother working night-shift jobs to keep the family together.

Nikki and I traveled the world widely, visiting five of the seven continents—and New York City many times, including attending that Emmy Awards ceremony. My life had come a long way from those "five-minute towns" and those cornfields in between.

Still, I can't stop thinking good thoughts about those little towns and places and the people living in them. I just needed to find my own path.

#

Now looking back through a distance of more than fifty years, I've always wondered how it ended. Who was the last Road Rebel? Was it down to one last guy wearing his Road Rebel club shirt or jacket showing up for the monthly meeting only to find that no one else came? Or was there a final meeting where a few guys showed up and decided that the club had reached its end and the time had come to call it quits? Or did it just fade away without a last meeting? And where did they all go, all those guys with their '51 and '53 Fords and '55 Chevys or Olds Rocket 88s?

From 1956 to 1959, we were a together bunch, all with visions of cool cars and good friends doing car-guy things: road rallies, car shows, and picnics. We were Ford guys and Chevy guys, with the occasional Plymouth or Buick thrown in, and we all got along no matter what the ride, be it an old '36 Ford or a sleek new spaceship-finned Buick. We just wanted to have cool cars and look cool—wearing our Road Rebel shirts and Road Rebel jackets with that Road Rebel plaque hanging from the rear bumper and doing things as a club.

There were a lot of things we had in common, and those things held us together for those few years. But there were no new kids coming in to keep things going, and honestly, we didn't seem to think much about it. Maybe we were too insular to let sixteen-year-old, fuzzy-cheeked kids join up. Maybe it was because they didn't have cool cars, and maybe they didn't even know how to tune a carburetor yet—or maybe we were too arrogant.

Another possibility is that parents didn't want their kids hanging out with us. For the most part, we weren't the best students, the best athletes or class presidents weren't involved, and we probably weren't the best role models for high school sophomores. Or maybe younger kids just weren't interested in cars. By the early 1960s, buying a twenty- or thirty-year-old Ford V8-powered car, hopping it up a little, dropping it with lowering blocks, hanging dual exhausts with glass packs, and "borrowing" a set of Oldsmobile Flipper hubcaps was too old school. They could buy a '59 Tri-Power Chevy and didn't need to do all that other stuff to make a street rod feel fast and look cool; the newer cars were faster right off the showroom floor. Why bother with doing all that greasy, busted-knuckles, hot-rod stuff?

And we probably just assumed that we would all be around together for as long as we could imagine. At that age, we really weren't even thinking about long-term concepts like what the club would be in ten years or who would be there to continue it. We were living in the moment, one day at a time.

Whatever the cause, the Road Rebels ceased to exist sometime after 1960.

But the Road Rebels always have slipped back into my mind from time to time over the past fifty years. A few of us exchange e-mails occasionally, some are gone forever, and some are whereabouts unknown. I can't watch reruns of *American Graffiti* without thinking about the Road Rebels. The music was the same, the kids looked the same, many of the cars were the same, and Curt (Richard Dreyfuss) flying off to college, leaving Milner (Paul Le Mat) standing there at the airport, feels too familiar. I'm sure I'm not alone with those feelings, though. Tens of thousands of people who lived in the same era, with the same experiences, must watch that movie and have the same electric feeling run up and down their spines and through their hearts. Along with a little sadness.

And it's clear that I wasn't the only teenage graduate who ever experienced that lost feeling. It was all captured a few years later:

> *I'm eighteen*
> *And I don't know what I want*
> *I'm eighteen*
> *I just don't know what I want*
> *I'm eighteen*
> *I gotta get away*
> *I'm eighteen*
> *I gotta get out of this place*
> *I'll go running in outer space*
> *Oh yeah!*
> (Alice Cooper, et al., "I'm Eighteen")

No one can have lived through their eighteenth year without having memories of what it was like to be leaving those teenage years: out of high school, losing contact with friends, and needing to move on. Readers might think that I thought the Road Rebels and New Bremen were a dead end. I didn't; I thought of myself as being at a dead end—at eighteen. I couldn't see how things would change if I didn't change.

Now, living in California, I still see Road Rebels everywhere: at car shows; at Friday, Saturday, Sunday driving nights; at swap meets; or just solitary rods driving along the highways. The car clubs are still around out here, and the guys all look like me: graying, balding, wrinkled faces, busted knuckles and grease under their fingernails—just like it was supposed to be all along. For me, what it took was the realization that there had to be something bigger, something that would still let me keep doing that Road Rebel thing but with a little more going for me.

October 2013, Southern California

Looking out at the road rushing under my wheels …
—Jackson Browne, "Running on Empty"

I rocketed up Interstate 15, northward from San Diego in my Mazda RX8, its smooth rotary engine effortlessly pushing me along at eighty-five to ninety miles per hour. I was trying to ignore the early morning, headachy drowsiness I usually cleared by walking my dogs around the neighborhood for an hour or so after breakfast. That morning, I was trying to get to Corona, around ninety miles north, by 8:30 a.m. to join up with a group being guided through the Tom Malloy Garage containing a fabulous collection of American race cars from the golden years of American racing: the '50s through the '70s.

I had just cleared the summit where I-15 nestles in the saddle between Palomar Mountain and the low range of mountains to the west, with Temecula spreading out on the plain below. I thumbed the right-hand paddle shifter to drop down to fifth gear to keep my bright silver car's speed from creeping up to one hundred miles per hour on the long, downhill run. A strong Santa Ana wind was blowing, and even my Mazda's low profile would be vulnerable to the side winds at that speed. And while in normal daily traffic, a car traveling at eighty miles per hour would not stand out as speeding on this freeway, where a driver is usually being passed by cars on both sides—simultaneously—at this speed, at 7:30 a.m. on a Saturday morning, it was likely to stand out as an easy mark for any nearby California Highway Patrol (CHP) officer.

I didn't want to be dealing with the CHP that morning—or any morning, really, but especially that morning—so I slowed to seventy-five miles per hour, which wouldn't even get a second look from them. After the beautiful highway drive through the rolling hills and sweeping curves of the green, low mountains of north San Diego County, the dry, boring terrain in the Temecula region north to the Riverside County area flattens out, and I knew my speed would be creeping back up again. I didn't want to miss the tour or even be late for any opening comments.

I was irritated that I had missed this opportunity the previous week when a friend and neighbor had invited me to join him for this same tour, which had been arranged by a San Diego car club. Based on the vague description he had been given, it didn't sound interesting to me. I know of most of the important car collections in the SoCal area, as well as the rest of the state, so I had declined.

But that same Saturday afternoon, probably within minutes of his return, my friend Bruce was on the phone. "Bob, you shoulda been there! It was the Tom Malloy Garage. Man, we saw some of the neatest race cars you could imagine!" Bruce still used *neat* as a main adjective in conversation, even though he was my age. We don't outgrow some things: cool cars and *neat* have always been used in the same sentences—including mine.

"Tell me about it," I said, my interest suddenly awake.

"There were Indy cars from the old days—you know, the '50s and '60s and '70s. There were dirt-track cars, short-track cars, and there was even something called a NOVI Indy car. And he has some fabulous road-course cars; you know, Can Am racers. He has everything!"

Instantly, I felt depressed. I had known about the Tom Malloy Garage for some time and had been wanting to visit it. I had even previously met Tom at the annual Coronado Speed Festival a few years before when he had several cars there for the races. But his garage/collection is a private affair and only open to the public on special request, so I had missed an opportunity to be there. The name Tom Malloy hadn't been mentioned.

And I knew Tom had number 21, the HOW Special. I had been on a quest to see that car since I had seen photos of it, sitting in all its restored glory in the Malloy Garage in a magazine article months before. I had first seen one of the HOW cars at that racetrack in Ohio in 1953 or 1954, when I was in my early teens. Its young driver and crew, with its young woman owner, were locked in my memory by a photograph my mother had taken at the track that day. My younger brother rediscovered the photograph in a photo album he found when sifting through our parents' house just after Dad died several years before.

That car and the memories it represents have always been a portal back to my youth and my years in Ohio. Talking to Bruce, I had become frustrated with myself for missing that tour and being able to enjoy it with a good friend to whom I could have described so many things related to the racing in those times. I had been there as a witness to those days, up to sixty years ago; not many people living today could say that. Not many people living today can talk knowingly about those days.

So I was in a hurry to get there and determined to not miss anything. I pulled into Tom's parking area just as he arrived. I introduced myself as he opened the main entrance to his building and explained that I had called the previous day and had arranged with his secretary to join up with a group that had already been scheduled for the tour that day. Tom was very friendly and graciously opened the inner glass doors, allowing me to wander alone through his amazing collection of historically important race cars for a few minutes before the official tour group arrived.

I walked in—and stopped. I stared transfixed at one of the first cars my eyes focused on, as if my subconscious had purposely sought it out: Number 21, the HOW Special. Hulman, Ober, Wolcott—names from the past. Names of some of the most important people in the Indianapolis racing scene in the '50s and '60s. Names I still remembered, so many years later.

It was one of the black-and-white beauties that had been owned during my teenage years by Mary Hulman, the daughter of the owner of the Indianapolis Motor Speedway. And the driver's name painted near the cockpit was one of the most prominent racers who had driven that car, Elmer George. The same Elmer George, our technical inspector for the Road Rebels Tri-State Rod and Custom Car Show. Even though other men had driven it, Elmer George was the right and the only name for that cockpit. HOW team cars, Mary Hulman, and Elmer George were all synonymous to me. My mind flashed back to that Sunday in Dayton when my parents had taken me to that race, one of the first big-time races I had ever seen.

That particular day, as well as other race days from that era, swirled through my head as the official tour group began arriving. I heard them long before I saw any of them: a low rumble, squealing tires, gears being shifted, superchargers whining. Then flashes of chrome, glittering colorful paint combinations, gray beards, balding and receding hairlines, ladies' scarves fluttering in the slipstreams. Deuce coupes, deuce roadsters, Model T rods, and '33 and '34 coupes and roadsters all pulling into the parking lot and shutting down, men and women exiting from cockpits barely above the parking lot pavement.

I was reeling, standing there next to number 21, surrounded by other racing machines I also had loved to watch as a kid back in Ohio, with the parking lot filling with the California rods my friends in the Road Rebels could only dream about back in those days.

The emotions flooding through me at that moment combined with the headache and a little nausea from the low-angle sunlight that had flickered between eucalyptus trees in strobe-light-like fashion in the final miles of my drive all mixed together in some way that made me unsure of where I was at that moment. California in 2013? Ohio in the '50s? I had to walk away from the assembling group so that I could regain my balance; I didn't want to meet the group and introduce myself in that moment. I wanted to let a memory that was pushing its way to the forefront come into full focus and fill my mind.

I went completely into the past, my mind's eye bringing back a late September Sunday afternoon in 1957, sitting with some of my own car club's members at our hometown New Bremen Speedway. We were watching another HOW team car carrying the number 21, a successor to that first number 21 in that earlier Dayton race, blasting around the track, carrying its driver, Elmer George, to that year's United States

Auto Club National Sprint Car Championship. Dust and clods flew back from the race cars' spinning wheels as they strained for traction as ear-shattering blasts from the unmuffled exhaust pipes pounded our ears, nearly deafening us, and the drivers sawed their steering wheels left and right, trying to keep the cars in the fast groove—or even just on the track.

We yelled and screamed and pounded one another's backs as one favorite driver after another made daring moves to advance their positions, diving to the low line under another car or driving around the outside into the curves in the high groove, getting there slightly before the other driver, who then had to back off or risk a serious accident. It was death-defying stuff, and it was happening just yards away from where we sat. Big-time drivers in big-time machines risking it all in our little hometown.

Watching half-mile, dirt-track sprint car racing in the days of cars with no roll cages and only a skinny roll bar behind their heads for imaginary protection—if even that—was watching men who had left all caution and reason at home and had decided that they were going to be the bravest and fastest that day. It was truly frightening but somehow inspiring to us at that time—not inspiring enough to make any of us want to do it as a career, but it was inspiring that men could sit in those cockpits with everything happening in split seconds at speeds of more than one hundred miles per hour. The noise and confusion, vision limited by dust and jarring car motion, surrounded by cars with wheels just inches away, and still maintaining control over their race cars—and their emotions—while slipping and sliding and bouncing through ruts and bumps in the track was beyond brave. We all knew we were seeing a different breed of man, doing what only they could do, and to hell with the consequences if something went wrong.

"Jesus Christ, did you see that? He almost hit the wall!"

"He's gonna kill himself!"

"Bullshit, that's normal for Larson!"

"I think he's gonna win!"

"He's not gonna get by Branson today; he's too hot!"

We yelled at each other over the roar of the blasting cars, trying to predict what would happen and who would win but not really caring who or how; they were all heroes, and all deserved to win. Anyone who could do what those guys did, week after week, deserved nothing but success—and to live to race again another day.

Finally, when it was all over and we were hoarse from yelling and screaming for our favorite driver and limp from the excitement—and fear—we stayed to finish a last beer or soda and talk about what we'd just seen. It would be time to decompress a little and also plan what was next for us: a race somewhere next weekend, a club event, or something happening in town. Hoping for a fun evening before the weekend was over, I asked, "What are you guys doing tonight?"

"I have a date," Lee said with his friendly smile.

"Me too," Jack added.

"So do I," Don said proudly.

"I do too," said Red, flashing his huge, toothy grin.

"Oh," I mumbled.

"What about you? What are you doing tonight, Gilly?" Jack asked, using the nickname I always hated.

"Oh, I think I'll just take a drive with the top down, maybe out around the lake, listen to some music, and watch the sunset from the park," I whispered, mostly to myself.

The other guys were all out of high school by then; they had jobs and girlfriends, and some were even engaged. I was the youngest member and one of only three Road Rebels still in high school.

"Where's Joanie? Aren't you still seeing her?" Lee asked.

"No, she's going steady with McCullough now," I had to admit.

"Pat or Jean? What about that other Minster girl, Barbara?" Don wondered.

"They're all going steady too."

"Can't help you, then. So you've just started into your senior year this past week, Gilly. What are you going to do after you graduate?" Don asked.

"Leave town so I can lose that nickname," I joked. Then I added, my voice taking on a serious tone, "I'm hoping I can go full-time at STAMCO as a draftsman and work my way up as a designer." I was working part-time in the blueprint room, making copies for the engineers and refiling engineering drawings in the vaults.

I remembered how hope was my major asset at that time. I was hoping that the company would give me a job I really had no training for, and I was hoping I'd find a girl so that I wouldn't have to spend weekend nights driving around alone.

#

After a few minutes of this reminiscing at the car museum, I regained my presence of mind and listened to the comments Tom was making to the assembled group. I tagged along at the back as the group moved through the garage. But I was really only half there; the other half was back in Ohio—again—in the '50s and '60s, with my friends, my parents and family, my hometown, and my life back then. That memory of standing at the track that day with the guys, elated after the day of racing but then having those conversations and the feeling of disappointment—and that hope had been my only asset—had me thinking about how things had changed.

Driving back to San Diego that afternoon, within the speed limit, I couldn't shake that feeling of déjà vu. I wanted to feel it; I wanted to taste the racetrack burgers again, I wanted to smell the sweet perfume of Alky racing fuel, I wanted to have my ears blasted by roaring Offenhauser racing engines … and I wanted to hear the old music.

These days, I know how to get my racing fixes nearly whenever I need to. I can go to one of the many events where classic race cars are not really raced—because they are too valuable and too dangerous—but gentlemanly driven as a way of letting today's crowds see what it was all about back in the glory years. It's not the real thing by a country mile, but I can settle for it. I had attended the Coronado Speed Festival a couple of weeks before and had temporarily satisfied my recurring need to immerse myself in racing nostalgia. I had smelled the scent of Alky racing fuel, and I had eaten "track" burgers—the best food in the world.

And I had just seen many of my old friends in August at the New Bremen reunions.

But an empty feeling that had always been with me through all these years was the result of not knowing anything about the lives of the special girls I had such strong feelings for back then. No matter how our relationships ended, they had been an important part of my life, and I've had only good feelings for them all since. I had no ideas about where they were or what had happened to them, and I didn't even know some of their married names. I had begun to understand that, for me, a girl I had once embraced and carried in my dreams—even if just temporarily—should not be lost as though she had been just another casual acquaintance.

The trip back to Ohio had been great fun, but I realized that reexploring and retouching my past would be incomplete until I discovered at least a little about the ones I'd had no contact with for decades, including those old girlfriends. I wanted to try to find them, if for nothing more than just to say hello but hopefully to find something out about their lives over the past fifty years.

I ignored the maddening traffic through Lake Elsinore and on into Temecula, thinking about the searching I would spend the next several days and even weeks in, if necessary.

Epilogue 2014

Hello, stranger, seems like a mighty long time ...
—Barbara Lewis, "Hello Stranger"

Most of the people in these stories probably have had a life that has been pretty close to what was imagined in 1958 or 1959. I've always wondered, though, how many of them have had that life-changing experience, the epiphany that transforms everything, or some personal shock that made them do something completely out of character relative to who they were at the time and what they were planning on doing in the next weeks or months—or for the rest of their lives.

Carol had happened into my life and made me look closely at myself—something I had probably already started to do with the first pinion gear from that oily bucket—but her unexpected touch gave me the lift I needed to try to make something good happen.

A fortunate man, or boy, will find that girl who has, for him, the gift of bringing out the best in him, if he just listens. It is possible that any or even all of the other girls—but certainly Nikki, the girl I married—in these stories might have played the role of Carol at that time back in 1958. In that case, it was just a matter of circumstance: the timing and luck, that farewell evening, and my awakening and knowing I had to do something.

Doing something was everything.

#

Where Are They?

Would they remember me? What would I say? How would I open the conversation? And, after my well-practiced opening lines, what do we talk about? Will they even want to talk? Would they have the same feelings about those days that I was having? Or had they shut them out of their minds forever?

But why not call? There's nothing to lose!

I found Carol just as this book was being completed. It took a bit of searching, but I always felt that it was a search I had to do. I had to find her to tell her about, and thank her for, all the difference she had made to me, even though I knew she wouldn't have any idea of what I was talking about. I felt that the circle needed to be closed.

"Hello, Carol. This is Bob Gilberg … from New Bremen."

"Hi, okay … do I know you? I do remember New Bremen."

"I thought you might ask that; I'm the guy who drove you down to your aunt's place near Dayton before you flew back to New York back in the summer of 1959."

"Yes, I did have an aunt there."

"Well, look, the reason I'm calling is to tell you how much you changed my life when …"

And I told her the story.

"That's a really nice story, and I'm happy for you, but I can't …"

We talked for an hour and a half during that first call and many more hours in following calls. I know she realized that I wasn't making the story up, but I believe she probably has had difficulty putting it in the context of the life she's lived since. I've been glad to at last be able to catch up on her life following those days. And I'm also glad that she learned a little about me—a person she didn't realize she once knew.

It turns out that she had met and married a premed student at Ohio Wesleyan. And, just as imagined, he was *a frat guy from a well-to-do family*—but he drove a TR-3 instead of a Corvette at the time. But he did—later on—become a Corvette aficionado. Unbelievably, they had both transferred to Ohio State, where he could finish his medical degree and Carol continued her studies.

I was amazed to hear that Carol was on campus at Ohio State for some of the same years I was. How many times did I pass her between classes or walking along Neil Avenue or crossing the Oval in front of the library? Or did I unknowingly slip past her while working my part-time job in the library, restacking books? But with thirty-five thousand students on campus, the odds of seeing and recognizing her were probably minute. In my deepest instincts, though, I know it had to have happened. Two ships passing in the night.

She is now married to a different man and lives in Florida. And she is still as beautiful and as friendly as I remembered. I can't really blame her for not remembering me—she must have had hundreds of guys throwing themselves at her over the years. It's easy to get lost in that. As Graham Nash wrote in "Wasted on the Way," *so much water moving underneath the bridge.*

I told her that I felt very lucky to have met her at the time I needed something, or someone, to jump-start my going-nowhere life.

She insists that *I really didn't deserve to be painting that basement.*

Pat, my first-ever date, went on to teach and become vice principal of a high school in Miami, Florida. She married the baseball coach, Tony, and for years, they spent their weekends in the Florida Keys, scuba diving and hunting lobster. They still live in Florida, and she still has that mischievous smile and look in her eyes—and that great sense of humor. And she is still dubious about that carnival-ride torpedo event—not to mention my judgment. I've had ringing and reduced hearing in my left ear ever since that carnival ride, and I may still owe her $2.50.

Judy eventually married after the events of her tragedy, and along with her husband, raises Arabian purebreds in South Carolina. Judy was born, like I was, in a small, rented New Bremen residence with Dr. Fledderjohann and our mutual aunt Ruth in attendance—also in 1940. Aunt Ruth was aunt to both of us: to Judy from Ruth's husband's family and me as my father's sister.

After that visit to see her in Chicago, I didn't see her again until thirty-five years later at our fortieth class reunion in 1998 and then again at later class reunions. We always had a brief hug, an exchange of smiling eyes, hellos, and a short, pleasant conversation. The old friendship was still there.

At our fifty-fifth class reunion in 2013, when I finally tried to apologize to her for my ineptitude on that day of Larry's death in 1962, she insisted that she had not noticed and asked me to forget it. She smiled and we hugged; I am now finally at peace with it.

Jeanne, who offered a helping hand to Judy when she needed it badly, still lives in Chicago but spends her winters in San Juan Capistrano, California, around sixty miles from my home in San Diego. We met for the first time in fifty-five years, as this book was in its final stages prior to publishing. We had a long lunch in an upscale celebrity residential community area in Dana Point, above the nearby Pacific coastline—and a million miles from that muddy Ohio lake where some of the unforgettable events of this book took place. She had her "buck-an-hour" job too, at New Bremen's only bank, after she had graduated from high school in '59. After taxes and the usual ten-dollars-a-week rent that most parents charged their kids after graduation while still living at home, she had twenty dollars a week to do whatever she wanted: buy a car, keep a pretty, young girl in stylish clothing and cosmetics, and go places. Jeanne had her own something-has-to-change moment too, when on a flight returning from Phoenix, she had a casual conversation with one of the flight attendants. "Hello, TWA!"

Joanie married *him* (Bill) and is still married to him today. They live in Florida. I contacted her as I was finishing this book, fifty-seven years after that prom. She is still the sweet girl I've remembered for all these years. She remembers me as the thoughtful (!) guy who ordered the catch-of-the-day, baked fish surprise dish along with hers at the prom dinner that night. I'd always been suspicious of baked fish dishes, but I knew it was the right thing to do that night. (Actually, I'm pretty sure my mother suggested it.) Guess it wasn't enough …

We discussed the religion issues of those days that never became a problem for us. And it didn't become an issue for her and Bill, either—he converted—as I probably would have back then. That's what guys will do for a beautiful, worthy girl.

Linda, of the memorable full-body-kiss, married Charlie—the same Charlie of the carbide cannon incident—who did decide that school just wasn't his thing and dropped out before the rest of us graduated in '58. Charlie and Linda were married for their lifetimes, still together at the time of their deaths, just months apart, in Arizona in 2012. RIP, Linda and Charlie.

Dianne was still at OSU during my last quarter there; I just didn't look hard enough to find her. She married a well-known artist and settled in New York City. (What is it about New York?) She had difficulty remembering me too, but the mention of Fred and Don brought things back for her. I always knew I wasn't the most exciting guy in the room, but …

Don was the hardest of all these friends to track down, and I didn't get to have the fun of finding and calling him. He had passed away in the Chicago area in a nursing home in 1996 at the age of fifty-seven. He died too young; somehow I always knew that Don lived too fast to live long. RIP, Don.

Fred spent his career as a navy officer and is now retired—also in Florida. (What is it with my old friends and Florida?) And he married Kay, a girl from Minster, Ohio!

Cousin Paul recovered from the Corvair crash and his severe facial and dental injuries, along with a broken knee and a place under his kneecap where the Corvair's ignition key fit nicely. He and his wife are still living in New Bremen, but he has been dealing with lingering hearing and vision damage following a scooter accident shortly after his retirement.

Cousin Joe, survivor of the Dead Man's Curve accident, married and started a family but was nearly electrocuted working as an industrial electrician in the late '60s. The severity of his internal injuries gave him great difficulties as he grew older and finally added to the complications that led to his early death.

Cousin Bill is now in an elder care home. He had been his old self when I talked with him at that Road Rebels reunion just the year before. I visited him there on a recent summer day to show him a photo Road

Rebel Harold had sent me of the Oldsmobile Bill owned during his Road Rebel years. His face beamed with a rare smile.

Aunt Ruth Ritter, my birth nurse and the mother of my cousins Paul, Bill, and Joe, lived her lifetime in New Bremen and died at the age of ninety-eight. Nurse to everyone, unfailing visitor to anyone sick—at home or in a hospital—and the birth nurse to countless New Bremen babies. She was also the family sage to whom my parents went for counsel on nearly everything. She is sorely missed by her large family of children, grandchildren, and great-grandchildren, as well as the town where she spent her entire life. She was the Florence Nightingale of the town.

Cousin Ann Lynn no longer lives in that farmhouse near the intersection of those Ohio country roads where the Corvair met its end, but she is still living in the area. She is surrounded by an extended family of children and grandchildren. I hadn't seen her in the more than fifty years since that accident, and I realized while writing these stories that I couldn't remember ever having thanked her as much as I should have for being home and saving my life that night. In the summer of 2013, I called her to make sure that I'd done that as well as I could. She remembered it all: my yelling and pounding on the door and looking frightful, and her holding my scalp together, sitting on the front porch, both of us anxiously waiting for the ambulance.

I think I found at least one way to make a girl remember me.

We had our first in-person meeting since that Thanksgiving weekend in the summer of 2014. This time it was a kiss rather than a scream.

Ray joined the air force immediately after high school graduation (where they shaved off his ducktail hairdo) and married Joanne after her graduation. He spent a full career in the air force and retired in Alaska. They are still married, summering, hunting, and fishing in Alaska and wintering in—New Bremen, Ohio! Ray, still being true to his natural love of the outdoors and wildlife, now has salmon and Alaskan big game to chase, replacing those squirrels and muskrats.

Ted married Terry, his steady girlfriend since high school. He graduated from the University of Cincinnati in mechanical engineering—avoiding all things chemical—and spent his career as an engineer working in manufacturing businesses in the New Bremen area. They are passionate about ballroom dancing. They live within a few hundred feet of the cistern where the carbide cannon story ended. The area is calm now, the birds have returned, and that cistern has a new cover.

Betty originally married a Road Rebel, Don, who died young of a heart attack. Always resourceful, she remarried to the man who robbed the New Bremen bank the year we graduated, in 1958—after his release from prison. She always said, "I just wanted to get my money back." Betty also passed away at an early age.

Sissy, our goddess of swim, now lives in Alaska, where she probably never goes swimming.

Jim still swears all those girls were there in Oxford that weekend, but unfortunately we just went to the wrong places. He married his Miami U sweetheart but sadly lost both her and then his second wife to breast cancer. But now as then, Jim is a great optimist and has a wonderful new lady friend. He claims he never bought the Trojans.

Ethel, my classmate and the first African American student to graduate from New Bremen High School, has not been located or contacted since graduation. Classmates from the class of '58 are still trying to find her.

Fred eventually sold the Lone Pine and took a job at one of the manufacturing companies in New Bremen. He is gone now, but his young daughter, Wendy, whom he was able to spend more time with because I "held down" the Lone Pine on his breaks, still remembers the legend of the little race car.

The little race car, to this date, has never been found.

Harold, who started the Road Rebels, still has a residence in New Bremen and also spends time in Florida. He says he has never been able to satisfactorily reconcile the contradictions in our choice of the club's name and the “Safety Club” words embroidered on the shirtsleeves. Well, we had good intentions, and we were safe—most of the time, anyway.

Most of the Road Rebels still live in and around New Bremen. We had our first club reunion in August 2013, fifty-seven years after becoming a car club … just because.

The Road Rebels: Bob B., Bill, Dick, Don, Ferd, Frankie, Hap, Harold, Harry, Jack, Jim, Lee, Louie, Ray, Rich, Red, Roger, Ron, and Bob G.

Stan Bowman, our ace driver who won that first race in the Road Rebels Hobby Stock car, went on over the next few years to a promising but far too brief career as a highly competitive driver in USAC’s top flight National Sprint Car Driving Championship circuit. Stan won the first-ever USAC race at the not-yet-famous Eldora Speedway and finished second ahead of A. J. Foyt and other top drivers in another big race soon after at New Bremen, but he was killed later the same year in another dirt-track race at Terre Haute, Indiana. He had been signed up for a top ride at the Indianapolis 500 in the next year.

Thankfully, there has been no corpse-like figure in a Road Rebels jacket enclosed in cobwebs in a rear corner of the Hotel Hollingsworth’s basement, found sitting there for these five-plus decades—waiting for the guys to come back. We all moved on to the lives we wanted.

A half-smoked Pall Mall and an empty Bud can were reportedly found on the floor of an abandoned, locked janitorial closet, though, when the building was recently being remodeled.

#

I have fond memories of all the people and times in this book and will never forget anyone or anything: the adventures, the fun, the failed loves, the music, the screwups, the disasters, and growing up and moving on.

I consider myself very lucky to have met and married Nikki. It was *so easy* to fall in love, and it’s funny how I had always imagined it was supposed to be just that—*easy*. If it wasn’t natural, if it wasn’t there from the beginning, if we both didn’t know it right away, if it had to be forced—pushed—persuaded, how good was it going to be? It was unconditional for both of us; there were no other considerations, and there was no hesitation. The Platters had it right when they sang, *"Only you can make this world seem right."* When people are right for each other, they simply are right for each other—and the world is right for them.

Nikki is a dedicated bridge life master, a wonderful cook and gardener, and mother to our long succession of cocker spaniels and fox terriers—and Cosmos: the parrot that came to live with us in 1967, the year we were married, and stayed with us for the next forty-six years. Nikki has been the best traveling companion I could have hoped for: knowledgeable, capable, calm, and ready to cope with all the challenges international travel presents. She is my essential life partner.

She even drove my Jag.

We live in San Diego, having spent the majority of our professional lives here. I now have too many cars, probably trying to make up for all those years without wheels in my college days—no Buicks, though.

Now, I'm no longer trying to persuade trillions of electrons, using millions of transistors on an integrated circuit chip, to do certain things. Instead I write, play guitar—a little—and play with cars—a lot. My 1970, 428 Cobra Jet, Mach 1 Mustang is out in the garage waiting for me to change the balky, old carburetor. And my '65 Jag XKE—the one from Dayton, Ohio, purchased in 1966—is sitting there, next to the Mustang, waiting for me to decide where I'm going to get the needed body and upholstery work done.

#

Life is an infinite series of decisions, events, and luck—mostly little things, but some huge. Among mine were that oil spraying off those pinion gears that first day in my shop job, meeting a beautiful girl from New York, Sputnik, that bad wheel bearing in my Alfa Romeo, and then meeting *the girl* from New York. And, years later, going to work for a little company in San Diego named Linkabit, the mother ship of high technology in San Diego that employed the key people I worked with in the development of digital TV, HDTV, and antipiracy technology for thirteen fabulous years.

Afterword

Will the circle be unbroken, by and by Lord?
—"Will the Circle Be Unbroken?" (A. Habershon and
C. Gabriel) "Will the Circle Be Unbroken?"

Integrating the stories of the people and events in this book, rather than leaving them as unconnected short stories occupying space on my computer's hard drive and only occasionally sending them to a friend or cousin, seems a far better use for them. *The Last Road Rebel* is my attempt to share them with as many people who can relate to the time, place, music, and events as possible. And hopefully it will also resonate with the sixteen-, seventeen-, and eighteen-year-old kids who haven't yet figured things out for themselves.

The process of writing this book set me on a magical journey of reconnecting with these wonderful people who were part of my life in those times. That journey itself has made it more than worthwhile. It has been valuable to reflect on how people I had known for just a few years or a few months or even just a few weeks, decades ago, are still with me—influencing in unknown ways, small and large, how I think, feel, and live today. Truly, we should not forget.

With thanks to the Nitty Gritty Dirt Band, the Carter-Cash families, the Allman Brothers Band, and hundreds of other musicians who have kept this old song "Will the Circle be Unbroken (By and By)" alive.

I've tried to keep our circle unbroken.

New Bremen 2014

New Bremen remains much the same as it was back then in the '50s: still very much a small town, now with close to three thousand residents. There are still just a couple of bars and a few gas stations, but now it has seven churches, most being the same ones from the '50s. Education levels are even higher; according the 2010 national census, for residents older than twenty-five, 96 percent have high school degrees, and 23 percent have college-level bachelor's degrees or higher.

There still may be one or two high school students graduating without a plan, though.

The town has fared well over the last fifty years, with an average income level 30 percent higher than the state average, and an average home value 10 percent higher. Also, according to the last national census, it has a residential racial makeup that is beginning to look a little more like the rest of the country, with thirty-five Hispanics, ten Asians, and three African Americans. There is a Mexican restaurant and an Asian restaurant in New Bremen—but strangely, no German restaurants.

The movie theater (the Lock One Theater) is back after a long absence, but the racetrack now unfortunately seems to be forever gone.

The old racing surface is still there, but is now covered with grass and weeds. It is a ghostly place, haunted by the memories of great race drives and great times.

There is still a municipal swimming pool—a new one in a new location—for summer fun, giving boys and girls a chance for those special meetings. And the Lock One canal lock has been restored in its original location after a close call with demolition. Lengths of the old Miami and Erie Canal are also still visible in town, along with a stretch of the original towpath. The New Bremen Historical Association, with its publication, the *Towpath*, keeps the town's heritage very much alive for the town's current and former residents.

Amazingly, New Bremen and Minster seem to be at the point of converging into one another. They are both expanding toward each other, with homes and shopping centers and small businesses now filling in the spaces that used to be farms and cornfields. These two "five-minute" towns, with the ever-shrinking cornfields between, may become a single "fifteen-minute" residential and commercial strip. That feels not-so-different from California.

And will that "religion thing" finally be gone when those cornfields that acted as a proxy denominational buffer zone disappear and the shopping areas meet? It's difficult to say, since those prejudices die hard, and it's doubtful that a Protestant church will be built in Minster soon. One thing is certain, however—the basketball rivalry will carry on.

The S curve that challenged us—but somehow *allowed* us to survive those days—is also gone. It's probably for the better, but I miss it. Now the road between New Bremen and Minster is just another one of those boring, almost arrow-straight roads I tried so hard to avoid in those days.

At this writing, the old Boesel Opera House was under reconstruction and restoration by that same but no longer small company—Crown Equipment Inc., where I had that first full-time job. The structure had burned to a shell, but those old German-built brick walls survived the fire. Over the last fifty years, that small company grew into the industrial rock of the town. A wonderful company with a strong sense of community, they have purchased the opera house and are in the process of restoration, just as they have already done with so many of the old buildings around New Bremen. They have even purchased and restored the big brick home where my parents last lived.

All those restored buildings, while continuing to look authentic and original from the outside, are put to good company use by locating administrative, human resources, legal, and other similar functions in them—still in the middle of town. Their manufacturing operations are based in modern, industrial-style buildings on the edge of town. To the company's credit, it has embraced the town rather than centering its operations outside the city limits. And it also has not outsourced itself to the Far East as is so common these days. It is a company that should be a model for the rest of US industry.

The family who owns Crown Equipment has even created and located the Bicycle Museum of America in one those old downtown buildings. In my time, it housed one of our two drugstore–soda fountain businesses: the Schulenburg Drugstore, with its old-time soda fountain bar, high stools with heart-shaped wire backs, and a few tables with matching chairs. Now it is home to a wonderful collection of bicycles, ranging from the old high-wheelers through the streamlined Schwinns of our '50s and on to more modern two-wheelers. It features much of the entire Schwinn collection and has more than one thousand bicycles in all. It would be a fitting home for Ted's Schwinn, the one that served as our ambulance to transport Charlie to Dr. Fledderjohann's office that day of the carbide cannon incident. Just sayin'.

After all, that event was the first story, written in 2003, that led to all these stories and this book.

Robert Gilberg
San Diego, California
October 1, 2014

Acknowledgments

Tammy Greenwood and her Monday group at San Diego Writers, Ink: Shauna, Erin, Bridget, Jan, Chris, Kevin, and Dave

Larry Edwards

Laurie Gibson

My support group at iUniverse.com, Kathi, Traci, Sara, Amy, and Patty.

All the Road Rebels: Bob B., Bill, Dick, Don, Ferd, Frankie, Hap, Harold, Harry, Jack, Jim, Lee, Louie, Ray, Rich, Red, Roger, Ron.

My lovely and patient wife, Nikki, who can't wait for me to finally stop it with these stories and those "women"

Genevieve and Joyce at the *Towpath*, New Bremen Historical Association

New Bremen High School classes of '56, '57, '58, and '59

Carol, Joanie, Judy, Pat—love you all

All of my San Diego neighbors—who had to listen to these stories, especially Meg.

The singers, musicians, and songwriters whose music has meant so much to me over the course of a lifetime, only a few of whom could be included in this project

John Mellencamp and Alice Cooper music, with permission of Hal Leonard Permissions

Photographs with the courtesy and permission of Harold Stamen, Darrel Willrath, Genevieve Conradi, Mary Ann Olding, Christa Coles, Barb Huxley, R Gilberg personal collection, and the Polio Survivors Association.

Dayton Journal Herald news article with permission of Cox Ohio Publishing

Sidney Daily News article, used by permission of *Sidney Daily News*

Made in the USA
San Bernardino, CA
24 February 2015